LISTENING FOR CHANGE

Listening for Change

*Letting Native American Voices
Unsettle Our Avoidance*

M. B. LANG

☙PICKWICK *Publications* • Eugene, Oregon

LISTENING FOR CHANGE
Letting Native American Voices Unsettle Our Avoidance

Copyright © 2024 M. B. Lang. All rights reserved. Except for brief quotations in critical publications or reviews, no part of this book may be reproduced in any manner without prior written permission from the publisher. Write: Permissions, Wipf and Stock Publishers, 199 W. 8th Ave., Suite 3, Eugene, OR 97401.

Pickwick Publications
An Imprint of Wipf and Stock Publishers
199 W. 8th Ave., Suite 3
Eugene, OR 97401

www.wipfandstock.com

PAPERBACK ISBN: 978-1-6667-7806-9
HARDCOVER ISBN: 978-1-6667-7807-6
EBOOK ISBN: 978-1-6667-7808-3

Cataloguing-in-Publication data:

Names: Lang, M. B., author.

Title: Listening for change : letting native american voices unsettle our avoidance / M. B. Lang.

Description: Eugene, OR : Pickwick Publications, 2024 | Includes bibliographical references and index.

Identifiers: ISBN 978-1-6667-7806-9 (paperback) | ISBN 978-1-6667-7807-6 (hardcover) | ISBN 978-1-6667-7808-3 (ebook)

Subjects: LCSH: Indians of North America—Ethnic identity. | Indians of North America—Social conditions. | Indians of North America—Cultural assimilation. | Indians, Treatment of—North America.

Classification: E98.E85 L36 2024 (paperback) | E98.E85 L36 (ebook)

05/17/24

New Revised Standard Version Bible, copyright 1989, Division of Christian Education of the National Council of the Churches of Christ in the United States of America. Used by permission. All rights reserved.

For my father, John Edward Lang Sr., who evoked my earliest questions about Indian identity and who died a highly honorable death while in the pursuit of labor justice.

"Hear, O Israel"

THE SHEMA
DEUT 6:4 KJV

"He that hath ears to hear, let him hear."

"If any man have ears to hear, let him hear."

JESUS
MATT 11:15 AND MARK 4:9 AND 4:23 KJV

"Who can understand his errors? Cleanse thou me from secret faults. Keep back thy servant also from presumptuous sins. Let them not have dominion over me. Then shall I be upright, and I shall be innocent from the great transgression."

A PSALM OF DAVID
PS 19:12 KJV

Contents

Preface | ix

Acknowledgments | xi

Introduction | xiii

1	Our Secret Fault: The Problem of Not Listening	1
2	An Unusual Outsider Prepared to Listen	15
3	Social Analysis with a Twist toward Healing	26
4	Deliberate Deafness: A History of Non-Hearing	39
5	The Messages We Have Missed	65
6	Theological Reflection: Turning Their Messages at Ourselves	89
7	Listening: Saying Yes to Being Changed	119
8	Hearing, then Healing: Recommended Action	125
9	Sitting in the History until Avoidance Breaks	153
10	The Beautiful Breakthrough Moment That Is Reservation Dogs	157

References | 161

Index | 169

Preface

The texts highlighted in the epigraph above are presented in their renderings from the King James Version of the Bible, a translation commissioned by the then-reigning monarch of England in the year 1611. It is not an oversight that this translation is quoted, nor that these verses use male pronouns to refer to all humans, for this "secret fault" created a blind spot and a deafness to women in the culture that produced a grand translation of what it believed adamantly to be God's word to the—whole—human race. Let he that hath ears, and all they that have ears, hear.

    This book exists because almost ten years ago I asked what young Native Americans have been saying to the rest of America. What had the post-Boomer generations of those people indigenous to North America been communicating to the wider American culture? When I explain the topic of my inquiry, it usually elicits the question, "What *are* they saying?"

    In a concise answer, I sometimes paraphrase Vine Deloria Jr. and I tell these questioners, "Native Americans are saying that you are not listening to what they are saying, even when you think you are listening." I let people begin there, rather than answer with distillations of content from my years of attending to the matter—content which those who care enough to find out can read here, and can find more fully in indigenous sources.

    Deloria's words were the first to grab my attention as I followed the digital creations, poetry, legal writing, stories, and contemporary literature of twenty-first-century Native Americans. The next insight that arose was that not only were we White scholars and other well-meaning Americans not listening, we did not even know how to hear Native Americans. It explained a lot.

    I determined that I would be That White Scholar who would listen deliberately and respectfully. That became my methodology. I have secretly hoped that I might learn to listen. Whether or not I succeed the indigenous may judge.

This work, as a result of respectful listening, offers a theologically informed analysis of the social landscape that is White America's relationship with its indigenous peoples. Before rushing into an overview of the material—material that I dwelt with over much time and allowed myself to feel and respond to—I encourage my readers to pause and to consider how they will listen to it. The research material, comprised of the voices of indigenous people speaking, exhorting, condemning, laughing and exalting, is inextricable from history. That history is more than context; it is a social landscape. Presented in these pages is a rendering of what Native Americans communicate to the wider culture in which they live and have lived. It cannot be understood or received from any landscape other than history. Therefore, the "what they are saying" is presented alongside an overview of related American history.

Formed from this attempt at respectful listening are recommendations for White-established institutions. But most important are exhortations for real listening. Some may look for fast hacks. How will I know I have listened well and respectfully? Readers will miss the point if they expect five fast points and quick fixes for their bad listening habits—and even academics today fall prey to instant-answer culture. Yet the work of reconciliation need not be long or laborious. Healing, even cultural healing, has the potential to sweep in fairly quickly when we begin with our own selves, when small and committed communities are ready to be changed by what they hear from another.

Acknowledgments

St. Thomas University enabled me in this work with ongoing scholarship support throughout my time as a doctoral student and candidate. Thank you.

My committee chair, Mary Carter-Waren, DMin, provided encouragement and insight, always with patience. Thank you.

Chestnut Hill College professors laid the groundwork for my doctoral study and the Sisters of St. Joseph of Philadelphia offered a generous spirit that invited me to continue the pursuit of justice in my academic work.

Committee member Catherine T. Nerney SSJ, PhD mentored me graciously during the academic journey that culminated in this work. Thank you.

Committee member Beth Stovell, PhD, committed herself to this work despite the many demands of her own work as a scholar and mother. Thank you.

Janene Lang and James Antonioni liberated me from the need to teach full-time to pay rent, by housing me while I formed my scattered research into a written doctoral dissertation. Janene Lang also made me laugh. Thank you.

Many kind friends aided me with expressions of support, prayers, and money. Thank you.

My ancestors have guided me as their darling child and I acknowledge their presence and help.

Introduction

We in America can agree that we are failing to find agreement. Divisions apparently built into the fabric of this American cultural and political life feel deeper in recent decades. The advent of digital communication with its vast availability and democratizing effects has handed an old-fashioned soapbox to anyone who can set up an account on their chosen platform. The result is multi-sided. The opportunity to be heard for individuals and groups once ignored, marginalized, and therefore disempowered, brings astonishing agency. The opportunity to propagate any and all agendas with gatekeepers cast aside is possibly revealing the limits of freedom that generations past recognized as real and concerning. Truth and responsibility are arguably lesser considerations in world of online free speech. Soapboxes—a dated reference to improvised political speeches made in person on the equivalent of the tree stump platform that raised the speaker high enough to be seen and heard by an actual crowd of bodies—today exist as social media platforms. Digital platforms enable free speech and free digital shouting matches. And from this cacophony, a question emerges: Does more opportunity for expressing equal more listening?

This book is the result of a determination to listen, across media new and old, to one particular group of Americans historically ignored. Native Americans post-World War II issued a continuing statement. Those who had tenaciously forged academic and artistic platforms of expression within twentieth-century structures insisted the wider European-descended culture and its power-holders everywhere were not listening. Politicians and academics particularly had been ignoring the American Indian, ignoring them out of perceived existence, after previous attempts to somehow make them go away.

The determination to listen led me straight into the question of why White academics, ministers, politicians, and the otherwise racially privileged were so deaf and blind and willfully ignorant of the original inhabitants of the land on which they lived. I'd heard the most popular explanations. We White people are just all racist, on a level so deep that we don't even know it, and because we are comfortably privileged, we don't care enough to change things. We think we are probably fine and that those still screaming for change are at best inconveniences, at worst a threat to be silenced or removed or even killed. I, however, wanted to understand, and I knew a lot of others who shared a caring attitude that was open to going deeper toward understanding not just what Native Americans were saying, but toward understanding ourselves, our history, our beliefs. A caring attitude in White people is being criticized as self-hate, as liberal groveling, and otherwise viewed negatively. Social media enables all responses, with many quick and inadequate dismissals.

Listening for Change presents an attempt to answer questions around the failure to listen to Native Americans; it represents the messy unpacking of the connected issues, the history, and the voices sidelined. Dismissive labels and quick answers to complex questions will not suffice. I decided I would do the work of listening to what Native Americans said White people were ignoring. In the process, I found myself asking how the American culture's blind and deaf zones functioned. How did the dominant power structures, and those masses of European-descendants, manage to not hear or see or understand? What exactly was insulating them? How did the presumption of White superiority maintain itself among recent generations whose individual members insist they are colorblind? Particularly, how have White people managed to ignore indigenous people to such a dazzling degree?

Each chapter that follows serves a distinct purpose in unpacking the material connected to these questions and ways we might rebuild. Research means being methodical about asking and answering questions, something missing in the new thought habits we are forming in the new digital century. The chapters, taken together, I hope can bring a contextually responsible understanding. Forming such an understanding will require engaging both the mind and the heart and must find a readiness for the civic responsibility of healing our history and reconciling traumatically broken relationships. Inclusion and diversity are value-categories emerging as we recognize that White American power structures, as they have existed, were formed for the benefit of the Europeans who settled the land in North America upon which the American nation rests. How can we transcend the odious stance that we White people are at the center of all civic life? How can we heal the blindness that sees ourselves at last, graciously or forcibly "letting" other people—the not-white people, not-male people, not-Christian people—inhabit and co-own the places where decisions are made?

INTRODUCTION

Listening for Change is subtitled "Letting Native American Voices Unsettle Our Avoidance." Before we can "let" those on the margins of power form with us a diversity of engaged and shared political power that resembles justice, we will have to listen. In my determination to listen to Native Americans, beginning with their insistence that White people like me were not listening, I became convinced that listening is the only path out. I also found that it will be uncomfortable, that it takes attention beyond the perfunctory, and that it requires a letting go of things we think we cannot let go. This is the work.

I invite readers from every background to come along as I retrace my own research path, reflect, and point toward hope for reconciliation with our indigenous relatives.

1

Our Secret Fault
The Problem of Not Listening

IF A TREE FALLS IN INDIAN COUNTRY AND NO ONE HEARS IT, WHAT DID IT SAY?

Two things happened in 1969 that contributed to this book's publication fifty-five years later. That year I met my grandfather. I was told he was "an Indian." Irvin Royce lived on Menominee Nation land in Wisconsin. My father planned the car trip of less than two hours from our rented farmhouse to introduce me and my siblings to the father he knew of but had not grown up with. Irvin Royce looked just like my handsome father, but had browner skin. He acknowledged as his grandchildren me and my brothers and sisters, who filled our burgundy Buick, asking as he looked us over, "How many are there?" I was in the back seat as we drove in on a dirt road, transfixed by a small dark-haired girl about my age riding a tricycle nearby. She was one of several Indian children playing outside that June morning, running and screaming at the end of a dirt road. A circle of simple wooden houses had short two-step porches, women sitting on some, watching the children. "That little Indian girl looks just like me," I had thought. We could have passed for twins, but I would never learn her name nor see her, or my grandfather, again. I was growing up white in southern Wisconsin.

The year 1969 had followed two civil rights leader assassinations, tragedies of which I was unaware. That same year a Sioux leader, then a law student, named Vine Deloria Jr., published a collection of essays titled *Custer Died for Your Sins*. The American Indian Movement was underway as Deloria subtitled his book, *An Indian Manifesto*. As Americans of that time were being warned not to trust Communists in peace negotiations, Deloria said Native Americans were laughing and sneering, recalling the abysmal record of the American government in keeping its own promises. Treaties with tribes had been broken with impunity over and over, and a waft of insistence and resistance was in the air (Deloria 1969, 35).

When Vine Deloria Jr. died in 2005, I did not yet know his name. I was then a journalist in Chicago, writing a column that often remarked on politics and justice. The parade of injustices I'd investigated and reported on would lead me by 2009 to studies in spirituality and social justice, and then to practical theology. My years in contemplative living and study would bring an anamnesis, a sacred remembering as if outside time, of my visit to the Menominee Nation land, and a new asking of the questions that had been with me across adulthood and parenthood and professional life. What did it mean to be an Indian? What had Native Americans been doing since 1969, across my lifetime? What were they saying now? And: Am I an Indian?

I formed answers over several years, and as the work of reading, watching, visiting, and listening congealed, I found I was not the first white scholar to reach the conclusions I was finding. Scholar of history and literary editor Edmund Wilson had been writing across the twentieth century, even before I was born, calling out for awareness and awakening of complacent Americans. I'd read Wilson's *To the Finland Station* in college but had never heard of another of his works titled *Apologies to the Iroquois*. The Mohawk Band of Indians in upstate New York grabbed Edmund Wilson's attention in the summer of 1957. One of the six Iroquois Nations, the Mohawk were resisting alterations to the land and river route given them in a 1784 treaty. Wilson admits his ignorance to the matter but is keenly interested, as an owner of land that borders the reservation (Wilson 1992, 39–40). The superb historian begins his research with a visit to the village and its chief Standing Arrow. His investigations form a history of each of the Iroquois Nations written for an audience of white readers like himself, and with "apologies to the Iroquois."

Like Wilson, my humble inquiry left me with an urgency to speak to the European-descended American culture of which I was a part. I had listened to what recent generations of Native Americas, from Deloria to young YouTubers and rappers, were saying. I didn't want to speak for them: They were very capable of putting out their power messages. Instead, I hoped I could communicate to my well-meaning white colleagues, friends, and brothers and sisters in ministry, that we really have not yet heard. We are poor listeners, carriers of an arrogance subtle and insidious, the "secret fault" of which David spoke, a deafness unknown to ourselves. As Deloria wrote in 1969, "Before the white man can relate to others, he must forego the pleasure of defining them" (1969, 175). More than half a century has passed since Deloria issued that challenge. Ten years ago, I would have said that great progress has been made in the attitudes and understanding of white people about Native Americans. Academia especially has welcomed indigenous scholars. The U.S. government has likewise appointed a Native American woman the Secretary of the Interior, and the U.S. Supreme Court in 2023 upheld the Indian Child Welfare Act to support keeping Indian children in Indian homes rather than in white foster care or other situations. Native Americans are making pathways into popular media with films and series that are their own work, their own self-portrayals, their own literary expressions. The Smithsonian includes the National Museum of the American Indian. The U.S. Poet Laureate from 2019 to 2022 was a member of the Muscogee Nation, Joy Harjo.

Bravo? Harjo is in her seventies, part of a generation that began breaking into the consciousness of white America's baby boom generation. She and every indigenous voice that is expressed and recognized and respected are reasons for hope. But as someone who'd grown up with more awareness of American Indians that most whites, I wondered why I didn't know more. I wondered what the Gen-Xers among the indigenous were saying, and what millennials and those younger were producing in the digital age. What were they saying? Were they echoing Deloria, were they poets like Harjo? And who is listening? My working suspicion was that we white people—even those of us who considered ourselves alert with our education, caring, and conscientious—were not paying the right kind of attention. Our knowledge was not leading to much change. Students, I noticed, continued to conceive of Indians as either a bygone population or as possessors of an exotic and more hip spirituality than they'd been given. I suspected that I and my community functioned with secret faults that only God could show us. The psalmist writes, "Who can understand his errors? Cleanse thou me from secret faults. Keep back thy servant also from presumptuous sins. Let them not have dominion over me. Then shall I be upright, and I shall be innocent from the great transgression" (Ps 19:12, KJV). I suspected that before we are shown what is not detectable to us, we may have to, like David, ask to be shown.

Native Americans within the United States have explicitly over at least two generations identified the problem. It is they who tell the non-Indian culture around them: You are not listening. In a landmark publication that drew attention to Native Americans as few had done before, Vine Deloria Jr.

(1969) writes, "Rarely does anyone ask an Indian what he thinks about the modern world. So assured is modern man that he has absolute control of himself and his society that there is never any question but what Indians are moving, albeit slowly and inefficiently, toward that great and blessed land of suburban America, the mecca for all people" (222–23). Deloria goes on, "It appears to many Indians that someday soon the modern world will be ready to understand itself and, perhaps, the Indian people" (223). Proceeding with the hope that the late Native American scholar's "someday soon" can be now, this research asks the twenty-first-century Indian what he or she thinks about the world.[1]

To ask what the Indian thinks about the world, in hopes of understanding what Native Americans are saying now, many decades after Deloria made his assertion, and in deference to this "giant of all of American Indian scholars and intellects" (G. E. Tinker 2008, dedication), is the task at hand. This work aims to understand this "modern world" to address the problem stated: the failure of a colonizing culture to listen to the colonized, even while making claims of moving toward post-colonization. Heeding Deloria's 1970 title, *We Talk, You Listen*, research is dedicated to a social analysis followed by reflection on what is being communicated, and recommendation for action. Deloria stated clearly more than forty years ago the problem that persists: Americans, including academics, Christians, and members of a society who benefit from the fallout of colonization, have not listened to Native Americans. This chapter will provide evidence from Native American writing to demonstrate that across the twentieth century and into the present, the colonizing "Euro-American"[2] culture that persists in the United States in the forms of religion, government, education, and popular culture is one that suffers from an inattentive deafness, and a cultural blindness. It will show that there is a problem. Method will be discussed shortly, but it should be noted that to *hear* in this context of this work of social analysis, and theological reflection, may be understood as a single-word reference to the combined work of "seeing" and "judging" as described in Joseph Cardijn's "see-judge-act" method; the "act" portion roughly paralleling the pastoral planning portion of Holland and Henriot's (1980) social analysis

1. Vine Deloria Jr.'s publication of *Custer Died for Your Sins: An Indian Manifesto* was preceded by some of its chapters being published first, most notably "Anthropologists and Other Friends," in *Playboy Magazine* that same year.

2. A term used by Native American historian Roxanne Dunbar-Ortiz to speak generally about the colonizer culture particular to the United States. Because this work limits its scope to indigenous peoples in the United States, the term is useful. Further, it is used because the methodology of this work is one of respect for self-naming and for the terminology used by Native Americans not only for themselves (Dunbar-Ortiz 2014, 9).

(10). To *hear* what young Native Americans are saying means to attend to it deliberately when reading or viewing, and to then reflect upon it before rushing to certainty that one understands. It is to keep what is said, in the Marian sense, and ponder it in the heart.

Even scant attention to Native American voices, much less pondering, evokes this suspicion that few from the power centers of a American culture are really listening to the newest generation of Native American voices. Deloria would remind those that few really listened well in the last generation. The problem of not hearing Native Americans outlays a twofold task: First, to listen well and with humility and respect. This approach carries potential to reveal the cause of prior failure to hear, very practical information for those who aspire to justice and peace. The hope, secondly, is that out of this listening, a response can be formed to what is heard, one that brings healing where it is needed. It is implicit, in this author's understanding, that social relationships need healing and that Native Americans are working to heal their own communities from historical and ongoing trauma. Yet we who were born into a more comfortable white American existence may be most in need of healing.

Needed: Deliberate Attention to the Problem

The generation who were Deloria's students are respected scholars and artists speaking today, as are voices still emerging from Native American, or First Nations, communities. Together the message of a twenty-first-century indigenous generation in the United States is not exactly the message of its predecessors—the established Native American scholars, theologians, teachers and writers of the century recently left behind and today. What do the newest voices ask us to understand so that we may form more just relationships and move toward peace? Is this effort at listening justified? Clearly it is. Young writers and artists recognize a need for healing, both within their own communities and for those outside. They also point out that before progress can be made in this centuries-long relationship, Euro-America needs to pay attention with refreshed ears and eyes.

For example, Kimberly Roppolo (2003) (Cherokee/Choctaw/Creek), a Ph.D. in Native American Literature, explains how she receives a similar reaction every semester when she asks her community college students "what is in the front foyer of Applebee's restaurant" (188–89). Roppolo (2003) writes, in Moore's anthology of "new Native American writing," in a chapter titled "Indians as Mascots: An Issue to Be Resolved," that "None of [my students], not even if they work there, are ever able to tell me there is a statue of an Indian man, in non-specific tribal attire, often with a 'special of the day' sign around his neck. Applebee's claims this statue 'points to the next nearest Applebee's'" (189). Her example demonstrates the failure of both our wider corporate culture and average Americans dining at Applebee's to even notice or question the use of a Native American image, much less to experience unease or indignation over it. She continues, contrasting the Applebee's Indian to the degree of attention and awareness that arose around treatment of African Americans through the twentieth century, "I guarantee that if a major restaurant chain placed a statue of an African American man in supposed tribal dress in the front of each of its restaurants pointing to the nearest one, people would realize that these statues were inappropriate" (189). Roppolo's remarks also point to the awareness among the newest generation of Native American[3] writers, artists, and activists—students of Vine Deloria Jr.'s students—that there remain issues to be resolved, that not only was Applebee's not listening, but neither is the rest of the culture. The occasionally indignant tone of young American Indian writers suggests the problem addressed in this work: that relationship with the wider culture, if changed at all, has not changed enough, and where improved awareness has occurred, it does not represent a sufficient improvement over that of the last generation. Roppolo (2003) specifically suggested what change needed to occur, an issue identified repeatedly by Native American writers, and one which argues that there does exist a shared American Indian voice. She writes, "Racism against American Indians is so intrinsically part of America's political mythology, the truth a group of people agrees to believe about itself, that without it this country would have to do something it has never done: face colonial guilt. Everything we see around us was made from stolen American Indian resources, resources raped from this Earth that we consider sacred, an Earth in danger of global disaster from imbalanced greed" (189–90). As evidence from history for the argument that the wider White culture has not heard American Indians, and therefore the work at hand is a necessary work, Vine Deloria Jr. provided an essay in response to the Civil Rights movement and racism in America. Published in 1969, Deloria's words express what Roppolo and others felt compelled to re-express, three and a half decades later. Deloria (1969) writes, "But the understanding of the racial question does not ultimately involve understanding either blacks or Indians." He continues, "It involves the white man himself. He must examine his past. He must face the problem he created within himself

---

3. The designation "Native American" and "American Indian" used here are drawn from the title in which Roppolo's essay is published, *Genocide of the Mind: New Native American Writing* and from the writer's use in her essay. As will be discussed shortly, use of referential titles are based on self-reference, not assigned by the author here.

and within others.[4] The white man must no longer project his fears and insecurities onto other groups, races, and countries. Before the white man can relate to others he must forego the pleasure of defining them" (175). Both writers, across decades, point to imbedded racism arising out of a failure of white culture to tell itself the truth about itself. In between Deloria's radical scholarship and Roppolo's essay resisting the mindless portrayal of Indians by Applebee's, the generation of now-established scholars raised the same issue. George E. Tinker (Osage), then-Clifford Baldridge Professor of American Indian Cultures and Religious Traditions at Iliff School of Theology, in 1993 pointed to "America's unfinished business" (Tinker 1993, 5). In a work examining mission history in the United States, Tinker identifies the problem of well-intentioned Christian missionaries operating out of cultural blindness, having internalized "the covert 'lie' of white self-righteousness" (Tinker 2008, 4). Again, a Native scholar and writer called upon Euro-descended America to examine its assumptions. While Tinker's work has been noted by scholars working in cross-cultural ministry and theology, its impact fell short of reaching Applebee's diners, or marketers, a decade later, and Roppolo's call to "face colonial guilt" echoes Tinker, each evidencing the fact that white America has failed to listen.

While Roppolo's, Deloria's, and Tinker's remarks offer an unfolding example of at least one common theme and possibly of a collective voice, any scholarly consideration of a new generation of indigenous voices will need to proceed carefully and deliberately, constantly aware that no single voice can represent all indigenous persons or all tribal nations, nor can a collective consideration and analysis of Native publications be neatly summarized. An explanation follows of how this work navigates these issues.

With that noted, it can be said that today's young Native voices suggest actions which could facilitate healing and reconciliation, but as a new generation does so, it points to questions raised—and yet not fully answered—by its prior generation. MariJo Moore (2003) (Cherokee), editor of *Genocide of the Mind: New Native American Writing*, explains in the introduction to the 2003 collection, "This anthology is a response to modern-day Native people becoming more and more disgruntled with spurious representations" (xv). She says that each writer's essay serves as "a bridge between what has been 'presented wrongly' and what needs to be expressed accurately'" (xvi). The very existence of Moore's anthology argues that the wider culture listen,

---

4. The matter of damage done to the minds, self-esteem, and identity of American Indians is a theme echoed in nearly every source listed, every "voice" included in the data under consideration. But Deloria as cited here, writing nearly half a century ago, notes the interrelational quality of colonization's damage, in which the colonizer has as much work to do, toward truth-telling and healing, as do the colonized.

listen well, and listen *now*. While Moore aimed at gathering the voices of Native writers in a single collection, she does so as an insider assisting in the task of cultural correction, and bridging the tension between the individual voice and broad conception issues that are commonly experienced by American Indians as needing cultural correction. These issues are sometimes ongoing from the past, and as will be shown, are also found arising presently in time-altered contexts.

The research presented here heeds Moore's hoped-for correction, awaiting the "accurate expressions" she has gathered lest they be spoken to a "seemingly uncaring society" (xv). It will attend to what a new generation of Native American writers, academics and artists is saying about its own identity, about its relationship to the dominant "white European" culture in which it finds itself. It pays particular attention to how these voices suggest our culture remains mistaken about itself, as already exemplified, to the myths it tells itself, as well as to where correction is needed most. The core task here is to listen in a way that effectuates this cultural bridge between colonized and colonizer; to listen, analyze, and hopefully build yet another bridge, rendering communication to those who, for any number of reasons, might not otherwise hear. And very importantly, this work asks those who pride themselves on having already listened to listening again, more closely, and with an openness to the possibility that something was been missed.

Terms Matter, and Don't Be Smug

Before proceeding further, an explanation is needed of the terminology used. Sensitive readers and those familiar with indigenous matters at all are understandably concerned with dignity, respect, and with unmasking and changing the colonizing default mindset surrounding the problem at hand. To claim to "listen" while arrogantly naming those purportedly being heard would constitute both hypocrisy and academic irresponsibility. The key point of the last section—that those who think they have been listening may have work to do—was lived out in my own experience, relating to this matter of terminology. This anecdote provides a poignant illustration. Enrolled in a course in career counseling, I was tasked to create an updated resume, so that I could in turn help students and clients do so. The career center staffer who reviewed my resume made a point of correcting the description of my dissertation, the precursor to this book. The short description after the title's reference to "Native Americans" made reference to "American Indians." I was told to remove this because it was an offense term. This advice was perhaps not bad; if the very educated career center staffer thought this, surely others reviewing my resume might have a similar concern. "What a sloppy academic!" This kind of overcorrection is possibly better than no attention to how we name Native Americans, but it reveals a failure to listen to Native Americans themselves. Those who would have corrected my use of "American Indian" might do well to note that the very public Smithsonian has named its group of museums for our indigenous peoples the National Museum of the American Indian. This is a reference in plain sight for those who are looking and not merely repeating well-meaning talking points. The Smithsonian did not choose its title haphazardly any more than I did. It is possible to be so overly full of our sense of being the good, educated people of the world that we leave no room for new information. Smug might be an appropriate descriptor here. Listening and smugness may be mutually exclusive.

Two ideas, therefore, guide the use of terms in this work. First, the goal is to honor how indigenous people name themselves as opposed to assigning, a directive whose essence is already noted from Deloria; this work will "forgo the pleasure" of naming, labeling, defining, or assigning (1969, 175). Then, because this work's focus is limited to tribal communities in the United States, it acknowledges self-references from that context differ from those of other indigenous groups, even from its northern neighbor, Canada, where the term First Nations is used. While the term "First Nations" eliminates the non-indigenous national identity imbedded in the term "Native American," a reading of Native American U.S. writers shows common self-reference by this term, as well as American Indian, or just Indian, even in very recent publications.[5] It should be noted that the use of the specific tribal affiliation after the writer's name is now common practice and will be observed here on first reference.

No single authority or body among tribal communities is charged with determining how Native Americans will address themselves, nor with how they might properly be addressed and referenced by those outside their communities and culture. Usage in print and online varies. It is recognized, however, that outside the United States, usage of "indigenous peoples" is accepted usage when referring to peoples who populated a given geographic location prior to European colonization, and who often struggle to define their identities in a post-colonial world.[6]

---

5. One important exception to the frequent scholarly self-references of "Native American" and "American Indian" is Roxanne Dunbar-Oritz' usage in her work titled *An Indigenous People's History of the United States*. Despite this choice for her title, the historian notes that she uses '"Indigenous," "Indian," and "Native" interchangeably in the text' (Dunbar-Ortiz 2014, xiii).

6. R. S. Sugirtharajah offers a compelling collection of essays in *Voices from the*

The assigned name "Indian" is, of course, a historical error, yet many indigenous today self-reference this way. In the late twentieth century, the name Native American replaced "Indian" in respectfully intentioned company and among academics. This usage, however, is admittedly seen by some as a denial of tribal sovereignty, in making tribes "American." Importantly, George E. Tinker (Osage) titles his work on sovereignty, *American Indian Liberation: A Theology of Sovereignty* (2008), self-referencing with the term "American Indian" in spite of his explicit language-based resistance regarding nationalistic adjectives (1–2).

Admittedly, First Nations has grown in usage and is widely accepted among scholars outside the United States, thanks to the Canadian model. However, the term "Native Americans" continues to be used in indigenous-authored sources from the United States, and so, also, sometimes is simply "Native," without the "American" adjective. The research data are drawn primarily from the United States, and hence this work considers what is used by indigenous persons in that context.[7] This is not a comparative work of relations in Canada and the United States, with their indigenous peoples; that represents a worthy study outside the scope of this research. However, it would be remiss not to note that Canada's national relationship with its First Nations shows evidence of a level of respect and desire for reconciliation that is arguably greater than that of the United States government with its tribal nations. This will be commented upon in more detail later.

Working from a methodology of respectful listening, this work, then, heeds Deloria's directive and gives preference to the terms Native American and American Indian, as do many of the indigenous writers referenced. First Nations and tribal nations, as well as indigenous peoples are used where the context warrants use of their nuances of meaning.

Because Native Americans regularly denote their tribal affiliation after their name as a way of identifying the nation to whom they belong, so will this work, as does Steven Charleston (Choctaw). The tribal affiliation will be given on first reference. If a writer self-references as "Indian," that is respected also. Further, historian Roxanne Dunbar-Ortiz (2014) asserts, "all citizens of Native nations much prefer that their nations' names in their

---

Margin: Interpreting the Bible in Third World, showing how indigenous scholars the world over are working to decolonize the use of Scripture. So, while a scholar in Botswana writes of imperialism and the use of texts, he finds it unnecessary to name a particular people (R. E. Sugirtharajah 2006, 297), while a professor in Oklahoma self-names in his essay's title, "A Native American Perspective: Canaanites, Cowboys, and Indians" (235).

7. *Genocide of the Mind: New Native American Writing*, edited by MariJo Moore, includes two First Nations writers from Canada, among thirty-three contributors (2003, 341–52).

own language be used, such as Dine (Navajo), Haudenosaunee (Iroquois), Tsalagi (Cherokee), and Anishinaabe (Ojibway, Chippewa) (xiii; xiv). Dunbar-Oritz is white and also claims Native American ancestry, but has no tribal affiliation, so none is provided here. The insistence upon reference to tribal affiliation in the original language, not the tribal name assigned by the colonizer, represents a developing level of resistance. Tribal names rendered in their indigenous language is increasing in use by indigenous people. The underlying intent here is to honor, not assign, and it will be left to those whose work is being heard in this research and reflection to decide if this work has been respectful, as is intended. In short, this work names American Indians as American Indians name themselves, and secondarily, as makes meaning most clear.

Another set of terms that calls for clarification is "the church," as well as references to "Christianity" or "Christians." This may mean the Roman Catholic Church, specific Protestant traditions, or the church as the body of Christ that includes all Christians, or their usage may refer to Christian missionaries or Christian-influenced European cultural traditions. Encounters occurred between the church in the broadest sense, and indigenous peoples; yet they were and are specific encounters and therefore happened between Native persons and Catholic persons, or individual Baptist ministers, or others who came bearing what they believed to be the Christian gospel message. What matters for this work's intention to listen, is the question: To which "church" do the voices speaking refer? In some cases this is very clear, and when that is so, it will be noted. At other times, references to Christianity may apply to all and to any within the broadest definition of the church. This can be difficult for Christians, and for alert theologians, who may experience the urge to read defensively, and make mental notes about whether Catholics are being referenced, or Baptists, or some other group that is not ourselves. Some Native American scholars reference a specific Christian group, other voices speak more generally. As will be shown, these distinctions, while important to those from specific Christian traditions, are not always equally important to the evangelized and the colonized, and that evaluative element must not be overlooked in a work dedicated to listening. Academics may rush to the criticism that says, "what or whom do you mean by 'church' or by 'Christian,'" but in doing so, provide a glaring example of exactly what Native American voices insist is a cultural relationship problem, a lingering effect of colonization—that being the insistence on defining. Smugness may be present when academics and Christians balk at how they are being defined. This work's insistence upon respectful listening asks how the indigenous view, and name, Christians. This is the work of decolonization.

Musa W. Dube (2006) offers an explanation of decolonization: "Decolonizing . . . defines awareness of imperialism's exploitive forces and its various strategies of domination, the conscious adoption of strategies of resisting imperial domination as well as the search for alternative ways of liberating interdependence between nations, genders, economies, and cultures" (298). Dube, as Associate Professor of New Testament at the University of Botswana, in an anthology compiled by postcolonialism scholar R. S. Sugirtharajah, discusses imperialism as it manifests in texts and historic uses of texts in empire building. Academics generally do not consider themselves exploitive or imperialistic, and most would readily claim they search for the "alternative ways of liberating interdependence" of which Dube writes. Decolonizing action by academics, then, must defer to the colonized and respect their use of terms, what terms they choose to define and what details they find important. To self-define, and also *to define the colonizer*, is resistance to an academic power structure that has, in the experience of indigenous peoples, acted as a colonizing partner alongside Christianity and commercial enterprise.[8] In order to listen, the listener by definition cannot dictate what terms are to be applied to whom. This is not to deny the listener's responsive examination of historical, factual, and contextual usage of terms, as will be discussed later.

First, an example of decolonizing resistance in texts and terms used, is provided by Tinker's 2008 work reference above, titled *American Indian Liberation: A Theology of Sovereignty*. Tinker begins with a footnote explaining his chosen usage:

> My use of the lower case for such adjectives as "english," "christian," "biblical," and so on is intentional. While nouns naming religious groups might be capitalized out of respect for each Christian—as for each Muslim or Buddhist—using the lower case "christian" or "biblical" for adjectives allows readers to avoid unnecessary normativizing or universalizing of the principal institutional religious quotient of the euro-west. Likewise, I avoid capitalizing such national or regional adjectives as american, amer-european, european, euro-western, and so on. I also refer to north America. It is important to my argumentation that people recognize the historical artificiality

---

8. George E. Tinker details the cooperation of missionaries with economic and social colonizers of indigenous peoples of the United States, in his 1993 work *Missionary Conquest*. This work is an important conversation partner in the next chapter. His thesis is that missionaries of all Christian traditions, despite good intentions, made the disastrous mistake of confusing and equating the gospel of Jesus Christ with European culture.

of modern regional and nation-state social constructions. ...
Quite paradoxically, I know, I insist on capitalizing White (adjective or noun) to indicate a clear cultural pattern invested in Whiteness that is all too often overlooked or even denied by american Whites. Moreover, this brings parity to the insistence of african Americans on the capitalization of the word Black in reference to their own community (in contradistinction to the New York Times usage). Likewise, I always capitalize Indian and American Indian. (2008, 1–2)

Tinker's grammatical resistance exemplifies decolonizing action and resistance in the face of otherwise invisible forms of oppression embedded in language usage. It also explains, in part, why *Listening for Change* does not labor unduly to clarify Christian or Catholic or other such terms where those speaking do not do so. In short, we must consider that the ecclesial and doctrinal distinctions that we Christians make concerning what we mean by the church, and Christianity are not substantially or equally important to the indigenous cultures who were Christianized. Steven Charleston's (2015b) account of the complexities of being indigenous and Christian will speak to this in chapters to come.

Because this work is, primarily, addressing an academic audience it will where called for by those academic demands attempt to specify references to Christian traditions. It should be noted, though, that general references to oppression by Christianity are left as such deliberately, where they appear in the data; they are not neglected in ignorance of need for specificity that a different academic work might demand. Rather, the issue of defining one's own terms in speaking about one's own experiences exemplifies a key matter related to this work of hearing what Native Americans are saying to the wider culture in which they exist.

In cases where Scripture enters the conversation, again, it will speak as part of the Christian tradition broadly, and of the Christian church in the broadest sense, where not specified by those being heard. Once more, where a distinction of tradition is clear in the given context, or otherwise discernable, it is noted. Where it is important for purposes of scholarly clarity, it must be made clear what tradition is referenced. Where a Native writer's use of "Christian," or "church," or scripture is vague and general and thereby possibly offensive to Christians who may feel the criticism is appropriate only for a specific group, the generalization is part of the data and must be heard and received as such. A respectful consideration of a given piece of data demands respect for the lens through which Christians appear as one group to those outside Christianity, to the colonized to whom Christian culture's many distinctions and divisions are unimportant. Our distinctions are not theirs and this must be accepted if we are to listen with respect.

Dunbar-Ortiz, in *An Indigenous Peoples' History of the United States* (2014) applies the term "Euro-American" to the dominant culture within the United States. While it can be argued that American culture is not only Christian, Dunbar-Ortiz and others reference the historically dominant culture and beliefs that Europeans imported and implanted by force, in another word, colonization. This is useful as a means of discussing something that is generally seen, experienced, and understood by readers, but needs naming. This work uses the "Euro-American" designation also, with acknowledgment of Dunbar-Ortiz's use of it in her text. However, references to broad American culture will be clarified as is demanded by academic rigor, noting which areas of Euro-American culture are referenced.

2

An Unusual Outsider Prepared to Listen

THE PROBLEM REQUIRED AN UNUSUAL OUTSIDER, PREPARED BY LIFE TO LISTEN

My own story matters, as listener. The experience of the researcher is key to the method of social analysis used in this work, especially in the role of researcher as listener and reflective theologian. A garnering of hard data is of little value even if it could stand alone, untouched by human experience. Social analysis is required in a work addressing a human failure of listening, especially listening on a cultural scale. The human experience of the researcher, the listener, is key. The insertion of those being heard, and of the hearer, brings together the parts of a whole theological practice (Holland and Henriot 1980, 11). Hence, this insertion of the author's experience is as complete as is necessary to show my role here as "unusual outsider," a term I created to fit and explain my part in the whole of the pastoral circle of Holland and Henriot's method of social analysis, to be discussed later. As explained briefly at the start of the first chapter, my interest in Native American identity began in my earliest years and informs every observation made.

With the importance of any author's experience in mind, I invite readers to contemplate with me the way experience prepared me for this work of respectful listening. I am an outsider to Native American communities. It may be helpful to understand, however, that I might be classified as an unusual outsider; that is, while I do not qualify as an insider, based respectfully upon the boundaries of community set by most tribal communities,

I am not without any shared experience whatsoever. Reflection upon my own subjectivity in this work has yielded the conviction that life circumstances have prepared me to be an unusual outsider, with the accompanying potential to serve effectively in addressing the above-described problem. Who can break this stalemate of not-listening? It is not the burden of the Native American to make White Americans notice that they are present and speaking. The awareness of the problem—that non-Native Americans pay little attention to Indian communities—arises from years of reading, traveling, speaking with Native Americans in several states, and attending to online news, blogs, and artistic sources of indigenous voices. It began, though, in 1969, with my father taking me and my siblings to meet our Indian grandfather on the Menominee Nation reservation in Wisconsin. The inquiry into the problem, and the results of this research, will represent a culmination of attending to Indian-related questions across my youth and into adulthood. In multiple ways, my life circumstances have brought me to this very work, and have formed my "unusual outsider" status.

It was not immediately clear, as I began to form my experience and research into a formal work, how to answer the question: Am I an insider or outsider? The late twentieth century witnessed the movement of indigenous scholars into fields of study involving their own peoples, resisting and replacing the etic approach of the White anthropologist or social scientist observing the Native culture and religion (Grounds et al. 2003, 209). Insiders were being invited to speak, as the only persons who could rightly understand what it meant to be Native American; outsiders were being invited to listen and learn. As my own experience led to a growing awareness of the need for the dominant American culture to hear[1] what Native Americans today were saying, it was clear that I would have to do so as an outsider. Yet, it would not be honest or even accurate to claim that this work represents the listening, social analysis, and reflection of a fully objective, academic outsider. I have grappled with questions of Indian identity since childhood when on that summer day, on an unpaved road on Menominee Nation land, I met my grandfather, Irvin Amos Royce. Among the impressions I recall was seeing a little "Indian" girl about my age, riding a red tricycle like the one I had at home, and being observantly aware—and even surprised—that she looked just like me. I recall wondering "where the Indians were." All I saw was people who looked like me.

---

1. To "hear" in this context of a work of social analysis, including theological reflection, may be understood as one word referring to the combined work of "seeing" and "judging" as described in Joseph Cardijn's "see-judge-act" method; the "act" portion roughly paralleling the pastoral planning portion of Holland and Henriot's social analysis (1980, 10).

Questions of the meaning of Indian identity never left me. I have not attempted to claim tribal affiliation, the identifying line today between those who identify and who are accepted from within as Native American, and those who may make some other claim to Indian identity.

Historically, under federal policies of assimilation and termination (Dunbar-Ortiz 2014, 173–74), concealing one's Indian identity seemed for many the best way to survive or possibly thrive in a White-dominated society. Donald L. Fixico's (Muscogee, Seminole, Shawnee, Sac, and Fox) work, *The Urban Indian Experience* (2000) closely examines the "urban Indian identity crisis" and the policies that created it. He also describes many aspects that parallel my own experience (172–89). My non-Indian grandmother left blank on my father's birth certificate the box that should contain the name of his father. This happened in 1942, a time when attempts were underway to assimilate Indians, when American Indian identities were being systematically erased. By not documenting that Irvin Royce was my father's father, my white grandmother "killed the Indian but saved the man," a slogan used during the days of Indian boarding schools, but an idea still at play culturally when my father was born to a nineteen-year-old German-Jewish woman and a twenty-two-year-old man whose Indian identity still remains unclear. Saving the man, my infant father, from his Indian ancestry, may have seemed to her the best thing to do at the time (Pratt 1892).[2] This phenomenon persists today (Fixico 2000, 58). Children of indigenous birth who are placed in foster care, or adopted by non-Indians, describe similar identity issues, knowing they are descendants, but having not been raised in the tribe, failing that identifier (181).

There are multiple reasons indigenous peoples increasingly use legal tribal affiliation to define Native identity, not the least of which being that many tribal nations distribute assets communally to all members. This is a reasonable action, but with consequences and not without its critics. Native author and lecturer Gabriel Horn (White Deer of Autumn) refers to "greedy tribal governments" who are guilty of "paper genocide" (Horn 2003, 74). As someone who, despite knowing my grandfather, fails the tribal affiliation test, I have never gained anything nor tried to gain anything from my ancestry, likely Menominee or the Stockbridge Munsee Band of Mohican Indians. But neither, however, do I fit what Deloria describes as the stereotypically vague Indian princess story from someone with an "Indian-grandmother complex that plagues certain whites" as Vine Deloria Jr. (1969) describes

---

2. This usage makes reference to a quote from Capt. Richard H. Pratt, in 1892, regarding the education of Native Americans, especially children, as a means of severing them from their tribal memory in order that they might be "civilized," and "mingle with Whites" as a solution to the "Indian problem."

people of European ancestry who contrive a distant Indian identity (11). Those Native Americans who decry "wannabes" (Martinez et al. 2016, 98), derisive slang for white people who forge an Indian identity from vague and unprovable stories, describe a typical profile, which my Indian identity does not fit. I *met my grandfather*, face-to-face on a Wisconsin reservation an hour's car ride from where I lived. It was there, several miles from my father's birthplace in Antigo, Wisconsin, on a dirt road outside a plain box house with one front step, that my father introduced my siblings and me to this man who looked just like my father, but with slightly darker skin. My dad said, "These are your grandchildren." Irvin Royce, a handsome man less than fifty years old, looked us over as he answered, "How many are there?" My father introduced us each by name and our grandfather looked us in the eyes, one-by-one, as our father did so. He impressed me as a kind man, gentle in manner like his son, my dad.

The meeting impressed me in ways beyond just creating identity questions. I noticed the bleakness of the surroundings; I saw a quiet adult seated on the single stair to the box-house, I took in the apparent poverty. Our family was by no assessment wealthy. We were what is today called working poor. But the reservation seemed poor to me, as a child of a factory worker with five children. The only happy sound was some Indian children screaming and laughing, and I noticed that no adults smiled, including my grandfather. I felt something was not right in this place. The Indians seemed sad. My memory is clear, the experience a part of me that resides inside me, as I take my place as an outsider to listen.

Some among Native communities acknowledge that there exist those who cannot legally document their identity for reasons related to colonization: termination policies, removal of children from their tribal homes, forced relocation, and the cultural pressure to 'denounce their 'Indianness'" (Moore 2003, 63). Further, some insiders even criticize the "identity police" among Native and non-Natives alike, especially those who demand to know "How much Indian are you?" (Horn 2003, 71–73). I have always understood that the reason my father made the effort to drive us north to the Menominee Nation lands for our face-to-face meeting with his blood father was because he anticipated his children's adulthood questions. I can never say, "I think I am part Indian." That my grandfather was Native American is a story passed down from my own father and it is part of my own lived experience. Our meeting took place on wooded land shared by Menominee and Stockbridge Munsee, land over which the tribes disputed; the Menominee apparently provided a piece of their reservation after the Stockbridge Munsee Band of Mohicans had been driven west with no place to go.[3]

It was not until November 2008 that I published an account of my Native ancestry experience in a column, during Native American Heritage month. Before this I had never shared the story beyond my personal circle. I was a news editor and columnist, and this was written as part of my regular job. I was paid an extra $40 for every column, as column writing was not in my job description, and I wrote every week. That week, I decided to tell the story of my heritage, or non-heritage, as it were. My fellow editors told me I should turn the column into a full screenplay. I responded, "But that's all I have to tell. I didn't grow up on the reservation." I realize today that there is more to the story, but it is not my story. The more is the work of listening.

One of the primary content factors in tribal identification,[4] is that of being raised in a tribal community, being involved and participating in the community (Martinez et al. 2016, 99). It is in this upbringing that a child learns Native ways on a deep level. It is about formation. Honor for this, as stated, is a reason I do not approach this work as an insider. I've listened, accepted, and begun to understand the definition that tribal members make of Native American identity and I honor it, knowing that the boundary drawn to define their community is forged in pain and in pride (Owen 2008, 16). Further, this definition is not accepted grudgingly. I *am* an outsider, I was not raised in a Native community, and therefore I lack an insider perspective, regardless of the genes I may carry, and in spite of possessing some markers of being Indian.

It would not be true, though, to say I have nothing in my experience that overlaps the phenomenon of being Indian in America. Though I have inherited cultural privilege that comes with having white skin, I have, nevertheless, experienced disdain for being apparently Indian, if only in a comparatively small degree. I was not white enough for some white people: I have been ridiculed for looking "like an Indian" and even suffered violence related to it. I was told I had "awful straight Indian hair," I've been suspect for having black hair and brown eyes in communities of many blue-eyed northern European immigrants, growing up and in adulthood. I've been passively refused service in a supper club in northern Wisconsin, where wealthy white vacationers don't care to mix with local Indians, and was once

---

3. Historical accounts differ, but in the 1820s, the two tribes and the Ho-Chunk lived side-by-side in the area west of what is today Green Bay, Wisconsin.

4. Grace Sage (Oneida Nation of Indians of Wisconsin), cites Susan Lobo's list of "contributions that assist in the establishment and formation of an urban Indian identity." They "include ancestry, appearance, cultural knowledge, and urban/reservation Indian community involvement and participation" (Martinez et al. 2016, 99).

called a "monkey" by a sloppy white man wearing overalls in a department store. My father was unemployed the summer of 1972 and he found temporary work in the fields picking peas alongside migrant laborers. Blending in, he was called a "wetback." These and other incidents caused me to internalize the idea that my siblings and I were not as "white" as other white people. Like many on reservations, I grew up poor, and more so after my father's death when I was fifteen. My family received food stamps and I had lunch free at school. I remember sometimes being hungry at home those last few days of the month, until a check arrived on the first. This kind of poverty can be common to reservation life as Joel Waters describes, "It was always the same old worries: Are we going to have enough food?" (Waters 2003, 86). Still, I am routinely given certain advantages because I have white skin, and I know that. I was gifted with intelligence and the ability to write very well. I continue in awareness that there are forms of hardship and dehumanization I have not experienced and cannot.

There is another element of Native identity even more worthy of mention, that of a spirituality of community. I came to this work holding a master's degree in holistic spirituality, but a sense of inter-connectedness and caring for others has been with me since my earliest memory. This also is part of my aforementioned sense that I came to this work uniquely prepared to listen. As a child, I experienced myself, powerfully, as one with everything around me. My father made sure we spent much time outdoors and we didn't watch very much television. When I drew a simple house in kindergarten, I put three doorknobs on the front door at different heights. My teacher asked why I had done this and I explained, "So that everybody can reach." The spirituality of thinking of the whole community, of giving for it, seemed born with me, even though I have had to accept that there is no knob at all on the door to my Native ancestry. My grandmother removed it and those inside aren't opening to white, college-educated "plastic shamans," like some may categorize those without tribal affiliation (Aldred 2000).

As a young adult, I self-educated on Native American issues, again, intuitively defying the stereotypes decried by Native writers; I sought out the very materials that the 1491s comedy group (2013) offer as the antithesis of the faux Indian merchandise sold to seekers in "The Indian Store." A buyer wants books on treaty history and Indian law, or "anything by Vine Deloria," but the Native storeowners can only offer him books on New Age-style Native spirituality. This comedy troupe's work will be focused on later; they have since the time of my research gone on to create the FX Hulu series *Reservation Dogs*. I was good at discerning sources. I owned as an undergraduate the University of Nebraska's publication of *Documents of United States Indian Policy*, edited by Francis Paul Prucha; it was not required for any college course. I read most of it along with other primary source history and whatever literature I could find that seemed worth reading. I am familiar with popular Native spirituality literature and with Native American history and culture, to the best degree one might be without having a tribal affiliation or having grown up as part of a tribal community. A high school history book for Indians found me once, at a thrift store in northern Wisconsin. *They Taught You Wrong* was its title. I am unable to locate another copy or digital trail in order to give a reference. I spent time on reservations in the 1990s, while my brother lived there serving as a pastor of a long-existing Protestant church. I interviewed, for a college project, Ojibwe eldress Josephine Dowd in her home as she beaded moccasins for her great-grandchildren. I sat in on tribal community meetings and in Ojibwe language classes as the tribe sought to retain its language in the next generation. My self-education in tribal culture has spanned, then, four decades and it was never about trying to be Indian; it was about understanding what that identity meant, since I'd been told from my earliest memories that I was an Indian, and because I met and was acknowledged by a man whom I was told was my Indian grandfather, who lived on an Indian reservation miles from my father's birthplace.

And since that event, I have learned that by current definition, I am not an Indian. I am not alone. It was a surprise to begin this research and find that Ward Churchill, noted above, published in *Native Voices* as Keetowah Band of Cherokee, cannot prove the Cherokee ancestry he claims. His tribal membership is honorary based on his decades of activism for Indian rights, yet he and others are subject to the "wannabe"[5] criticism (Martinez et al. 2016, 98).[6] Churchill's situation is echoed in the voices that comprise the data here. It is no surprise that some cannot show their identity when a colonizing culture rewarded identity surrender, when whole tribal nations were scrubbed from official existence, as was the Menominee Nation in the "termination era," in effect from 1953 through the 1980s (Dunbar-Ortiz 2014, 173; 175). If this explanation of the writer's experience seems lengthy, it demands to be so out of respect for the legitimate indignation experienced by Native Americans; first their identity, their very existence, is under attempted erasure, then, in an evolving White culture shift, it became trendy

---

5. A derisive term used by indigenous people for white people who make nebulous claims of Native ancestry, or who attempt to take up Native ways without being Native by any of the definitions discussed, most importantly having tribal affiliation and having been raised in a tribal community.

6. *The Rocky Mountain News* published an investigation of Churchill's ancestry claims after he was fired from the University of Colorado, sued and won.

in the late twentieth century to claim you are Indian. To take Indian identity lightly and to make a claim to it lightly reveals ignorance, at best.

Indian Enough to Notice No One Was Listening to Indians

Having begun with questions of my own Indian identity, my attention to what Native Americans were saying led me, over time, to the very suspicion that informs this work. As stated above, I suspected that almost no one was listening, that a sense of superiority, privilege, and patronizing concern permeated words and actions on the part of the culture that had colonized the Americas and its indigenous land. As Paula Gunn Allen (Laguna/Metis) explains, "white-think is almost entirely unconscious; nameless, formless, unacknowledged, it exists as a powerful barrier to authentic communication across cultures" (Allen 2003, 307). White-think could be understood as proverbial cotton in American ears.

The Native American response to a recent affront and form of exploitation, the appropriation of indigenous spiritual traditions especially by the New Age spirituality movement, is telling. It seems incredulous that no precious thing is off limits, that there is seemingly nothing that cannot be taken from Native peoples. In the same way that the music of African American slaves was usurped by their oppressor's culture, so the sacred practices of indigenous peoples have been up for grabs. "White-think" seems almost too mild a term. The irony crosses over into the cynical when one considers that the very same practices that two generations of Whites have now embraced were, by previous generations of Euro-American Christians, denounced as evil, pagan. It is not surprising that these young American Indian writers—and the older ones—are indignant. This will be explored in chapters to follow.

Estranged for years of my adulthood from a fundamentalist Baptist upbringing, I re-opened myself to the religious tradition I had been given in Christianity and I discovered that my inborn sense of the sacred everywhere and *everywhen*[7] was, after all, present and practicable within the broad Catholic tradition. I found a way to be at home spiritually. I appreciated Native spirituality, and I "felt" like I understood it, but accept that it is not in my power to decide whether that is true. I have unwittingly used the same words as tribal spiritual writers, but I learned to ask to what extent I really mean what they do, or vice versus—and if we need to?

---

7. A term I penned to describe a spiritual experience, unpublished. "The Journal of Marlene Lang," 1992.

The list is long and strange of influences which prepare me as an unusual outsider, maybe starting with my grandmother's fateful decisions and the blank "father's name" birth certificate box. The influences continue across my father's life circumstance, his example of humility and service to his community—at his own expense—as he organized for just wages. My father was a U.S. Army veteran, active in the Wisconsin National Guard 32nd Infantry (Red Arrow) at the time of his death at age thirty-six, amid his union activism at the factory where he worked. He was a volunteer fire fighter and he was funny. In his twenties, John Edward Lang Sr. was ordained in the Baptist tradition and our family spent two years in training for missionary service under a mission organization which targeted indigenous peoples around the world who had never been "reached" with the gospel of Jesus Christ. This was the early 1970s and New Tribes Mission, headquartered in Sanford, Florida, represented a surviving remnant of the "missionary conquest" era examined deeply by Tinker. As a child in the first and second grades, I recall furloughed missionaries presenting slides of their work, the homes and dress of people indigenous to the Amazon, Papua New Guinea, and Venezuela. As part of bringing the gospel to these "new tribes," some New Tribes missionaries were also trained as linguists and specialized in developing grammars and writing down the tribal languages, in some cases for the very first time. At dinner, our family discussed the question of whether missionaries in the Amazon, who encountered a tribe whose dress entailed only a beaded string about the waist, should "teach" the people to wear clothing like ours—that of white missionaries. We giggled over the matter, but as a family, we collectively concluded that it was not the place of the missionaries to change how people dressed. The fact of being introduced to questions like this, and being taught to think critically about them as a Christian, I now recognize as an incredible piece of my formation, and of my preparation for the work at hand. These circumstances all have served to prepare me to listen.

Acting on an inherent inclination to reflection, I began a journal in 1986 which now consists of about forty-four blank books filled with theological reflection, drawn from considerations of Scripture, lay ministry as a young Baptist, and readings from my father's ministerial library—my inheritance after his death in 1978. A Baptist spiritual mentor gifted me with my first blank journal when I was twenty and suggested I "write down my insights, because they are good." I became practiced at reflection and I bring this to this work. My insertion, then includes this insight that circumstances to this point in life have prepared me to serve as a bridge-maker. This is not something one decides to be, nor is it a matter for which one might even contrive preparation. Questions that demanded to be clarified, in order to undertake this work effectively, pointed to an awareness of the larger questions related to Native American identity, history, and spirituality, and how those factors created the present relationship between indigenous peoples in the United States and the rest of its citizens.

My Christian faith also informs the direction of this work; Christians are called by Jesus to be peacemakers, and it seems urgent that the Christian church, first, learn better how to be a neighbor in a pluralistic world. But as Pope Paul VI reminds us, for peace we need justice (1965, 32). I am convinced that the wider White culture must listen to these Native American voices with humility, looking out continuously for a common good, as people who have inherited certain advantages, who are blind to their own needy spiritual state, and who stand in need of self-examination in many aspects. Self-examination is unlikely to be as easy as one might hope and, if we are truly listening, may entail identifying deeply entrenched untruths, cultural narratives, and outright lies. Many hear the call to change, many will agree it needs to begin with inner work; not so many enjoy when the inner work starts telling them they are not great human beings. I stand guilty of this non-enjoyment, yet persist.

I have not been completely comfortable as I've proceeded in this work. From the above described unique combination of personal identity questions, experience, and diligent reading across decades, there arose a need to address the problem, an insistence that I be among those to listen. Too few seemed to be serving in the work of respectful hearing, and I felt possibly prepared. My experience, curiosity, and the habit of reflection help me to move beyond what Donald L. Fixico (2000) of the University of Kansas points to in a chapter on "The Urban Indian Identity Crisis," which opens with an unattributed quote: "My soul is lost" (172). Being an unusual outsider represents a meaningful place in a work of social analysis that aims at social transformation. I hope that listening will change our state of lostness.

Am I Native American? It may be the hardest question I'll ever not be able to answer. But my soul is not lost. Not long ago I received a dream that I was outside a concrete and wood building with peeling paint. The landscape was flat and open and a warm wind was blowing dirt around; it seemed I was on a reservation. There was an old metal swing set nearby and the building, I thought, was a school and where I sat was the playground. There was little grass, mostly dust, as a few children ran around. I was seated on the ground between the building and the swings at the side of the playground, watching the sky and the children. One boy, about ten or eleven years old, walked up to me with two younger children staying steps behind him, letting him approach. He said to me, "Are you an Indian?" I answered instantly and calmly, "I am a grandmother." He seemed satisfied with this answer and we looked straight at each other before he and the children went back to playing. After awakening, it occurred to me that my dreaming self is not confused.

If eyebrows are raised at the inclusion of a dream in an academic work, remember that this dream story is part of an account of my own preparation as an academic to listen to what Native Americans are telling the wider culture in which they live. Native American readers are less likely scoffing. These ones may understand the inclusion of the dream account as possibly the best of the evidence here to show that I am prepared to listen. Scoffing is evidence of smugness and its settled, stale confidence.

3

Social Analysis with a Twist toward Healing

IF A TREE DROPS OUT OF INDIAN COUNTRY AND ONTO FX HULU, WILL WHITE AMERICA HEAR IT?

It has been suggested, above, that the dominant culture within the United States, including the church, the academy, and those interested in neither but who have gatekeeping power in media culture—none of the above have been hearing what voices from tribal nations are saying. Over several generations a Euro-American culture has not been listening well, and the questions arise: why haven't we listened, and how might we begin to listen?

Through the method of social analysis, consideration can given to what might have been missed, dismissed or misunderstood in the past century as Native Americans rose up, spoke out, and otherwise resisted the place, image, and history they had been assigned by a colonizing culture. Further attention will follow in pursuit of understanding how we have failed to hear, and what constitutes the cultural blindness and deafness creating the key problem. The reflective and pastoral elements of the social analysis method allow for the possibility of moving beyond the cultural stalemate of understanding.

Michelene E. Pesantubbee (2003) (Choctaw), Associate Professor of Religious Studies at the University of Colorado-Boulder and a student of Deloira, notes that the established generation of scholars of Native American religions, like herself, entered their field of study reading "histories of religion and anthropological studies of American Indian culture" which they knew "minimized and . . . villified our people's cultures and histories"

(209). Pesantubbee explains that she chose religious studies as the best means of changing "the way academics portrayed American Indians," and of helping others learn "about our traditions in ways that did not relegate us to specimens of evolutionary development" (209). Her word choice, "minimized" is a perfect expression of the problem addressed, an insidious *listening without hearing* of which, will be shown, indigenous people are accusing their white neighbors.

The social analysis made here in *Listening for Change* aims to discover whether the aspiration of Pesantubbee and fellow scholars that academics—and implicitly, the wider culture—is being met. It asks whether and how portrayals have changed or remain unheard and unheeded, doing so in the process of listening to the assessment and criticisms of the generation of up-and-coming American Indian writers and artists, on those questions. Such an effort can provide a window—or a microphone—into this transmission, this work standing in as a listener for other academics, Christians, and Americans who also genuinely care to understand what it is that Native Americans are saying today. Ward Churchill, an activist scholar included alongside Pesantubbee in a collection titled *Native Voices*, reflects on the generation who influenced him. Churchill draws upon Jean Baudrillard, who said, "A culture that is mistaken about another must also be mistaken about itself" (Baudrillard 1975, 107). Churchill echoes the problem his teacher Deloria decried, that no one really cared what an Indian had to say; yet Churchill adds the insight that our careless condition is of necessity accompanied by a willful blindness about ourselves, perhaps even delusion. This work will listen for what is true, knowing that truth and reconciliation are partners. A method of theological reflection upon what is heard, the voices that comprise the data, is part of the social analysis, yielding a pastoral recommendation for action.

Using the method of social analysis as developed by Joe Holland and Peter Henriot, S.J. (1980), this research aims for a pastoral response to the identified problem of not listening. More than three years were spent dwelling in the data, reading, considering and contemplating what First Nations, especially those of the younger generation, writers are expressing now, and Holland and Henriot's method of social analysis aids this work of bridge-building. Gathering these data and texts, social analysis will be the first step toward an effective understanding of the present relationship of Native American communities with the wider American culture, with a view toward justice and peace. An update on current developments from Native American voices and their success in breaking into large media platforms will follow the analysis.

Here is how taking the stance of "unusual outsider" is key to using Holland and Henriot's (1980) method effectively for this particular work: The method of social analysis places experience at the center of its "pastoral circle," and thus befits this inquiry (8). This is particularly important, as much of the data are comprised of young Native Americans describing their experiences, and further, these experiences have alerted the researcher *even during the research process* of the importance of her own insertion experience, as noted. The preparation of the researcher by experience for the work of listening to messages expressing experiences that have thus far been misunderstood, cannot be understated. Hence, the lengthy insertion of the writer's experience in the last chapter.

Holland and Henriot (1980) outline a method in which "facts and issues are no longer regarded as isolated problems. Rather, they are perceived as interrelated parts of a whole" (13). Social analysis has been chosen for this work out of the suspicion that the problem addressed persists because it has not been received in wholeness, the kind of wholeness which can possibly transcend social fragmentation. In the case of the failure of America's dominant culture to accurately hear its Native American neighbors, it is possible that a structured social analysis followed by the kind of respectful, reflective listening demanded by the method, can be a catalyst needed for social change; change that must begin with those embodying the problem. Holland and Henriot's method expects that "all the moments of the (pastoral) circle are part of an expanded definition of theology. All are linked and overlap." For this work, theological reflection is not merely the third step in the method, but an encompassing methodology that overlaps all stages of the work (14). It is possible that the "unusual outsider" status of the researcher, as described above, allows for listening with some measure of shared experience of both the outsider and the insider. It provides a small degree of overlap. The failure to hear may derive from a failure of concern, which can be the result of having not experienced what is being described. It may be that a long-missing piece for the work at hand is someone whose experience has created both a limited understanding of what is being spoken, and a concern that it be understood. Just as Pesantubbee looks for Native Americans to become the scholars of their own religions, so might practical theologians look for those with concern born of experience to serve as its reflective listeners, playing a part in the whole which may be *the part* that has been missing in relationship between Native Americans and the wider, Euro-white culture.

An insertion of one more experience-story will illustrate the value of experience creating concern for a social situation, which serves to drive the theologian to "seek creative paths that lead to new and better forms of society" (Holland and Henriot 1980, 40).

Joe Kennedy III was in 2008 Tribal Council President for the Western Shoshone of Nevada. The author was present at the University of Nevada in Las Vegas for a conference addressing nuclear waste issues as they affected Native Americans. Joe Kennedy was recounting the efforts of the tribe to obtain "affected status" regarding the construction of Yucca Mountain's deep geological storage facility for the spent fuel created by nuclear power plants across the continental United States. In public hearings on the matter, tribal nations were not allowed at the table, even though tribes like the Western Shoshone were geographic neighbors to the waste site.

I was not there as an academic. At the time, I was editor of Three Mile Island's hometown newspaper, in Pennsylvania. The 1979 nuclear reactor accident at TMI was living history, as one of the two reactors was still in use and the Exelon plant was an important employer in the area. The more I informed myself, the more aware I became that waste storage and disposal were serious national issues. After I'd published several commentaries on nuclear waste policy, the director of the Nuclear Waste Task Force in Nevada emailed me to invite me to attend an upcoming conference. I paid my own way. This is how, I, the researcher of this present work, came to be seated in a room at the University of Nevada, listening to a tribal leader of the Western Shoshone Nation explain how the federal government was not listening to his people. Later in the conference, the head of Canada's task force for nuclear waste explained the Canadian process of seeking a disposal site. In Canada, leaders from First Nations were invited to offer input. It was a dizzying display of the problem this work addresses. The Shoshone people were not the first group I'd seen, as a journalist, being systematically shut out of the public conversation about decisions that would affect their health and well-being. I had encountered, as a reporter, mobile home park residents fighting for code enforcement, African American housing project residents resisting police brutality, factory workers striking for benefits being discarded while CEOs received raises. Within a year of my visit to Nevada, I resigned as editor and began graduate study in spirituality. I knew something had to change, someone had to listen, and that effective change would take more than writing news stories. Holland and Henriot (1980), understand this, as they write, "It may be that we do not have any historical precedents for the transformation of advanced industrial capitalist societies" (40). This statement appears in the authors' discussion of the "radical model" for social change. The model "requires direct input from communities of ordinary people into the key decisions of our society" (38). The transformational change at which social analysis aims begins with hearing what people like Joe Kennedy III have to teach us. If a society—from those who are part of the structures of power to those who are distracted by some combination of earning a living and being entertained—fails to listen to its marginalized, who, then will hear? Such hearing begins with concern, and an active concern is formed in experience that creates an "unusual outsider" prepared for the task of listening.

Who Will Be Heard

The voices of a new generation of First Nations writers and artists are speaking, standing as those experiencing what it is to be Native American today, and offering insights for others to understand or respond to that experience. They will constitute a social context and will be seen as arising out of a complex historical context to be analyzed. The researcher will place these data within historical context, informed by her own experience as a descendant of Native Americans, a Catholic Christian, an academic and an American, all roles that drive the desire to understand this relationship and that serve as a bridge toward understanding and reconciliation. The very issues that reveal the need for healing and reconciliation arise in the researcher's experience, in that tribal communities reject their own descendants—grandchildren—so great is their need to reclaim the identity that was stolen, denied them, violently destroyed. Identity is today being regathered. Gabriel Horn's (2003) description, mentioned above, of the "genocide of (his) generation's identity," by cynical symbols and stereotypes, but also by "paper genocide" shows the identity theft turned on itself, as Horn calls out "greedy tribal governments" who "do not recognize many of these children, who are often born in urban hospitals, as Indians," and by this failure, "have assumed the role of oppressor and carry out genocide against ourselves" (74). Thus is illustrated the complexity of Native identity issues, a grasp of which is key to openness in hearing the concerns of the new generation of Native American voices. Holland and Henriot's (1980) "key questions" drawn from personal testimony such as Horn's and analysis of surrounding historical and social context provide a means of analysis that will not shortchange the issue by limiting the research to a claim of objective analysis. It will allow for a wholeness in "diagnosis" (15) as it moves on to reflect on the theological implications of what these voices are saying, and then to form a response.

Academic consideration of the encounter between Europeans and the indigenous peoples inhabiting the Americas five centuries ago is an encounter whose ugly fallout continues. The method of social analysis will guide the conversation through the complexity of this historical heritage and into practical action. The method calls for honest questioning of the structures that caused and continually fail to acknowledge past trauma, bravely inquiring where healing looks nearly impossible and where the voices speaking say it is we—the non-Natives—who perhaps need healing. Social analysis, then, is ultimately a method of faith and hope for justice.

Further, it should be noted that a methodology of narrative underlies this work. The data, discussed below, frequently take the form of stories. There are two reasons for this choice. First, stories have the ability to communicate in ways that quantitative methods cannot. The generation of respondents whose published work constitute data in this method often use stories to critique the culture out of their experience, which is multifaceted, contextual, and whole. Story conveys material which is lost in other methods. Stories are often the manner in which the subjects themselves choose to speak. As a means of communication preferred by those speaking, a respectful response would honor that means. It could be an offense and part of the very problem addressed in this work, to approach it with a poll or survey and ask tribal persons to complete them to help with research about themselves. Thus, this work accepts narrative as both a means by which data is conveyed and, in fact, a preferred means. The methodology is modeled in the inclusion of the author's insertion, above, in narrative form.

Native Americans, as fitting a conception of marginalized persons, are placed at the center of the analysis. This work gives a preference to hearing indigenous voices, in the tradition of what Gustavo Gutierrez (1973) first called the preferential option for the poor. The indigenous peoples of the Americas were in every sense a "crucified people" whose oppression and poverty were, in reality, their death (xxxiv). It is a requirement of faith, then, to prefer them in this work. It is time to listen to these "poor" and as Jon Sobrino (2008) suggests, perhaps find our own salvation in doing so (xi). Thus, liberation theologies inform this work, though the methodology is limited in its applicability to Native Americans as marginalized peoples. Gutierrez (1973) points to the "locus of reflection" from which criticism may be formed out of inductive approaches that "refuse to serve as a Christian justification of positions already taken" (xxxiii). He insists that reflection is "by no means secondary" and that we must ask what our Christian message means to a people in their present condition, and do so in dialogue (1973, xxxiii). Gutierrez echoes Deloria's well known indictment of "anthropologists and other friends" who "never carry a writing instrument . . . because he ALREADY KNOWS what he is going to find" (Deloria 1969, 85).[1] These aspects of the liberation theology tradition are useful, yet it must be borne in mind that

---

1. Emphasis using all capitals appears in Deloria's text.

indigenous groups are more than marginalized; they were also colonized, and this history of invasion, conquest, and cultural genocide means that the Exodus narrative of "liberation" that provides a primary metaphor in those theologies, is problematic for the indigenous. Robert Allen Warrior (2006) (Osage) offers a reconsideration of the Hebrew conquest of the promised land in his essay, "A Native American Perspective: Canaanites, Cowboys, and Indians" (235). Warrior finds the Exodus story to be "an inappropriate way for Native Americans to think about liberation" because Native Americans identify with the Canaanites, the people who were already living in the promised land the Hebrews receive following "Yahweh's command to mercilessly annihilate the indigenous population" (236–37).

Therefore, the method of placing marginalized voices at the center of an inquiry is useful, while the Exodus metaphor for liberation clearly is not. The method of social analysis undertaken here asserts the primacy of listening reflectively, and therefore, subjects itself to these marginalized voices as central and authoritative, without claiming prior knowledge of what they have to say, and further, very deliberately seeking to set aside those assumptions derided by Deloria and his students.

Research Data and Method

Research data for *Listening for Change* took the form of the published writing of young Native Americans, a new body of which is presently emerging. These works, representing the voices of a new generation of the indigenous in the Americas, are the texts which constituted the data. No single Native voice was considered a mandated voice speaking for all, since there are hundreds of tribes, individual sovereign nations, and there exists disagreement among them. However, this did not negate the possibility of hearing something significant for the research problem. By focusing on the body of recently published works from young Native writers, common messages could be discerned. The works of these young people have been published and are endorsed by elder writers, scholars and indigenous leaders. The act of publication indicates that in some manner these voices can be representative. As with any other set of data, these texts offer contrasts, similarities, and irregularities. The data also included venues of expression that the newest generation is using, such as blogs, social media, and film. It will include short videos from comedy-drama group "the 1491s" (the1491s 2013), including "The Indian Store" and the group's video reading of a poem by 1491s member Ryan Red Corn, "Bad Indians" (2011a), and others. Online venues like YouTube has made accessing their expressions possible in a way that it was hardly imaginable in the recent past. The indigenous artists who comprised the 1491s, with others, have since the time of this research created the FX on Hulu series *Reservation Dogs*, under the directorship of Sterlin Harjo (2022). The already acclaimed work will be given its own chapter for consideration, below.

The method of social analysis calls for drawing connections between what these data show and the historical context from which the voices constituting the data emerge. The voices, then, became more than individual anecdotes, but help form a web of connection of isolated data, enabling explanations of "why things are the way they are" (Holland and Henriot 1980, 10). Social analysis places the researcher in the role of observer as she considers the works of these Native American writers. All data represented voices who have in some way reflected upon the experience of being Native American today, in the United States, and who are making statements about their experience. In gathering individual narratives, I was alert for larger narratives and recurrent themes emerging from the texts—the term used in its broad academic sense—which constitute the data.

Data were selected for inclusion with a view to variation of form and content, tribal background, and social situation, with the intention of listening in a manner more broadly than narrowly focused. This study could not cover deeply all issues related to Native Americans and the wider culture; mascots, appropriation, sovereignty, urbanism, language loss, government policy, religious practice, even high suicide rates; each represents a topic which itself could serve as the subject of larger, separate research. Chosen data were selected with attention to those who speak to matters of history, identity, social structures, and who offer suggestions for change or action. The research looked for what topics Native Americans choose to speak on. It aimed to remain open to messages that constitute the unexpected, as one part of the problem is the matter of what has *not* been heard due to a failure to listen, due to the problem of feeling or thinking, even unconsciously, that we already know.

A primary inquiry of this work is: What does this Native writer or artist want his or her intended audience to understand? What does this writer seem to want me—whether as academic, Christian or a white American—to understand? Some sources are scholars at universities, while others are bloggers or artists and poets expressing something about being Native American in the twenty-first century. The researcher's responses to the data were reflected upon in informal writing first, held until all data were heard; responses were only then reviewed and considered for larger themes emerging.

Social science research, a broad category into which this research method falls, by definition, studies people and their communities. It is an unfortunate state when historical dehumanization of peoples leaves whole communities traumatized and wary of efforts to in any way study their culture. This is clearly the case, as was noted above in Deloria's (1969) scathing essay on anthropologists as cultural colonizers. The generation schooled by Deloria, represented by currently active scholars—a number of whom were his students, and others who are students of his work—echo their teacher's offense at "the fundamental thesis of the anthropologist, . . . that people are objects for observation . . . for experimentation" (86). A relationship of trust must be forged before any study of a community can be successful, accepted by the community as respectful in nature and beneficial to themselves. It was outside the means of this research to invest in the physical and financial demands that forming such a bond, over much time, would have required. Thus, "Living among the natives" whether as insider or outsider is not appropriate here, where colonization over centuries has left a trail of mistrust. When considering a young generation that is finding its voice in the wider culture, it seems respectful to attend and observe as one who does not know, and as one with no agenda other than to understand with an openness to self-examination, and perhaps to facilitate healing among all parties, but first for those who are bereft of the ability to listen. Again, as shown above, the researcher as "unusual outsider" may be what is demanded, due to an activated concern borne of experience. As Christian Scharen and Aana Marie Vigen (2011) note, theology "is not a system of thought . . . it is a visceral and sensual response to hurts and harms" (66). With this in mind, the research design aimed at hearing a group of persons whose expression it sought to understand, and whom it expected had something important to tell, rather than intending to observe research subjects.

In consideration of data selected among indigenous communicators, there was further cause for using data in the form of published writers; reasons also informed by respect to those speaking. Earlier generations of practical theologians and social scientists may have had to do the work of an anthropologist to gather these stories at all; the stories existed for the tribal community, not as data. Yet today's voices are clearly speaking to the academy, to the church and to an American society that can't seem to see past its own either romanticized or degraded images of the Indian (Deloria 1969, 10). Upcoming chapters will show this distorted view of the indigenous as a primary underlying theme heard from "these Native voices."

Today's Native American voice can be found in print and in brick and mortar galleries as well as on digital display, and now on digital demand. As the purpose of this dissertation was ultimately to deepen understanding through social analysis and theological reflection, online sources, especially social media, provided a valuable opportunity. The Internet also represented an appropriate distance, a hearing of those speaking not as academic eavesdropper but as part of an audience that the speaker has intended be present and receptive. This expectation of an audience, the invitation to see and hear that is embedded in any act of posting in online media, has made listening to Native Americans possible in a way that arguably has not existed before the twenty-first century. It is qualitatively different than being observed as the exotic other, which is not appreciated, but is resisted, and anything that even resembles it may be eschewed, due to "Native suspicion of all academic projects" (Owen 2008, 157). Problematic in collecting data then, especially anything akin to anthropological research of indigenous communities, has been mistrust of the White, outside researcher. Scharen and Vigen (2011) acknowledge this in *Ethnology as Christian Theology and Ethics*, pointing to the quandary of human research that puts the researcher in a seemingly superior position to the subject who is studied (22). Further, the ethnographer or social scientist stands to gain from the ethnographic research, and their subjects know this. The anthropologist in the end will publish the research and be granted a degree or recognition that means more power and status for them. Even when following what seem to be the most respectful practices possible, the fact of going in as a researcher to study tribes is an affront, given the traumatic history of colonization's exploitive relations with First Nations. As noted above, mistrust of the colonizer is deeply embedded in the tribal cultures, the degree depending on the community and its history of colonization. In terms of relationship, whether individual-to-individual, community-to-community, or culture-to-culture, as noted above, when there is a wound, it must be addressed. There is little to do on the part of the offender—in this case, any White, non-Native researcher—except to humbly listen. Expression online has shifted the dynamics of what it means to notice and attend to the indigenous is ways that this research recognizes and celebrates for the empowerment it facilitates. As noted earlier, listening has taken place with deference, exercising a preferential option for the speaker, but online publications, video data, have the ability to dethrone the researcher and put her in her place as listener.. As an unusual outsider, a researcher sensitive to the context and the historic crimes that created this mistrust, can accept that a one-way speaking of the data is appropriate and overdue.

By choosing data that appear online and are published, then, the research could proceed in deference for what the speaker is choosing to say, as opposed to placing questionnaires before a respondent. While questionnaire and survey research designs are perfectly valid and valuable in many other situations, it was deliberately abandoned here for the reasons stated, namely to allow for self-determination on the part of those speaking the data. The Internet enables platforms for expression undreamed of when Deloria's *Custer Died for Your Sins* was published in 1969. And again, it is presumed that those creating videos for YouTube and social media are inviting someone to watch, read, and listen.

Because the problem at hand is the relationship between indigenous peoples in the United States and the culture in which they find themselves—a relationship at once foreign and familiar—data sources were selected based on content; that is, voices that have chosen to speak regarding this American social-cultural relationship will be preferred as data for this very reason. This is not to run over self-determination, as discussed above, but rather, a necessary limitation of the scope of this work. Specifically, writers were selected from among recently published anthologies of essays such as *Genocide of the Mind,* and *Native Voices: American Indian Identity and Resistance.* Novelist and children's author Sherman Alexie, and Cherokee scholar Adrienne Keene, Ph.D., who created Nativeappropriations.com are considered. Also included is extensive attention to Indian Country Today Media Network, a popular tribal communities news and opinion website. Film data include a recent releases depicting Native Americans and a film titled *Songs My Brother Taught Me*, an award-winner at the 2015 Sundance Film Festival.

Conversation partners, accompanying these younger voices and providing a wider cultural context were the prior generation's widely accepted voices. These are respected academics and writers who are acknowledged by Native Americans as in some way speaking for American Indians. This will include the late Vine Deloria Jr. and scholars whom Deloria deeply influenced, including George E. "Tink" Tinker of the Iliff School of Theology. Theologian and Episcopalian Bishop and Native Elder Steven Charleston (Choctaw). Charleston's (2015b) work includes accounts of attempts to live between cultures and "religions" and of his own such crisis as a younger man (4). He published two more books in 2023, along with the work of Joy Harjo (Muscogee), who became the twenty-third United States Poet Laureate in 2019. Also among this group of academic and literary elders are novelists like Leslie Marmon Silko (Laguna Pueblo) (1977) and poet and literary critic Paula Gunn Allen (Laguna Pueblo) (1989). Tinker was among the editors of the *Native Voices* anthology and is also one of the essayists included. An essay from Silko is included in the *Genocide of the Mind* anthology. As such, she and Tinker represent a living elder influence upon the generation they are presently influencing, actors in contemporary Native history. This group of informants is set apart from the younger voices included in the data only by virtue of their already being influencers of culture, both that of the tribal communities out of which come the newest generation of writers, and the wider academic and Western culture to whom they also clearly speak. They attained their varied platforms from which to speak as Native Americans before digital platforms existed.

Historic voices such as Charles Eastman, and the popular rendition of what became a stereotypical "Indian voice" embodied in *Black Elk Speaks*, have been considered, as well as part of the context from which connections will be made. These elder voices reach into the present and must be included as conversation partners, but not as part of the research data constituted by the newer, less established voices who are describing a new experience of being Native in the twenty-first century.

Reflective Listening, the Essential Tool

The Christian church cannot declare when and whether it has done enough in response to its role in colonization, so culturally embedded has it been within the systems of power and repression responsible for suffering among those indigenous to the United States of America. Nor can anyone else partaking in a postcolonial cultural blindness and deafness evade responsibility while Native Americans continue to suffer from what some consider "genocide of a generation's identity" (Moore 2003, 63). All must listen for that affirmation that says, "Yes, you have heard well. We think you have begun to understand." The true insider, the colonized, must give this confirmation (Schreiter 1985, 41). We, Euro-descended America, are not there. The church is not there, nor is the American academy, nor U.S. government agencies. Neither are consumers buying plastic-wrapped dreamcatchers from chain retailers or eating at popular chain restaurants that use ceremonial Indian items as decor. Listening must be done with respectful attention to the voices of the newest generation of Native American writers and artists. Scholars, Christians, and caring Americans might possibly begin to see themselves more clearly, and may find a new way of understanding their relationship with Native Americans. By placing the experience of these young First Nations people at the center of this inquiry, by attending to the insights they offer, and by utilizing the method of social analysis, an answer can emerge to the question: How, in the twenty-first century, might a continuing estrangement be healed between a colonizer American culture, and the indigenous peoples whom our ancestors colonized?

In any effort to understand the issue of relationships with Native American communities, those embedded in the wider culture—however well informed we consider ourselves to be on the issue—are likely functioning with outmoded models. This is, of course, an inescapable condition, in the sense that social conditions are constantly changing (Holland and Henriot 1980, 17). Academics, pastors, and socially conscious leaders and citizens may have moved beyond the old stereotypes of feathered-and-painted Indians on the Plains, and discarded the "exotic other" model, and the suggestion that Native American spirituality is to be sought out as "hipper" and deeper than "irrelevant Christianity" (Tinker 2008, 85). However, the experience of today's Native American, as currently expressed, requires a renewed, rigorous social analysis. A renewed understanding can begin with a backward look in order to grasp the history that formed each of the above ways of understanding—or of not understanding—Native Americans, as well as comprehending the present experience of indigenous peoples. This phenomenological aspect exists both for the colonized and the colonizer: it is possible both need to throw off internalized lies about themselves.

4

Deliberate Deafness
A History of Non-Hearing

"THE CRIME SCENE THAT IS NORTH AMERICA" (2014)

History shows a series of action plans mutating over decades as one approach to what was called the Indian problem created new problems, as the newcomer colonizer found the Indian still has not disappeared. Awareness of a Native American understanding of history and consideration of the present social situation of Native Americans in the United States is imperative. It is needed if one is to attend to what new Native American voices are saying in the twenty-first century. This chapter considers both. Historic relations between the indigenous peoples inhabiting North America and Europeans who arrived and colonized the indigenous might be imagined as a long series of attempts to, in a word, get rid of Indians. While "the physical extermination of Native Americans was never an official policy of the United States government," the fallout of practice and policy resulted in death on a massive scale. Further, there is, in fact, evidence of intent to eliminate indigenous peoples on a large scale, even if this intention does not appear in legislation, and on the contrary, the language of public policy often expressed an intention to "protect [the Indians] from the depredations of its own citizens" (Bordewich 1996, 37).

Awareness that there is an indigenous perspective in historical narrative provides context for contemporary expressions from indigenous voices. Presuming familiarity with American history as received by persons educated in the United States, this chapter points to the radical retelling of United States history as a history of violent colonization and attempted genocide. That retelling comes from established Native American scholars whose work represents the decolonization of dominant narratives. These scholars—historians, theologians, religious studies scholars, attorneys, and artists—invariably give acknowledgment to Vine Deloria Jr., their predecessor, teacher, and mentor in scholarly resistance, an attorney and academic who was among the first indigenous voices to demand that Native Americans define themselves. He led by example. Leslie Marmon Silko (Laguna Pueblo), author of *Ceremony* (1977), writes of her teacher: "No one who reads Vine Deloria Jr.'s books remains neutral. Vine's books influenced our generation and are as important to U.S. cultural history as are books by Normal Mailer and Tom Wolfe. This will be appreciated by future generations when U.S. history ceases to be fabricated for the glory of the white man" (Deloria 2003, vii). This chapter considers the work of Silko's generation as students of Deloria who were mentored in decolonization and who serve as teachers of the emerging generation of Native scholars and artists. For these conversation partners, subverting the dominant narrative is crucial to the decolonization process.

While revisiting what non-Natives may consider established history, it must be kept in mind continually that there exist other narratives that include events, stories, and facts largely omitted from, or diminished in, the dominant narratives surrounding the arrival of Europeans on the North American continent. Indigenous revisions of history name events from the dominant historical narrative differently, and in doing so, call for a radically altered understanding of that same historical context if one is possibly to understand contemporary Native voices. The arrival of Europeans is not, for the Native American, understood in terms of discovery, conquest, and expansion; it is, for those who were already living on the land, a "european [sic] invasion" followed by an attempted genocide (Tinker 2008, 5). Historian Roxanne Dunbar-Ortiz (2014) concludes her *Indigenous Peoples' History of the United States* with a section titled "North America Is a Crime Scene," which serves, with that acknowledgment, as the subtitle of this chapter because it so well illustrates this radical recasting of the common narrative. It exemplifies the lens through which this chapter suggests looking (228).

Dunbar-Ortiz demonstrates how the very language used, the choice of words in presenting that dominant narrative, is overwhelmingly problematic even apart from facts and events. When describing the rise of Andrew

Jackson to the U.S. presidency, she titles the section "Career Building through Genocide" (2014, 84; 92). In this direct and unapologetic style, Dunbar-Ortiz renames White "settlers" as "squatters" on Indian land and refers to the "successful settler intrusion" into Georgia (94–96). The historian foreshadows the telling of Jackson's career rise in a previous chapter by calling him a "genocidal sociopath" (94). That assertion is not made without evidence. She provides justification for use of the label in the next chapter, recounting Jackson's "brutal war of annihilation of the Muskogee (Creek) Nation" when "hundreds of settlers were squatting illegally on lands of Muskogees" (97–98). The language can seem combative in tone to a first-time reader of indigenous writers, to those immersed in a prevailing narrative that "[wrote] Indians out of existence" and who have not asked critical questions like whether Lincoln's "free soil for settlers" was a victimless giveaway (8; 114).

Dunbar-Ortiz (2014) is not alone in what must be considered a radical re-telling of United States history, nor is she alone in her choice of unsettling language. This chapter references her work heavily, however, for several reasons. *An Indigenous Peoples' History of the United States* is significant among recent historical scholarship by Native Americans about their own history. Six years in the making, the work insists on the non-Native "settler society" coming "to terms with its past" (xxi, 229). In this intention, its author offers a guided tour, so to speak, of the past, with a goal similar to that of this chapter; to consider how the story reads through an indigenous lens. Dunbar-Ortiz asks readers to look squarely on a past they may not want to recall, and she does so with little concern for niceties in presentation. She offers the narrative she finds necessary to the task, and thus serves well as a conversation partner for the limited account of history offered here for an audience not unfamiliar with American history or revisions of it, but perhaps one that has yet to take time with a wholly insider view.

Elizabeth Cook-Lynn (Crow Creek Sioux), Native American Studies professor, is likewise a critic of the American historical narrative. In her essay, "The Lewis and Clark Story, the Captive Narrative, and the Pitfalls of Indian History," Cook-Lynn (2011) criticizes the "romances, the thrust of adventure, and the clash of cultures that many white Americans early on expected would eventually coalesce into a celebration of the making of a greater America, a democratic community that other nations of the world would envy. As the bicentenary of the Lewis and Clark moment (1804–2004) approaches, this kind of fanciful history writing will surely continue, but not without a nagging reality check by its critics" (41). She defines decolonization against the assumption that it is an attempt to return to a pre-colonized past. Instead, Cook-Lynn calls it "a process designed to shed and recover from the ill effects of colonization. Indigenous communities and nations decolonize their collective identity and their institutions, and individuals decolonize their minds and their ways of interacting and participating in institutions" (34).

It is also important to understand the methodological distinction that indigenous scholars make, as one approaches their work. As founding editor of a scholarly journal of Native American studies, *Wicazo Sa Review* (Miller and Riding In 2011, 269), Cook-Lynn's work aims at developing scholarship and discourse from an "indigenous paradigm," using research methodology that serves indigenous communities by working from a radically emic view. Lynn's approach allows its own categories for language and for privileged knowledge determined by indigenous scholars, a view which places indigenous communities at the center of its study, and which presumes a cosmos that is alive and responsive (9–18). Her work will be considered more closely in the next chapter, but here Cook-Lynn serves as another example of the scholarly resistance to colonization that informs the generation coming up. The move to resist being defined and to create a Native American Studies field rooted in something other than European academic traditions seems almost unimaginable, but scholars like Cook-Lynn are showing academia otherwise.

Historian Susan A. Miller (2011) also discusses "the indigenous historical paradigm" that arose in the 1960s and 1970s, fueled by Deloria and Clyde Warrior (Ponca) (26). Miller emphasizes the formation of an American indigenous historiography, which defined "indigenousness" as "a way of relating to everything else in the cosmos" (27). Miller continues, "People are seen in relation to their families or communities rather than as individuals... Because everything in the cosmos is sacred, all human activities are sacred: government, education, agriculture, hunting, manufacturing, architecture, recreation—nothing is secular" (27–28). Miller and co-editor James Riding In (Pawnee), in *Native Historians Write Back* (2011), aim to free Native American history both from the dominant narrative that serves a colonizing culture, as well as from methodology that disallows indigenous intellectual freedom. The editors, like Cook-Lynn, insist upon "the right of an indigenous community to apply its own standards to the use of its knowledge" (16). Such a right extends from language usage to decisions about privileged knowledge and intellectual property. Every story encountered by a scholar of Native American life is not necessarily appropriate for sharing, writes Miller. The collection of Native-written essays decolonizes history, or "writes back" by, for example, re-naming reservations as "concentration camps" and by referring to population removals as "death marches" (23; 117). It is critical to understand the presence of a scholarship of decolonization coming from American Indian scholars, in order to consider current expressions from younger Native voices. Chapters following this one will show these themes emerging from the data.

Another key elder voice in this effort to re-conceptualize Native American history and enable a hearing of today's young Native voices, is retired Iliff School of Theology professor of Native American Studies George E. Tinker (Osage/Cherokee), mentioned previously. Tinker writes as a theologian applying indigenous methodology, insisting on the radically altered perspective of his teacher Deloria. Tinker (2008), in *American Indian Liberation*, aims at a comprehensive decolonization, beginning with language and punctuation, but extending to radical truth-telling, an unmasking of the dominant Euro-American narratives that support continued cultural colonization of indigenous peoples, as well as "a theology of sovereignty" (57). Like Miller and Dunbar-Ortiz, Tinker shuns using terminology with which readers from the dominant culture are comfortable and consider standard. Summarizing colonial settlement of North America, he writes, "North America became a settler colony almost immediately, unlike south and central America where the settlers remained a minority of the population. . . . Hence, there was a more persistent and concerted effort in north America to deal in decisive ways with *aboriginal landowners*. The result was a persistent *ethnic cleansing* of the continental territory that became the United States" (12).[1]

The dominant cultural understanding of westward colonial expansion does not include Native peoples as "landowners" of any kind. Tinker well knows that "aboriginals" held no deeds or documents when Europeans arrived, and were considered under the Doctrine of Discovery to be occupants of their lands, not owners (Miller and Riding In 2011, 41). Tinker dares to appropriate the colonizers' conception, and apply it against them. Likewise, "ethnic cleansing" is not a term applied in the American narrative to the removal of indigenous peoples to make room for colonial expansion. Ethnic cleansing is something of which the dominant culture finds other rogue nations guilty, but in the American narrative, the Indians' numbers just dwindled or they altogether "disappeared" (Grounds et al. 2003, 290). In an essay titled "Yuchi Travels: Up and Down the Academic 'Road to Disappearance,'" Richard A. Grounds (2003) (Yuchi/Seminole) recounts doing graduate research in which he discovered a dictionary of Indian tribes that defined his own tribe, the Yuchi, as "extinct" (290). From passive constructions in history books to popular literature and film like *The Last*

---

1. Italics added.

of the Mohicans,[2] Grounds reveals the convenient narrative that provides "one of the bottom lines of the Amer-European justification for continental conquest: that Indians are disappearing" (293). He traces the published trail of his tribe's history, which he calls "the mummification of a living people" whom he says were assumed, if not dead, assimilated into the dominant culture, and thereby "extinct" (298). Grounds' resistance and decolonization takes the form of exposing language that disguises and renders indistinguishable the death by extermination and cultural genocide of his people, as well as challenging the insidious narrative of Indians disappearing as settlers moved west, as if their disappearance were a natural event.

Debate: Extermination or Civilized Cultural Erasure?

Likewise, Tinker (2008) points out that "in the post-U.S. Civil War era . . . at this late date in the colonization process," the debate in American newspapers in the East over the "humanity of the Indian" and how to proceed with western expansion, was one in which "both sides held to different but equally genocidal solutions" to the Indian problem (13). By this he meant that colonizers were divided between "justified extermination" and the liberal solution of "civilization," a broad term for clusters of reform constituting "yet another persistent (and self-conscious) attempt at Indian genocide" (13). As this chapter subsequently looks at some of those reforms and their language, one should recall Tinker's refusal to sanitize his own language in order to soften the factual edge of United States history or to make anyone comfortable. Tinker's resistant language is representative of the tone of much Native American scholarship post-Deloria. One of Tinker's earlier works, *Missionary Conquest: The Gospel and Native American Cultural Genocide* (1993), provides primary source documentation of the intertwined and often indistinguishable efforts of missionaries, military, and trader-capitalists, the unifier being "civilization." Even as he repeatedly acknowledges the good intentions of missionaries, Tinker shows the complicity of four historically revered missionaries in what he argues constituted and continues to constitute "cultural genocide" (Tinker 1993, 79).

Tinker's decolonizing examination includes history, theological methodology, and politics, and yet even as he resists every discernable form of colonization, he reveals his aim in his 2008 work, *American Indian Liberation: A Theology of Sovereignty*: "I write with the hope that we will be able to

---

2. Grounds refers to the 1992 film that featured Native American activist Russell Means, who lead the American Indian Movement and criticized other popular films, such as *Dances with Wolves* (Grounds et al. 2003, 292).

initiate a symbiotic healing process whereby Indian poverty and devastation can find healing even as White America begins to find healing from its ongoing history of violence and the resulting culture of violence that seems to have captured the north American present" (5).Tinker, himself a Protestant minister, uses examples from both Catholic and Protestant tradition in his critique of missionary "conquest," and yet, in his desire for healing, insists without apology on the necessity of "White America" looking squarely on its history, even if history irrupts conventional narrative.

This chapter's necessarily general historic overview, then, in conversation with Native scholars insistent on a radical recasting of the American narrative, will prepare for discernment of what Robert J. Schreiter (1985) calls *indigenous theologies*, or local theologies. That is, history as told by its indigenous participants provides a context out of which one may discern "patterns of production of meaning" formed by the people experiencing the events, as subjects of the history told (4; 5). This chapter's backward glance at those events and experiences will provide a framework out of which to hear the local theology arising from the data, the voices to be considered and heard.

Essential History

As part of a work of practical theology, this chapter will not go into great detail about specific historical events, nor will it offer a complete chronology. Rather, it shows a broad contextual landscape of points necessary to the purpose, events and policies that when in view bring into focus the contrast between a Native rendering of events and the dominant narrative of American history; yet this overview will focus in on a few specifics that inform the purpose at hand. History shows a series of action plans mutating over decades as one political or ecclesial approach creates new problems, as the colonizer finds that the Indian still has not disappeared.

Dunbar-Ortiz's (2014) *An Indigenous Peoples' History of the United States* offers a history of the United States as experienced by indigenous peoples[3] and re-conceives as well as documents United States history through an indigenous lens, all the while insisting that those who survived this genocide have done so by and with resistance. Dunbar-Ortiz writes, "Non-indians must know this in order to more accurately understand the

---

3. *An Indigenous People's History of the United States* by Roxanne Dunbar-Ortiz (2014) represents rigorous scholarship as a work that dares present its own narrative framework, re-telling the story and uprooting what she calls the "unconscious 'manifest destiny'" most Americans have learned (2).

history of the United States" (xii). She asserts that the evidence is mounting in support of the use of the word "genocide" and her work places the term prominently as the partner of colonialism and its "path of greed and destruction" (1–2). Dunbar-Ortiz re-categorizes documented "policies of genocide" into "at least four distinct periods: the Jacksonian era of forced removal; the California gold rush in Northern California; the post-Civil War era of the so-called Indian wars in the Great Plains; and the 1950s termination period" (9). Her central contention of genocide as tacit U.S. policy makes for unsettling reading; her argument is rigorously documented. Writing for academic and more general audiences, she reveals a history that needs no revisionism but only requires some dusting off, so to speak. In other words, this genocidal stance toward indigenous people is not cryptically hidden from view; it has merely been ignored. White America has been deliberately and selectively deaf and blind. The facts are there for those who will look, Dunbar-Ortiz shows, even if no one used the word *genocide*.

A scholar asserting Native descent, Dunbar-Ortiz (2014) acknowledges, as does this work, that there is no "collective Indigenous peoples' perspective" of history, or religion, or of politics (13). Still, a record exists that departs deeply from the popular American story of history and this is the narrative that Dunbar-Ortiz provides. Key points from the periods of U.S. history that she discerns give a helpful context for understanding the work of late twentieth-century scholars whose work references these themes from fields other than history. Scholars such as Dunbar-Oritz and Paula Gunn Allen are among the influencers of the present generation whose voice is here under consideration.

In a condensed account, Allen, who is both a Native American scholar and a literary critic, provides a general overview of the history of relations between the colonizers of North America and the peoples who existed there prior to "discovery." In her introduction to *Spider Woman's Granddaughters: Traditional Tales and Contemporary Writing by Native American Women*, Allen recounts those most crucial events that continue to inform today's situation. In summarizing the themes that arise in her selected literature, Allen notes the influence of war stories, "death, mutilation, indignity, and community destruction" (1989, 20). She anticipates transformation coming out of either defeat or victory, as loss seems pandemic in the women's literary works. Allen's perspective, then, offers an appropriate introduction to the historical context on which this chapter draws as a foundation for understanding a new generation's messages (1989, 20).

Alongside Allen's general view, though, Dunbar-Oritz presents the detailed work of a historian. Together, their works can help to navigate the landscape of indigenous American history. Dunbar-Ortiz (2014) gathers and places the pieces regularly left out of the popular North American narrative and identifies a broad cultural inheritance of ideologies that activated the bloody means by which Indigenous peoples were not merely put off their lands to make room for settlement, but were destroyed with malice (77). Allen's historic summary points to the key events of which one must be aware in order to begin to comprehend present-day Native voices, as her intent is to help readers understand Native-authored literature. Dunbar-Oritz gives the horrific close-up. It is useful, then, to use Allen's overview points to sort through the larger landscape provided by Dunbar-Oritz, and to note the emphases of Dunbar-Ortiz on events that have been de-emphasized by the wider colonizing culture. It is instructive to see where the alternative spotlight is focused.

Both scholars attend to the conditions in Europe that drove people overseas into the Americas (Allen 1989, 9–10). Bearing in mind the wars, poverty, and persecution that existed on the White man's first continent seems important before looking to what happened later in the Americas. Dunbar-Ortiz (2014) points backward to a "culture of conquest" that began in the Christian Crusades against Muslims, continued post-Reformation with England's invasion and attempted extermination of the indigenous peoples of Ireland.[4] The religious wars of the Crusades were transformed, she insists, under the influence of Social Darwinism, into a "genocidal mode of colonialism" which, it should be noted, was not a new idea at the time of colonial settlement in North American (39).

From the perspective of indigenous peoples, the massive trans-Atlantic migration and subsequent "encounter" are not neutral facts. The intent to take inhabited land cannot be so, for Dunbar-Ortiz. The historian poignantly reminds her readers, "People do not hand over their land, resources, children, and futures without a fight, and that fight is met with violence" (Dunbar-Ortiz 2014, 8). The historical fact of an element of indigenous self-defense must be kept in mind if one is to gain any deeper understanding of the present and move beyond the framework of understanding that sustains tense relations between indigenous Americans and the American descendants of Europeans. People were living on the land, raising children, existing, functioning, flourishing, when Europeans arrived in the Americas.

4. In her chapter "Culture of Conquest," Dunbar-Ortiz offers a rigorously documented history of the popular science and literature that considered the Irish "biologically inferior," a "lower species," and that justified an English invasion by means of sending colonists from Scotland and Wales to settle Northern Ireland. She argues that this prepared a population of settlers to do the same work on the American frontier, exterminating the next "inferior" indigenous population, and that the Scots-Irish comprised a disproportionate number of those frontiersmen glorified in the popular American narrative (2014, 38–39).

The arrival of foreigners who intended to inhabit and own their homes must be considered from the view of those already inhabiting the land. In such a situation, most people will prepare to fight the invader, and Dunbar-Ortiz (2014) points out that any resistance from indigenous inhabitants was met with the violence that was institutional to European colonizing culture: "In the United States, the legacy of settler colonialism can be seen in the endless wars of aggression and occupations; the trillions spent on war machinery, military bases, and personnel instead of social services and quality public education" (229). It is important, then, to bear in mind that the distant European past, the history of colonization, and the present are one history of violence and exploitation in her "crime scene" account.

Once more, a historical context is needed out of which to answer the question: What are contemporary Native American voices telling us that, we, the wider culture in which Native American communities exist, have not heard? Some essential eras in the historical context include: Removal and expansion, allotment of land and formation of reservations, the boarding school movement and other attempts at assimilation, tribal termination, the rise of resistance, and urbanization. These will be discussed here, accompanied by some primary source material, to make room for a broadened hearing of the history that confronts the established narrative.

Removal and Expansion: Scrubbing Violence from the Story

First among general movements to be understood are removal and expansion, that is, the forced removal of indigenous people from the places in which they were living, and the expansion of European colonist settlement into those same places. Removal is crucial as the backdrop to all Native history in what became the United States. America was built on removal, a term which, it must continuously be borne in mind, is a sanitization of history. To speak of "removing" an object from its place does not necessarily bring to mind violence. Yet, removing populations of human beings from their homes is hard to imagine without an element of coercion if not blatant violence. Also, a key idea that non-Native persons, no matter how educated, may need to re-cast from the abiding narrative is the belief that Europeans came upon a mostly "pristine wilderness," uninhabited, virgin territory, there for the taking (Dunbar-Ortiz 2014, 45–46). While one may be aware that the land was inhabited, the degree of indigenous management and cultivation of the land is largely absent from history, as are accounts of travel networks, political systems, and towns. According to Dunbar-Ortiz (2014), "Had North America been a wilderness, undeveloped, without roads, and uncultivated, it might still be so, for the European colonists could not have survived" (46). Donna Martinez et al. (2016) points out that "American Indians built the first cities on the continent at such places as Cahokia, Mesa Verde, Chaco Canyon, and Taos Pueblo. When the Spanish first found it, Tenochtitlan [today Mexico City], with an estimated 200,000 people, was larger than London, England" (vii). These facts of history demonstrate some measure of the degree of our mythic narrative; even Americans who consider themselves educated in United States history may find them surprising.

The survival of the descendants of North America's indigenous peoples represents an affront to a narrative that either ignores them, claims they "disappeared," or otherwise dismisses their existence as fully human inhabitants of the land that was to be settled. With the first colonies established, expansion of White settlements followed into the nineteenth century. As one government document vaguely informs the public, "American settlers pushed west" (National Park Service, n.d.). This commonly applied verbiage can be the beginning and the end of the popular image, allowing for a few imagined encounters between wagon trains of European settlers and Indians. In 1826, James Fenimore Cooper's novel, *Last of the Mohicans: A Narrative of 1757* presented an official public narrative, plainly named "mythology" by Dunbar-Oritz (2014), of the supposed disappearance of indigenous peoples, a "disappearance" that made way for the settler "pushing into" new territory (71). Even prior to the "push west," rival empires competing for land acquisition varied in their means of enabling expansion, overstepping one another, but treating the indigenous inhabitants as something less than civilized nations to whom they owed proper diplomacy, as essentially non-existent except for the fact that their homes, villages, and bodies were in the way of settlement. For example, it is noteworthy to recall that Jefferson's $15 million Louisiana Purchase of the "homelands of several hundred tribes" was a purchase made "not from the tribes themselves, but from France" (Allen 1989, 10), and came after the territory had been jostled between European empires for a century. What is known as the "Doctrine of Discovery" has provided a veil of legitimacy for the taking of land, or, "vacant soil," from indigenous peoples, based on Supreme Court Justice John Marshall's decision 1823 in *Johnson v. M'Intosh*. University of Colorado associate professor of political science Glenn T. Morris (Shawnee) argues that Marshall's decision was made under "extravagant pretenses without any basis in fact," and yet it established a legal basis for future decisions through Marshall's "occupancy of title" concept (Morris 2003, 110–13). In a word, Marshall used a theological appeal to create a foundation for supposedly objective legal decisions, harkening back to the charter of English explorer John Cabot, which claimed the right of Christian nations to land title over that of non-Christian heathens (Morris 2003, 109). Once *Johnson v. M'Intosh* was in place, the Doctrine of Discovery prevailed.[5] Its implications for issues of tribal sovereignty continue to this day.

While legal and judicial action moved forward around the idea of "vacant soil," removal of people from the supposedly vacant land continued. Removal, settlement, and expansion happened amid disagreement between powers; policy, law, and action unfolded but not smoothly or without contention. President James Monroe found the use of force against "civilized tribes" like the Cherokees "entirely unjustifiable" (Bordewich 1996, 44). The Cherokee Nation who dwelt in what is now the southeastern United States had adopted European "civilization" in many aspects; they had governing structures and laws, and sought peaceable co-existence and even co-operation with surrounding European settlers. But this did not prevent the Cherokees from losing their home. Journalist and historian Fergus M. Bordewich in *Killing the White Man's Indian: Reinventing Native Americans at the End of the Twentieth Century*, describes the 1828 discovery of gold in Cherokee territory, followed by the election of Andrew Jackson as president, dissolving any chance of continued Cherokee nationhood on Cherokee land. First, the colony of Georgia began the takeover of Cherokee land, then other states followed, nullifying Cherokee law, making a practical case for the 1830 passage of Jackson's Removal Act. The Cherokees sued Georgia, appealing to the authority of federal treaties. Despite a Supreme Court ruling that said the Cherokee nation was a self-ruling political society, and thus federal treaties apply, Georgia ignored the decision handed down by Justice John Marshall. Andrew Jackson did likewise; he contemptuously challenged Marshall to enforce the Court's ruling. The Removal Act, though it offered reimbursements, forced the Cherokees onto the infamous Trail of Tears, a removal of the Cherokee people to Oklahoma. Federal troops assured they left in the fall of 1838, a decade after the first gold was found on Cherokee Nation land. Thousands died in the removal, even as White farmers rushed in behind the exiting Cherokees (Bordewich 1996, 44–47).[6] In

---

5. The Doctrine of Discovery represents first a theological claim established decades before the voyages of Columbus by Pope Nicholas, then a legal claim forged from the papal bull. The Truth and Reconciliation Commission of the Canadian Conference of Catholic Bishops in 2016 issued a statement of response to the "errors and falsehoods perpetuated" by the Doctrine of Discovery (Canadian Conference of Catholic Bishops 2016). The United States Conference of Catholic Bishops has not similarly repudiated the Doctrine of Discovery.

6. The work of Fergus M. Bordewich (1996), while not formally academic, represents the highest caliber of researched narrative journalism. Bordewich traveled between Indian reservations throughout his childhood, in the 1950s and 1960s (400), and his work examines closely many of the key issues raised by Native Americans. For

1803, President Thomas Jefferson negotiated the Louisiana Purchase from France, but it was Jackson who a few decades later expedited the removal of the Cherokee and other Southeastern tribes in order to open the way for expansion of the new American nation. There were similar forced removals of Indians from the New England colonies who traveled through the Ohio territory, west (Dunbar-Ortiz 2014, 71).[7]

Removal must be understood as simultaneously physical and cultural. Forced removal cannot be lightly acknowledged if one is to understand the Native perspective of United States history. Removal includes both the physical, violent removal of indigenous peoples from their homes, and also as an ongoing, insidious use of cultural tools to "remove" Native identity, history, and existence on every level. These perhaps less obvious aspects are equally part of indigenous history. Insistence on the continued dignified existence of Indian peoples is a means of decolonizing language that subtly suggests a gradual disappearance of the Indian, a slow dying out, or as Richard Grounds writes of his own Yuchi people, the "extinction" of the Indian (Grounds 2003, 290). Grounds' essay, "Yuchi Travels: Up and Down the Academic Road to Disappearance," will be considered even more closely below.

For purposes of identifying key events across Native American history, "removal" must be noted as key, then, both as event and as idea, and both aspects of removal must be treated as present, not just historic, concerns. For example, a public government document published by the National Park Service, found online in 2016, extols Jefferson's "foresight" in closing the Louisiana Purchase deal, paving the way for unhindered expansion and trade routes in the Caribbean without foreign interference. The document offers praise for the political acumen shown by Jefferson: "The Louisiana Territory, purchased for less than 5 cents an acre, was one of Thomas Jefferson's greatest contributions to his country. Louisiana doubled the size of the United States literally overnight, *without a war or the loss of a single American life* and set a precedent for the purchase of territory. It opened the way for the eventual expansion of the United States across the continent to the Pacific, and its consequent rise to the status of world power"

---

example, he takes up the issue of Indian identity in "We Ain't Got Feathers and Beads," and recounts an attempt by a white property owner, whose interests were threatened by tribal recognition, to "pin (Vine) Deloria down" on the definition of a tribe (68–69). Bordewich's writing style is engaging, as well.

7. Among those removed from Massachusetts were the Stockbridge Munsee Band of Mohicans, who settled on Menominee land in Wisconsin. This is where M.B. Lang's grandfather lived, as noted in the author's insertion in chapter 2. It is likely his ancestors were part of this removal. The Menominee Nation is one of the few tribes in the United States that never suffered removal but remains on its own ancestral land.

(National Park Service, n.d.).[8] The above excerpt offers an example of the cultural removal of the Native American: Not a single American life was lost in the acquisition of the Louisiana Territory, yet hundreds of tribes were displaced and thousands suffered horrible deaths in the removal process. Native Americans are erased from this narrative, discounted as "Americans" and not deemed worthy, either, of mention as humans who are Indians, and some of whose lives were lost. This "innocuous" federal government document, written in 1991 but accessible and downloadable from a federal U.S. government website in 2017, represents a version of history that clouds and distorts our collective understanding of United States history, and of Native Americans as human beings. Jefferson's purchase and Jackson's physical removal to make room for White settlement were accompanied by an ongoing cultural removal of the Indian—both in the minds of American settlers and in the minds of Indians themselves.

Reservations and Allotment: War with Indians Is Inconvenient and Land Ownership Makes Settlers of Savages

Removal opened land to White settlers in the nineteenth century, as accompanying legislation made way for land acquisition by the United States, both by means of the reservation system and land allotment. Continued war with the Indians was not cost effective. An advisor to President Grant in 1870 had suggested it would "be cheaper to feed every adult Indian now living" for the rest of his or her life, and to educate Indian children "to self-support by agriculture, than it would be to carry on a general Indian war for a single year" (Nabokov 1999, 171). The new Indian family, modeled on European norms, was "given" a portion of land under the General Allotment (Dawes) Act of 1887 that divvied up the Indian Territory; each household was expected to set up farm life like the White settler (Allen 1989, 10, 11). The General Allotment Act of 1887 divided reservation land into family farms for Native Americans, but also managed to acquire treaty-given Indian reservation land by conveniently leaving "surplus" land for the United States (Dunbar-Ortiz 2014, 12). The Allotment Act remained in effect until 1934 and made for the "transformation of free Indians into dependent 'wards'" (Nabokov 1999, 171). Peter Nabokov (1999) describes the reservations created under the Jackson administration as "a holding tank for society's unwanted," in the same manner as "the prison, the poorhouse, or the mental asylum" (171).

---

8. Italics added.

DELIBERATE DEAFNESS

A telling example of how reservations and allotment served to enclave Native Americans both physically and culturally comes from an 1838 report to Congress by the Commissioner of Indian Affairs, T. Hartley Crawford. Not only does Crawford's report show the unquestioned entanglement of Christian mission with government policy, it reveals an ulterior motive in allotment, and in United States' policy; that of creating in the minds of Indians the desire to own land. Until "given" land by the American government, the indigenous viewed it as common to all, owned by no one (Prucha 1990, 74). Crawford early on advocated for allotment, equating civilization with the desire to accumulate individual property. An excerpt of his report shows this aspect of allotment policy coming to birth. It stands as a centerpiece to this chapter, so revealing are its words to the matter of understanding today's Native expressions. Crawford, in 1838, tells Congress:

> Unless some system is marked out by which there shall be a separate allotment of land to each individual whom the scheme shall entitle to it, you will look in vain for any general casting off a savagism. . . . Common property and civilization cannot co-exist. The few instances to be found in the United States and other countries of small abstracted communities, who draw their subsistence and whatever comforts they have from a common store, do not militate against this position. Under a show of equality, the mass(es) work for two or three rulers or dictators, who enjoy what they will, and distribute what they please. The members never rise above a certain point, (to which they had reached, generally, before they joined the society), and never will while they remain where they are. But if they should, these associations are so small and confined as to place their possessions in the class of individual estates. At the foundation of the whole social system lies individuality of property. It is, perhaps, nine times in ten the stimulus that manhood first feels. It has produced the energy, industry, and enterprise that distinguish the civilized world, and contributes more largely to the good morals of men than those are willing to acknowledge who have not looked somewhat closely at their fellow-beings. With it come all the delights that the word home expresses; the comforts that follow fixed settlements are in its train, and to them belongs not only an anxiety to do right that those gratifications may not be forfeited, but industry that they may be increased. Social intercourse and a just appreciation of its pleasures result, when you have civilized, and for the most part, moral men. This process, it strikes me, the Indians must go through, before their habits can be materially changed. (Prucha 1990, 74)

Crawford's argument is rich in its political forthrightness. He purports to show how communal sharing of land will create laziness among the Indians, but how land ownership will give rise to a conservative urge in the Indian, a moral compulsion that will serve the new nation. So revealing is this passage that its quoting banishes any contextual confusion about what he is saying. The indigenous ethic of common property, and a communal existence of any kind, is disparaged, while private ownership of any sort of property is equated with morality. This serves as an example of what "cultural genocide" looks like. Paula Gunn Allen summarized the intent of policies forming in Crawford's day; She finds they essentially advocated for cultural genocide, and without apology (1989, 14).

Crawford continues his report to Congress:

> If, on the other hand, the large tracts of land set apart for them shall continue to be joint property, the ordinary motive to industry (and the most powerful one) will be wanting. A bare subsistence is as much as they can promise themselves. A few acres of badly cultivated corn about their cabins will be seen, instead of extensive fields, rich pastures, and valuable stock. The latter belong to him who is conscious that what he ploughs is and will descend to those he loves; never to the man who does not know by what tenure he holds his miserable dwelling. Laziness and unthrift will be so general as not to be disgraceful; and if the produce of their labors should be thrown into common stock, the indolent and dishonest will subsist at the expense of the meritorious. *Besides, there is a strong motive in reference to ourselves for encouraging individual ownership.* The history of the world proves that distinct and separate possessions make those who hold them averse to change. The risk of losing the advantages they have, men do not readily encounter. By adopting and acting on the view suggested, a large body will be created whose interest would dispose them to keep things steady. They would be the ballast of the ship. (Prucha 1990, 74)[9]

Treaties reveal how "allotment of reservation land in severalty to individual Indians" led to the United States taking land given to tribes by treaty. An example is the 1854 Treaty with the Oto and Missouri Indians, in order to make room for White settlers in what is now Kansas and Nebraska. The two tribes ceded certain lands to the United States; payment amounts, method of payment and other conditions are described in the treaty, which reads, "Sums of money shall be paid to the said confederate tribes, or

---

9. Italics added.

expended for their use and benefit under the direction of the President of the United States, who may, from time to time, determine, at his discretion what proportion of the annual payments, in this article provided for, if any, shall be paid to them in money, and what proportion shall be applied to and expended, for their moral improvement and education; for such beneficial objects as in his judgment will be calculated to advance them in civilization" (Prucha 1990, 88). The provision for allotment and reservation reads as follows:

> The President may, from time to time, at his discretion, cause the whole of the land herein reserved or appropriated west of the Big Blue River, to be surveyed off in lots, and assign to such Indian or Indians of said confederate tribes, as are willing to avail of the privilege, and will locate on the same as a permanent home.... And if any person or family shall at any time neglect or refuse to occupy and till a portion of the land assigned, on which they have located, or shall rove from place to place, the President may, if the patent have been issued, or if not issued, cancel the assignment, and may also withhold from such person or family, their proportion of the annuities or other moneys due them, until they shall have returned to such permanent home, and resumed the pursuits of industry; and in default of their return, the tract may be declared abandoned, and thereafter assigned to some other person or family of said confederate tribes, or disposed of as is provided for the disposal of excess of said land. And the residue of the land herby reserved, after all the Indian persons or families of such confederate tribes shall have had assigned to them permanent ones, may be sold for their benefit, under such laws, rules, or regulations as may be hereafter prescribed by the Congress or President of the United States (Prucha 1990, 88–89).

Reservation Hoaxing: From Treaty with Sovereign Nation to Gift We Give You

The reservations had been created for those Natives who'd been removed, initially from Cherokee territory into what was then the Oklahoma Territory, also referred to as Indian Territory, until it was not. Dunbar-Ortiz (2014) placed the word "created" in quotes as she describes this move by the United States to "reserve a narrowed land base from a much larger one in exchange for US government protection from settlers and the provision of social services" (11). The reservation system must be understood as an inadequate solution among many attempts to address the White man's "Indian problem." But Dunbar-Ortiz emphasizes that the formation of reservations is today conceived in a way very different from its early meaning in United States history. She writes, "In the era of US treaty-making from independence to 1871, the concept of the reservation was one of the Indigenous nation reserving a narrowed land base from a much larger one in exchange for US government protection from settlers and the provision of social services. In the late nineteenth century, as Indigenous resistance was weakened, the concept of the reservation changed to one of land being carved out of the public domain of the United States as a benevolent gesture, a 'gift' to the Indigenous peoples" (11). The historian decries the cultural results of this shift in meaning, as the term reservation morphed to mean land being given, or "gifted" to Indians, which will be important in understanding Native Americans today. It is important to have viewed at least a sample of the actual treaty content and language in order to receive Dunbar-Ortiz, Tinker, and other writers as appropriate in their tone, language, and radical approaches. The subtle shift of meaning around the establishing of reservations undermined the perception of Native Americans both as independent persons with dignity, and as sovereign nations who agreed, by treaty, to the borders the reservations represented. Dunbar-Ortiz writes, "With this shift, Indian reservations came to be seen as enclaves within the states' boundaries. Despite the political and economic reality, the impression to many was that Indigenous people were taking a free ride on the public domain" (11). The matter of sovereignty is a complex and unsettled issue, but it should be noted here that the groundwork for current conceptions and related conflicts over treaties and sovereignty were set in place with the creation of reservations, as described.

Tribes from the Southeast and Plains continued gathering in Indian Territory following the purchase of the Louisiana Territory and Jackson's removals, or death marches. Indians made their way to Oklahoma Territory, or "Indian Country," as settlers followed under the Homestead Act of 1862, taking advantage of the chance to stake a claim on what was now federal land. This close look at samples of the rhetoric and policy that enabled the move of Indian land into the possession of the United States and its settlers opens the way for understanding Native American resistance in the century that followed. One must view, up close, what is being resisted.

The land grab that was removal and allotment was followed by another level of cultural genocide, the removal of Native children from their homes, and their re-education.

Boarding Schools and Assimilation: Patriotic and Christian, in English Only

Removal west was followed by the physical removal of Indian children from their Native homes, in a cultural move intent on assimilating them to White culture. Indian children were sent to boarding schools in the decades following the major removals. "To use educational warfare effectively you have to have your enemy in captivity. Thus, the Indian school system was developed to aid the military and 'legal' establishment in processing the resigned, defeated young Natives who fell into its hands" (Allen 1989, 12; 13). Treaty conditions, as shown above, required tribes to cooperate with government education programs, as deemed beneficial, or lose their land and annuities. Boarding schools represented the move toward assimilation of indigenous people into American culture, as Richard H. Pratt (1892), the early proponent of the movement infamously stated, "Kill the Indian, save the man."

Again, Christian mission was so entangled in this government-funded movement as to make the two indistinguishable in practice (Nabokov 1999, 213–15). Educating for assimilation was not a new idea, of course. The earliest missionaries in the Americas intended to educate the indigenous, and as George Tinker shows in *Missionary Conquest*, those Christians did so in a manner that equated the Christian gospel with Western European culture (1993, 4). While missionaries and the United States government undoubtedly had divergent intentions, overlapping interests supported the efforts of both systems, and amplified the effects on Native Americans. The boarding school movement was built on the ideas put forth in the above report of Commissioner Crawford, that Indian boarding schools should teach "industrial" skills, and use rigorous discipline on the undisciplined Indian student, under a methodology of immersion in White-European culture and a radical denial of indigenous cultural practices for students (Nabokov 1999, 215). A boarding school education was a Christian education, an English language education, and a patriotic education. In a report on Indian Education in 1889, Commissioner Thomas J. Morgan underscores the requirement of Christianity as part of the civilizing of the Indian:

> Of course, it is to be understood that, in addition to all of the work here outlined as belonging to the Government for the education and civilization of the Indians, there will be requisite the influence of the home, the Sabbath-school, the church, and religious institutions of learning. . . . Just as the work of public schools is supplemented in the States by Christian agencies, so will the work of Indian education by the Government be

supplemented by the same agencies. There need be no conflict and no unseemly rivalry. (Prucha 1990, 180)

The cultural education of the tens of thousands of Native American children who attended "Indian Schools" of this era also included by requirement the "inculcation of patriotism" which called for observation of the anniversary of the "Dawes bill," requiring remembrance "for (the United States) giving to Indians allotments of land" and instructing Indian school teachers to "use that occasion to impress upon Indian youth the enlarged scope and opportunity given them by this law." The same document, issued by the Commissioner of Indian Affairs in 1889, notes that while encouraging good character, teachers should also "carefully avoid any unnecessary reference to the fact that they are Indians" (Prucha 1990, 180–81).[10]

This history is not unheard of by an educated reader; yet regardless of a person's education level, the knowledge of most is shallow and scant on detail concerning the United States' government's historic relationship with Native Americans. Assimilation is presumed, embedded in the policy without necessarily naming it as such. United States history as taught and popularly portrayed has long placed Native American issues as an interesting sideline, with a sad nod that says the Indians "died off," as though by some force of nature other than human beings murdering one another, the Indians disappeared. The violence by which so many died is glossed over, Indians written off (Dunbar-Ortiz 2014, 9). Assimilation, whether by boarding schools and language deprivation, forced farming, or outlawed religious practices, must be seen as part of an attempted cultural genocide. Even for the urban Indians of the twenty-first century, the success of assimilation is not a given, in the sense of Native culture erased.

Assimilation became federal policy for addressing the "Indian problem," after World War II. The Bureau of Indian Affairs administered the Relocation Program beginning in the 1950s, by which Native Americans would be given the resources they needed to move from reservations and settle in urban areas. Donald L. Fixico (2000) offers a collection of stories based on the experiences of those "relocated," showing the program as a failure, and devastating to most of those who made the move and participated in job training. Fixico writes that of the 100,000 Native Americans who relocated under the program from 1951 to 1973, the majority "suffered socially, economically, and psychologically. In many cases, urban

10. Reference to many primary source documents was made possible by the late Francis Paul Prucha, S.J., professor of history at Marquette University. The 1990 second expanded edition of *Documents of United States Indian Policy* gathers more than 200 historic documents that thanks to Prucha's editing and scholarship, in themselves tell a story.

Indians... traded rural poverty on reservations for urban slums" (25). And while, it will be shown, urban Native Americans are finding ways of living off reservations and retaining an Indian identity, assimilation as a policy must be looked back on as a policy of colonization. Upon the official repeal of assimilation in the form of the Wheeler-Howard Act in 1934, Indian Commissioner John Collier told Congress the legislation would end "the long, painful, futile effort to speed up the normal rate of Indian assimilation by individualizing tribal land and other capital assets ... it also endeavors to provide the means, statutory and financial, to repair as far as possible, the incalculable damage done by the allotment policy" (Prucha 1990, 225).

Termination: You Are No Longer a Sovereign Tribal Nation, You're an American

Termination policy replaced allotment and in the decades following it, sought to end federal "wardship" of tribes and to make tribal members merely American citizens. Termination aimed to do so by eliminating tribal nations' status as sovereign nations with whom the United States would be required to keep treaties. Among the arguments for termination was the impression that assimilation was well underway already, in the 1950s. Utah senator Arthur V. Watkins, writing in 1957, explains, "Virtually since the first decade of our national life the Indian, as tribesman and individual, was accorded a status apart. Now, however, we think constructively and affirmatively of the Indian as fellow American.... He or she stands as one with us in the enjoyment and responsibilities of our national citizenship" (Prucha 1990, 238).

What sounded like an expansion of freedom or rights, or, again, like some sort of gift to the Indians, in fact, dissolved tribes and "abrogated all treaty relationship with each terminated tribe, resulting in significantly reduced treaty-obligated financial expenditures by the government and the hope of fewer complications in terms of land rights and future acts of indigenous resistance," writes Tinker (2008, 22). As seen earlier in this chapter, in the language of legislation that created reservations and allotment, the United States government obligated itself to provide many services to Indians as part of an exchange for Native Americans ceding land. Termination dissolved many of those obligations along with tribal political identity. In 1954, the Menominee Indian Nation of Wisconsin was terminated by an act of Congress that "provided for the withdrawal of federal jurisdiction from the tribe" by ending the tribe's legal existence as a tribe (Prucha 1990, 234). Legislation that went into full effect in 1961, reads, "The roll of the tribe...

shall be closed and no child born thereafter shall be eligible for enrollment" (Prucha 1990, 234). Further, termination changed the status of tribally owned, shared assets and enterprises. The example of the Klamath tribe of Oregon demonstrates how shared tribal assets became private businesses under termination, and the pressure to sell often proved too great for many poor tribal members. The Klamath's lumber business was worth $100 million in the 1950s. Previously a shared enterprise, tribal members now had the option of selling and splitting the profits. One tribal member described the temptation to sell, "It was like throwing steak to the dogs" (Walker et al. 1995, 362). Members received cash settlements, which were usually spent rather than re-invested, and soon found themselves in poverty, minus their tribal profit share.

The Menominee operated a lumber mill and the effect of termination was devastating. For example, "Termination of the Wisconsin Menominee tribe in 1961 proved equally traumatic. . . . By 1968, 50 percent of the Menominee people who stayed behind were on welfare" (362). Like allotment and reservation policies, then, termination and relocation served to benefit White capitalists more than it did the tribal peoples whom it purported to serve. This twentieth-century history offers insight into present indigenous concerns in the United States and can help explain the resistant and strident tone of much Native writing. The Menominee Nation serve as one of many examples of tribal peoples who resisted termination and won back their rights as a recognized tribal nation in 1973.

Sovereignty: Pesky Treaties and AIM

The matter of sovereignty is difficult to clarify, and few who have not paid deliberate attention to the question can correctly unravel the status of indigenous tribes in relation to the United States government. Questions persist such as, are Native Americans still wards of the government, are they independent nations, and if so, how are they still American citizens? The status of tribes is yet another manifestation of the persisting "Indian problem," another way of asking, How might we make them disappear, politically? Termination failed, as did every other attempt to "kill the Indian but save the man," as said Pratt (1892).

The Menominee Nation of Wisconsin provide an example of the historic path out of termination, and into the present situation, and of successful resistance. United States President Richard Nixon in 1973 signed the Menominee Restoration Act and restored their right to a sovereign tribal government. The tribe also contended for its right not to be bound by state laws in the case of certain tribal practices promised under treaties. Under termination policies, some tribes were denied hunting and fishing rights given in prior treaties. Arguing that these treaty-granted rights stood apart from the laws of the states within which their reservations existed, the Menominee appealed to the Supreme Court. These rights had been established in the Wolf River Treaty of 1854, but a legal issue arose around whether termination dissolved these rights along with nation status, or whether tribes now had to comply with state regulations, as American citizens. In *Menominee Tribe v. United States,* the Supreme Court in 1968 determined that rights granted in treaties and not specifically abrogated in termination legislation must be honored. The United States Constitution in Article Six, Clause 2, known as the Supremacy Clause, establishes that treaties, along with federal statutes and the Constitution itself, are the "supreme law of the land."

The matter of the sovereignty of tribal nations is one that is difficult, and thus remains; to remove a tribe's status as a nation is problematic policy. Questions continue, unclarified, as to the meaning of sovereignty because tribal nations exist within the United States, geographically located inside states' borders, while tribal members are also American citizens. The Civil Rights Act of 1968 included sections on the "Rights of Indians," defining "Indian tribe," and "powers of self-government" as well as defining boundaries of "Indian court" jurisdiction, and the effort to clarify continued into the late twentieth century (Prucha 1990, 250).

Yet, even as these questions remain far from settled, University of Arizona law professor S. James Ayana (Purepecha/Apache) explains that Native Americans over the twentieth century increasingly determined they would partake in creating their own history. For example, "During the 1960s, armed with a new generation of men and women educated in the ways of the society that had encroached on them, indigenous peoples began drawing increased attention to their demands for continued survival as distinct communities with unique cultures, political institutions, and entitlements to land" (Ayana 2003, 165). Concurring, in 1970, President Richard Nixon acknowledged in an address to Congress that the time had come for Native self-determination. He admitted then that the conditions of "the first Americans" ranked at the bottom for health, education, and employment, and that this was a result of a "heritage of centuries of injustice.... From the time of their first contact with European settlers, the American Indians have been oppressed and brutalized, deprived of their ancestral lands and denied the opportunity to control their own destiny. Even the Federal programs which are intended to meet their needs have frequently proven to be ineffective and demeaning" (Prucha 1990, 256). Nixon goes on to argue that the policy of termination was wrong; he admits that termination is no "act of generosity" but rather, that the United States government has "solemn obligations" to the Indians. Further, he points to the harmful effects of policies past: "In the past, this relationship had oscillated between two equally harsh and unacceptable extremes," referring to termination and its harmful fallout, and policies that created dependence as opposed to self-determination (Prucha 1990, 256–57).

Native activism in the 1960s and early 1970s aimed at action to follow official expressions of the need for policy revision. What appeared to be "a conglomerate of local complaints" by Indians was actually a connected movement led by Native Americans to raise awareness of the importance of "restoring old ways and raising the question of people and their right to a homeland" (Deloria 2003, 7). The American Indian Movement (AIM) formed in 1968 in Minneapolis, Minnesota, harnessing and building political resistance that included a cross-country march called the Trail of Broken Treaties, in 1972 (Martinez et al. 2016, 77). AIM's formation led up to an occupation of Wounded Knee in South Dakota in the summer of 1974 (Deloria 2003, 19). Tinker (2008) writes, "American Indians must also see liberation, or freedom, as our principal goal, as indeed it was in the hearts of 1970s Indian activists, for instance, involved in the American Indian Movement and in the hearts of our ancestors who struggled with the immediacy of the colonial invasion" (2).

The elder Native scholars referenced, but who do not constitute the data for this work, represent a generation to whom allotment and termination are in the past, and who carry forward the work of decolonization, marking a path for the new Native American generation. Deloria stands as a grandfather scholar and teacher to the generation of now-seasoned academics. These, in turn, are among the teachers of the newest voices, evaluating their own history.

As this chapter's overview of pertinent American Indian history concludes, it should be underscored, again, that no understanding of the last half century of Native American identity, history, or relations with non-Native culture can be formed without an awareness of Vine Deloria Jr.'s work. No conception of the current situation and of the messages emerging from the youngest generation of Native Americans can be formed without grasping the influence of Deloria, called "the current dean of all American Indian scholars" in 2003, two years before his death (Grounds et al. 2003, vii). Inquiries into Native studies may not intend to focus on the work of Vine Deloria Jr., but almost any reading of scholarship by Native Americans brings one to the feet of this "giant"(Tinker 2008, iii). Collections of work, such as *Native Voices*, begin with acknowledgement of Deloria's singular

DELIBERATE DEAFNESS 63

influence. Individual works, like Tinker's *American Indian Liberation,* is dedicated to Deloria (Tinker 2008, iii). *Genocide of the Mind,* an anthology of new Native voices, contains a foreword authored by Deloria. He is nearly unavoidable if one is to "listen," in order to understand what Native Americans have been saying in the last and the present century. Those only casually familiar with Native American scholarship but inclined toward a deeper understanding must take note of Tinker's 2008 dedication, which reads: "This book is dedicated to the memory of the giant of all American Indian scholars and intellects, Professor Vine Deloria Jr., who passed to the spirit world on November 13, 2005. He was a mentor, a friend, a critic, and a constant source of encouragement to me and countless other younger Indian scholars" (iii).

Deloria spoke as both insider and outsider; he advocated for his own people while possessing academic prowess and the audacity to apply it with wit and even biting sarcasm. His works address Native American social and political relationships in a singular manner, pointing to sovereignty as key, criticizing White methodological assumptions, calling for resistance. First published in 1969, Vine Deloria Jr. clarified Native history, called out misrepresentations and distortions, and upheld the human rights of the Indian in an authoritative voice that "spoke for generations past, and generations yet to come," as wrote Leslie Marmon Silko (Deloria 2003, vii). Deloria's importance, then, is hard to overstate, as it emerged from the very history described. His influence informs what the youngest Native Americans are saying now.

Author Diane Fraher (2003) (Osage) gives a broad-sweep summary of past-into-present Native experience in *Genocide of the Mind.* In a conclusion to the anthology, she writes:

> Native American culture has been exiled between nineteenth-century vanishing-race theories, which supported inevitable disappearance of indigenous cultures in the western hemisphere through assimilation, and entertainment-industry-generated images that made claim to authenticate the one true noble Indian. As a result, Native peoples' genuine voice has been silenced and their mere existence erased from the national consciousness since the close of the frontier in 1890. (337)

Writing about American Indian artists, Fraher continues:

> But Indians refused to accept their cultural banishment and there is now a spirit of empowerment that is ever growing in Native communities throughout the Americas. The prophesies of the elders are unfolding as Indian peoples reaffirm their

sovereignty and turn inward to listen to their own voices for revitalization and renewal. Cultural sovereignty is at the heart of identity. *What it means to be an Indian must now be portable* as contemporary Indian people move seamlessly between the two worlds of reservation and urban communities. (337)[11]

Fraher's observation that Indian identity is now "portable" points to the increasingly urban condition of the Native American in the twenty-first century. Contemporary indigenous people, the next chapter's data will show, are increasingly urban, responding to what Richard Nixon called "oscillating" (Prucha 1990, 256) policy extremes by forming Native identity in urban communities, by assimilating without annihilating their Native culture or connections to the reservations, while themselves influencing the larger culture in which they exist (Martinez et al. 2016, viii). In their 2016 publication, *Urban American Indians: Reclaiming Native Space*, Donna Martinez (Cherokee), Grace Sage (Oneida), and Azusa Ono together trace a profile of the twenty-first-century Native American, whom they note is most likely living in a city. In fact, 78 percent of American Indians are urbanites (xi). Bearing in mind, then, both this history of "the Indian problem," how it was addressed and how it was experienced by indigenous peoples, as well as the present urban condition of a majority of Native Americans, the next chapter will look to the data, those voices of a new generation of Native Americans.

---

11. Italics added.

5

The Messages We Have Missed

"MY LONG BRAIDS ARE A MIRACLE" (BECKER ET AL. 2015)

In an opinion column for Native American Heritage month, 2017, Ojibwe (2017) writer and political activist Winona LaDuke told readers, "I'm tired of being invisible to you all." It is clear, as shown, that for generations Native Americans have been speaking, but they have rarely been heard in any way that has resulted in respectful action by a colonizing Euro-American culture in which the indigenous find themselves. Even narrowing the listening focus to the late twentieth century and forward, it remains pitifully clear that policy and legislation have advanced the interests of the colonizer and not the colonized Indian, despite possible intentions to help and not harm. A history has been traced of efforts to manage the inconvenient fact of an indigenous presence on the land that was to become the United States of America. The term "manage" is, of course, a polite and euphemistic term of the sort that elder Native American scholars decry as part of the sanitizing of a grisly history of attempted extermination and cultural genocide. It is time, for those who recognize this history as one in dire need of change and who know that the time is now to form new relationships within a larger American culture, to very intentionally look and listen. *Listening for Change* set out to facilitate that work, dedicating years to shutting up in order to render a starting point for those who agree with Vine Deloria Jr, "We talk, you listen." It is time.

This chapter identifies common themes arising from the newest generation of Native American voices. The word voices here refers to writers, essayists, poets, musicians, comedians, photographers and videographers as well as contemporary scholars. The distilling of the messages spoken through varied medium into common themes represents part of the research process, toward a social analysis of the data for this work.[1] The sources read, heard, and viewed are here categorized into themes that appear consistently. The recognizing of these themes, then, represents the first step in respectful listening, an action taken in response to the problem of historic non-attention to, ignoring of, avoidance, or deliberate dismissal of indigenous voices.

To look ahead and summarize but not yet fully analyze, a few points should be made. Native Americans are more urban than not, yet very often maintain connections to reservation life. Many are forming communities of indigenous peoples in urban places. Further, young Native Americans are finding meaning in, and drawing strength from, group activism for social justice, and especially environmental justice (Supaman 2015). Concerned with the high suicide rate among their generational peers, young Indian leaders have emerged with a sense of responsibility for their own people— whatever their tribal affiliation—and for the earth. It was young Native Americans coming together in pursuit of their own healing who formed the beginnings of the gathering to protest the Dakota Access Pipeline in 2016 (Elbein 2017). Young tribal leaders, the data will show, are becoming educated and returning to their reservation and urban communities to bring encouragement and hope to even younger Native Americans, to those who cannot imagine a life without the devastation they know as reservation life. This emerging generation of Native leaders knows how formidable the task is (Becker et al. 2015). Native American youth have the highest rate of death by suicide among cultural groups in the United States, according to the federal Indian Health Service (2017). Unemployment, alcoholism and other addiction is commonplace, leaving children to raise themselves or be placed in foster care, usually with non-Indians. Native American women suffer violence at a higher rate than non-Native women (Rosay 2010). The sources that comprise a new generation of Native American voices have these concerns and others, and yet as they speak to the present situation, the past is never absent from their expressions. The history described in the previous chapter will continually inform what is expressed.

Each of the voices listened to for purposes of social analysis has been published in some form. This approach, as opposed to personal interviews or surveys, was chosen as a means of filtering, of addressing the problematic of determining so-called representative voices. Since no single source, whether writer or artist, can be said to speak for all of its generation, or for

1. The sources that comprise the data are referenced and summarized by theme.

its tribe, or even less for all indigenous people, publication serves here as a vehicle for selection. Written publication, particularly, means, for the data used, that established Native scholars and editors had a part in the process, in discerning that published voices are either representative, or singularly important, or both. Most of data that appear on YouTube are sources that are widely viewed, and some are versions of produced, edited programming, such as an MTV (Music Television) "Rebel Voices" episode. In preparation for the next chapter's social analysis, this section will also consider the influence of digital culture on the relationship between the newest generation of indigenous writers and artists, and the wider culture. The transformative influence of digital communication on these youthful voices—both on what they may be saying and how they are saying it—suggests the use of a radical interpretive model, as offered by Holland and Henriot (1980). As noted earlier, "The radical model . . . requires direct input from communities of ordinary people into key decisions of our society—those in the political, economic, and cultural arenas" (38). As the data are considered, as voices that are emerging from a community that has largely been ignored, the radical model of social analysis looks for a creative move of Holland's and Henriot's "conflicting forces" into the formation of new relationships. In the case at hand, "conflicting forces" may be conceived of as conflicting *narratives*, and the presence of the Internet and digital communication represent a force for transformation of that narrative that has not previously existed for this context of Native Americans speaking. Part of this chapter's aim will be to show the participative quality of digital voices that may open "creative paths" and which could provide a basis for structural transformation, as will be taken up in a subsequent section (Holland and Henriot 1980, 38–39). This chapter will prepare for a social analysis by considering this crucial element of context, the present technological revolution that is changing relationships on every level. The themes identified appear consistently in the data, and while this research is qualitative, not quantitative, it looks for shared messages emerging from the varied media by which young indigenous people are expressing themselves. This approach of identifying themes is consistent with the methodology of respect identified above; Native American communities emphasize an ethic of community that rejects the individual deliberately aiming to be a star. While some of the young artists, like Frank Waln or Inez Jasper, can be classified as celebrities, their messages make clear that their concern is their people. Celebrity is incidental. With that in mind, it is appropriate to listen for collective messages.

To listen to the newest generation of American Indian means being prepared to hear from both urban youth and those living on traditional reservations as well as understanding that travel and relocation between the two is common. Three out of four American Indians now live in urban settings. While statistics vary slightly, all agree that there are many more Indians living in cities than on reservations, about 78 percent, as previously noted (Martinez et al. 2016, xi). Diane Fraher's summary of past-into-present Native experience, cited above, frames well the content of the data; Fraher points to a spirit of empowerment, a portable identity, and a reaffirmation of sovereignty (Moore 2003, 337).

The research data gathered is presented by theme, with specific content samples offered that support each theme as one that is common to and in some sense representative of what young American Indians are presently speaking. The degree to which a given theme is common or representative will be discussed. The themes, of course, will overlap in the discussion, but an effort is made to present each as its own concern within the body of work presented by younger Native Americans—presented to an audience that is not always identified. The identification of themes drawn from data further represents long-term attention to the writing and other work of Native Americans, and to works identified even during the writing process. Each theme is presented in the form of a statement, and these short statements represent a distillation of what is being expressed and what is "heard."

"Indian Identity Is Confusing, Even for Indians"

The first and arguably most predominant theme that is echoed across sources considered is that of Indian identity; what it means to live as an Indian, to be Indian. Many of the themes to follow are in some manner related to the identity question, and so it is considered first.

Native Americans, especially younger indigenous people, find it a challenge to navigate the distorted images of the Indian that have been propagated for centuries and that still exist in the minds of those with whom they interact. The wider culture is experienced as ignorant, at best, about contemporary Native Americans, and often not merely ignorant, but also resistant to having common conceptions challenged or recast. Further, despite ignorance, members of the colonizer culture often insist upon defining identity for indigenous peoples. This is a recurrent subtheme to Native identity. Retired teacher Virginia Driving Hawk Sneve (Rosebud Sioux) tells the story of third graders debating the Indian identity of the teacher and of one girl in the class. The students have difficulty accepting that the teacher or the girl are Indians because neither lives in a teepee. One blond boy refuses to accept that the girl can be an Indian if she does not live in a teepee and he pronounces the girl not Indian (Moore 2003, 298). In today's popular usage, this might be called "whitesplaining," a term used by non-whites for the sort of audacious presumption of a superiority of understanding the condition of the non-white, by the white person (Decoded 2015).[2] What is possibly most distressing in Sneve's story—presumably drawn from her teaching experience—is how the "blond boy" has so fully internalized his colonizer privilege at such a young age that he even questions his teacher and makes fully confident assertions about Indian identity.

Educated persons who would never insist that Indians live in teepees nonetheless sometimes reveal predetermined definers of Indianness. Like many young Native Americans, journalist Kathryn Lucci-Cooper (2003) (Cherokee) struggled to find identity and community out of her mixed Cherokee and Sicilian ancestry, and within her urban situation. Like the girl in the teacher's story, she finds herself in college under fire about her Cherokee identity, scrutinized by a Lakota Greek Orthodox priest who finds non-reservation Indians to be less Indian. Encouraged by her Cherokee grandmother to simply ignore this, she continues looking for an urban Indian community identity, as an adult. She writes, "I threw myself into political activism," even as she reflects back on her Cherokee mother's "cultural bargain" to identify primarily with the Sicilian community (5–7). Lucci-Cooper's Cherokee grandmother had been a Christian yet had taught her granddaughter Cherokee tradition alongside Christian songs like "Jesus Loves Me." Lucci-Cooper finds herself and her own children attempting to forge "the same reconciliation of traditional self-identity" as her Native elders, but amid challenges even more complex (11). Her mother and grandmothers—a name for varied elder women relatives—shared the stories of how the Cherokees were removed from the mountains of North Carolina, the exact paths taken, the rivers crossed. She accepts these "sacred stories" as "a way of establishing a connectedness between the universe and ourselves," despite living an urban existence that would otherwise not remember (8–9). Native identity in the United States is complex for Native Americans themselves, and it is only with close attention that non-Natives can possibly begin to grasp the struggle it is for the American Indian to identify herself and to find a place of belonging between cultures, even sometimes against the scrutiny of other Native Americans.

Perhaps some of the most significant Native voices speaking right now are a group of young YouTube video artists. The 1491s call themselves a sketch comedy group. Most of the group's extensive content deals in some way with the question of what it means to be Indian, alongside other

---

2. A white writer attempting to explain "whitesplaining" is at risk of whitesplaining, as the video referenced shows, again underscoring this work's methodology of respectful listening as possibly the only way out of the conundrum.

questions. In "I'm an Indian Too," Ryan Red Corn (Osage)[3] opens, dancing in a headdress and loincloth; he looks very white in this parody of a segment from the 1946 musical *Annie Get Your Gun*. He sings his version of "I'm an Indian Too," moving through an urban shopping area, and then standing in a shop entryway, between two wooden cigar store Indians. The word "Hipster" is tattooed across Red Corn's chest as images flash of seductive white women in traditional Native garb, and of dogs dressed in "Indian" costumes. People stare at his somewhat lewd gestures. The hip-hop style song offers the original song's litany of tribal names as the crowd sings along, "Like the Seminole, Navajo, Kickapoo, like those Indians, I'm an Indian, too" (2012). The song is often edited out of contemporary stage productions of Irving Berlin's *Annie Get Your Gun*, but it did not escape the attention of these young artists (Berlin 2016). It's not apparent who is Indian. Ryan Red Corn looks like a white person trying to act Indian, but he is actually a mixed-blood Osage, who explains he comes from "a long line" of Indian men who fathered children with white women (1491s 2016, 00:40–00:58). His appearances in the 1491s videos is a source of confusion for many viewers, as noted in almost any of the comment threads, and this is part of the artists' message, as noted in this section's theme, Indian Identity is Confusing.

The flashing images continue in "I'm An Indian Too," offering historic images of Indians, those embedded in White culture and in American minds. The Three Stooges are seen, dressed as Indians, followed by romance novel covers, with a handsome, shirtless Native man. *Lakota Surrender* is the title. This display of images, song and dance, aims at the persistent cultural image of Indians that is frozen, left over from the past and not real, therefore not fully human. Members of the 1491s comedy troupe have gone on to create an FX Hulu series, to be noted below.

Young indigenous people are using photography to resist colonization. Ryan Red Corn's photographed portraits include a calmly defiant young woman wearing a shirt that reads "Not a Mascot" with the hashtag #notyourmascot (2015). The very existence of a need to insist on this right shows the depth of distortion of justice within White culture. Red Corn's photographic work, like the video, shows a struggle to decolonize by the insistence of Native persons on their right to define themselves and to define what it is to be Indian. The photographs are featured in an online article in

---

3. Ryan Red Corn's last name is published most often as two individual words, but in some instances is published as RedCorn. In this document, it appears as Red Corn in the text, and the citation lists the names as one, RedCorn, only so that the electronic program keeps them together and does not reference him as Ryan Corn. Red Corn is a professional photographer and published writer and speaker apart from his participation in the 1491s.

Indian Country Today (2015), a leading indigenous digital news publication. As a photographer criticizing photography of Native Americans, Red Corn decolonizes the work of nineteenth- and twentieth-century photographer Edward S. Curtis, whose photography is nearly ubiquitous in Euro-American culture as visual representation of the indigenous peoples of North America. Curtis' work represented a monumental effort to document the way of life of Native American peoples, a well-funded enterprise that provided twenty-five volumes and more than 500 images, including portraits of tribal leaders such as Geronimo, Red Cloud, Medicine Crow, and Chief Joe. White-European culture considers Edward S. Curtis a master and an artist who made a great contribution to cultural history by his documentation of the native way of life; a way of life that had already been "irrevocably altered" at the turn into the twentieth century (King 2012). A contention with Curtis' work is that none of Curtis' subjects smile. The well-recognized photographs show Native Americans in ways that helped create and continue to reinforce the impression that Indians stand apart, stoic, frozen in the past. The 1491s video "Smiling Indians" offers no verbal arguments to counter the image of the Indian who does not smile, but rather displays a corrective series of video clips of smiling indigenous faces (2011c), responding in kind to Curtis, whose work also made its impressions without words. Funded by J. P. Morgan, Curtis' work is acknowledged as historically valuable in some Native American publications. However, as noted in the title of an article in *Indian Country Today*, the work, no matter how artistically beautiful and anthropologically valuable, nevertheless "defined a race of people," and in doing so represents a work of colonization, asserting the privilege of defining the other (Allen 2013). The term "Smiling Indians" offers a redefinition, a portrait that resists Curtis' images.

Indian Country Today also reported on an indigenous photography exhibit called "As We See It." The works of Native artists and photographers show contemporary Indian life, as expressed by artists such as Wendy Red Star (Crow), who states that she wants "to show people what has happened to Indian people in the past and how native people are living today" (Asenap 2016). It is noteworthy that in her quote, Red Star's reference to "people" appears to mean non-Native, probably White people, in contrast to her reference to "native people." This is an example of the deeply embedded Native secondary-ness, which many of the sources here decry and say they are resisting. Overlapping into the next theme to be considered, genocide as not merely physical death, this form of colonizing invasion of thinking is intertwined with matters of identity.

The theme of Indian identity arises from new Native literary figures, also. Well-known author and poet Sherman Alexie has earned a National

Book Award for his fiction, which spills over with questions of Indian identity. *The Absolutely True Diary of a Part-Time Indian* and *The Lone Ranger and Tonto Fistfight in Heaven* are among his popular titles, works that have made him something of a media celebrity. Like the 1491s, Alexie (2000) dispels images of Indians from static stereotypes, showing Indians as they are, now. His characters, for example, in *The Toughest Indian In the World* are men still in love with their ex-wives, jealous of their old girlfriend's new lesbian partner. Alexie's Indians are prostitutes and Catholics, sons of fathers dying of diabetes, on the reservation, in Seattle, soldiers, drummers, and teachers. Many are urban, some live on reservations. They are college students and carpenters. In the final essay of *Toughest Indian*, titled "One Good Man," Alexie's fictional protagonist repeatedly asks himself, "What is an Indian?" The answers come in question form, never the same. "*What is an Indian? Is it a child who can stroll unannounced through the front doors of seventeen different houses?*" Alexie answers his character's query with questions that reflect aspects of Indian life, like this one that points to the communal aspect of Indian life, the sense of everyone belonging to everyone, but he refuses to give any one a definitive answer (217). "*What is an Indian? That's what the professor wrote on the chalkboard three minutes into the first class of my freshman year at Washington State University. What is an Indian?*" Alexie's essay tells of how the professor questions the character's Indian-ness, despite the student having black hair that "(hung down past my ass and I was dark as a pecan!) I'd grown up on my reservation and with my tribe. I understood most of the Spokane language, though I'd always spoken it like a Jesuit priest. Hell, I'd been in three car wrecks!" (225). Alexie's poetic repetition of the phrase is powerful, as he recounts being asked to leave the class for offering responses to the professor that caused the whole class to laugh uproariously. His character recalls his dead mother's advice to him, "Don't take any shit from anybody" (226). He is convinced his mother would hold the professor with contempt "not because he was a white man who wanted to be Indian (God! When it came right down to it, Indian was the best thing to be!), but because he thought he was entitled to tell other Indians what it meant to be Indian" (226–27).

The identity question is so complex for Alexie, that the asking goes on. "*What is an Indian? Is it a son who brings his father to school as show-and-tell?*" (227). The narrator tells how his father, after removing his dentures in front of the class, takes a seat and humorously challenges the professor on Indian identity. The professor points to his participation in Native protest occupations at Alcatraz and Wounded Knee and asks the father where he was while the protests were happening. "I was teaching my son here how to ride his bike," the father answers. "*What is an Indian? Is it a son who had* always known where his father kept his clothes in neat military stacks?" (230). Alexie's (2000) writing style provides layers to the expression of the complexity of Indian identity, the resistance to being assigned a definition of it, and even the beauty in the process of finding out (224–29). Along with the 1491s, Alexie also demonstrates that humor is embedded in Indian identity.

Sherman Alexie (2016) even addresses the identity question for indigenous children, in a 2016 publication, *Thunder Boy Jr.* The work tells the story of a boy who declares, "I hate my name!" Named for his father, Thunder Boy, Thunder Boy Smith Jr. wanted a "normal" name like Sam. Referred to as "Little Thunder," the boy wants his own name, not a name drawn from his relationship to his father. This childhood identity crisis is resolved after a discussion with his father, in which he is renamed "Lightning," and he and his father, together, will "light up the sky." The subtle lesson runs deep, revealing Indian identity not only as a matter of Indian-sounding names like "Mud In His Ears," or "Star Boy," but Native identity as being a member of a community and working toward good with others, not as an individual star (2016).[4]

"Genocide Is Not Just the Killing of Bodies"

The next theme that arises consistently, almost ubiquitously, from the data is that of cultural genocide, that is, an attempted killing of a culture by a colonizer. It follows closely the matter of identity, as Gabriel Horn (2003) shows in the title of his essay, "The Genocide of a Generation's Identity." Horn argues that Native identity is captive to a culture in the United States that relies upon denial of its genocidal history. Indian identity must adhere to images like Savvy Seminole; Horn is suspicious the word "savvy" may not be a reference to being "business smart" as claimed, but may be short for savage, like Florida State University's "Savage Sam." If Indian identity were not tied to these images, he writes, "the foundation of the United States would crumble" (Horn 2003, 65–69). This connection between historic denial and Indian identity distortion should be borne in mind as the matter of cultural genocide is considered.

Entwined in the matter of Indian identity are history, culture, language, and spirituality. "New Native American Writing," as collected by MariJo Moore in her 2003 anthology, touches on each of these areas. As just

---

4. As a work for children, the illustrated pages of *Thunder Boy Jr.* are not numbered, thus pages numbers are not provided in citations. The illustrator is Caldecott Honor winner Yuyi Morales.

referenced, Horn's essay shows how cultural genocide in the form of Indian mascots represents an ongoing, insidious assault on indigenous persons. He writes:

> When I look back to forty or fifty years ago, those images and names pained me in ways I cannot even know now. What I do know is that I became aware that this was how I feared the white man's world would always see me even though at the same time what I still longed to be more than anything else was an Indian like my elder uncles.... Savvy's face was just another Indian face plastered all over town, but he did not resemble my uncles. He did not resemble me any more than Savage Sam or Chief Wahoo or any other Indian mascot resembles my beautiful daughter or my handsome sons. They do not resemble my wife. Such racially and culturally demeaning images cannot reflect what I have seen in the physical features of any young or elderly Native American living today.... Such racism degrades not only the victim but also those not intelligent enough to recognize and respect the beauty in other people or even other forms of life." (Horn 2003, 69–70)

Horn offers specific details of how his own interactions with white persons is influenced by these symbols. Teachers, bankers, potential employers, he finds, do not see him as he is. Recognizing this pervasive prejudice as a young man, Horn says, resulted in "hating myself and hating them" (70).

The 1491s addressed the mascot issue in a 2014 segment of Comedy Central's *Daily Show* with Jon Stewart. The team and logo in question is the Washington Redskins, a reference to the derogatory use of the term, especially its historic use for a bounty paid for "dead Indians" during the expansion of settlement in the nineteenth century. The skin of an Indian was evidence of a kill, required to collect the $200 bounty (1863).[5] Native American groups have issued statements on the offensive and damaging use of mascots, while local polls ask whether Native Americans think it is a slur, results suggesting that many Native Americans have no problem with the usage (Associated Press 2013). Owner of the National Football League team, Daniel Snyder, insists his team's name is intended to respect and honor Native Americans (Stewart 2014). So contentious is the issue that the surprise introduction of a group of Native Americans—including three members of the 1491s—to respond live to Redskins fans who defend usage of the name, turned combative and required a disclaimer from Jon Stewart prior to its

---

5. A photograph of the newspaper page advertisement for the bounty can be viewed as a PDF at the link cited.

airing in 2014. It is noteworthy that *Indian Country Today*, in a headline about the program, refers to the team name as "the R-word" (Moya-Smith 2014). Stewart is apologetic in tone as he explains some of the participants who were Redskins fans did not appreciate the surprise appearance of Native Americans, said they felt "misled," and that it was a bad experience for them (Shapira 2014).

The aired version of the encounter edited out the more combative portions of the surprise meeting, and one of the 1491s group, Migizi Pensoneau (2014), later shared in a blog on the *Huffington Post* his experience of the meeting and what had been cut out. Pensoneau explains that the Native Americans group enters the room after the pro-Redskins panel has spoken. Then, he says, after the first pro-Redskins panel member speaks, "everything derailed." Pensoneau discusses what, of the meeting, was omitted in the final aired segment. He writes of one of the pro-mascot panel members, a white woman, who started to cry, and recounts how 1491s member Bobby Wilson offered her a handkerchief. The woman called the confrontation an "ambush." She addressed the Native panel, "How dare you?" She later told other media that she felt she was in danger. Pensoneau said that footage of the 1491s walking around among tailgaters was not used, and he regretted the lost opportunity to show Indians as "real people not relegated to the eternal myth of history," and "to show our humanity" (Pensoneau 2014). He concludes the *Huffington Post* blog by pointing out the privilege evoked by the woman's sobbing and claim of being afraid. "I thought she was crying because she was caught unawares and was afraid. But I realized that was her defense mechanism, and that by overly dramatizing her experience, she continued to trivialize ours. It was privilege in action. And as I realized these things, something else became incredibly clear: she knew she was wrong" (Pensoneau 2014).

A reflection that follows below will consider more closely what is happening in this very public encounter in which a group of young Native Americans confront what they consider racism and are met with dismissal and invalidation from those who propagate the racism. In considering here themes that arise from contemporary work of Native Americans, prominent from these voices is the idea that genocide continues; the bounty hunting of Indians may have occurred a century and a half ago, but the failure to acknowledge the horror of the mass murder of indigenous people diminishes the dignity, now, of those who survived the attempted genocide, who exist now, as the living affront to casual use of names like Redskins. Genocide continues when a people's history continues to be colonized. While *The Daily Show's* arranged meeting produced tears, these were not tears of shame or repentance, according to Pensoneau, who says the white woman's tears seem to serve instead as a diversion from hearing what the Native panel members have to say.

The Daily Show episode is only one example of young indigenous men and women pointing out a continuing cultural genocide and traumatization. Mike "Witko" Cliff (Oglala Lakota) is an activist with "Native Lives Matters" in South Dakota, where the group claim hatred of Indians is rife and police profiling of Natives in Rapid City, S.D. mirrors the racist treatment of African-Americans in other locations. "It hasn't changed," he says in the MTV Rebel Music episode. He continues, "They're still killing us. They're just killing us in different ways. Nothing's changed between the cowboys and the Indians" (Becker et al. 2015). Cliff and Nataanii Means travel among reservation schools, bringing suicide prevention workshops to children. Mike Cliff points to how damaging police treatment of Native peoples is to young minds. Cliff states, "[It] shows kids on the reservation that we aren't human. It dehumanizes us" (Becker et al. 2015). Canadian pop singer Inez Jasper (née Point) opens the MTV episode with the statement, "I'm a valuable indigenous woman" (Becker et al. 2015). Jasper speaks of her work with indigenous teens, helping them identify their own value in music workshops. She says that indigenous youth "need to be reminded that they're valuable, that they're gifted, and that they have a lot to offer the world" (Becker et al. 2015). The First Nations celebrity is dedicated to raising awareness about murdered and missing indigenous women. When one community began looking for the missing women, forming their own search groups and networks to find those who've disappeared, Jasper states, "It makes me feel really good to know our people are taking this work into our own hands" (Rebel Music 2015).

Cultural genocide can take the form of this internalized sense of inferiority and shame related to being Indian, the data suggest. Mitaka Wilbur discusses the cultural images that form identity for indigenous children. Her "Ted Talk" video begins by showing a Native American girl watching videos and other media on a mobile device, with images of Native Americans provided by movies, advertisements and Disney. These images distort the image of what it is to be Indian not only in the minds of ongoing generations of a colonizer culture, but also in the minds of the colonized, who must struggle with the incongruity between what they see in media and what they know of the indigenous people among whom they live and are a part, including themselves.

Wilbur is a photographer, activist, and founder of Project 562, an artistic effort to counter media images of Native Americans by photographing people of all 562 federally recognized tribes and territories in the United States (2017). She hopes to show the diversity that comprises what it is to be

Native American, and to provide a positive alternative image of which children can be proud, rather than confused or ashamed. She says, "My prayer is that this experience stops. My dream is that our children are given images that are more useful, truthful, and beautiful" (TEDx Talks 2014). Wilbur's portfolio depicts strong people, powerful figures, men and women who appear proud. Together the mascots, the movies, the Halloween costumes, the wooden Indians at Applebee's all furnish an insidious undermining of confidence that leaves Native Americans in the frozen past, not quite real, and always in danger of internalizing the distortion. Wilbur's work represents a young generation that recognizes this warping of self-images, this cultural genocide, and she is working in positive ways to build healthy, real images for the youngest indigenous youth. She demonstrates, as well, an approach that is common among the young indigenous voices being heard here. Wilbur chooses to work from love, setting anger aside in order to make room for healing.

"Loss of Language and Culture Has Crippled Us, but Has Not Destroyed Us"

Again, closely related to the question of identity and cultural genocide is the loss of indigenous languages. Tribal leaders recognize the importance of language to cultural preservation, and yet the struggle to revive the use of tribal languages seems nearly insurmountable. As a testament to this connection between loss of language and cultural genocide, Moore's (2003) anthology of "new Native American writing" dedicates a full section to language in a volume titled *Genocide of the Mind*. The section "Native Languages" begins with an estimate by linguists that all Native languages could be lost within fifty years if "they continue to dissipate at the rate they have over the past hundred years" (103). As shown in previous chapters, deliberate historic efforts to eliminate Indian language usage was embedded in assimilation policy, most notably the boarding school movement that removed children from their indigenous homes and raised them in an institutional environment that forbade use of the child's tribal language, often under threat of corporal punishment. A movement is active among tribes now to revive use of indigenous languages. Moore writes, "For the remaining Native languages to survive, concentration must now center on 'how to keep our languages alive' instead of 'who is to blame for the decimation'" (103). The task falls on the few elders who know some of the language, and those younger members who are willing to learn and use it. Young tribal members feel the loss, "My father knew his name but he never gave me mine," writes H. Lee Karalis

(2003) (Choctaw), a "mixed-blood Choctaw-Irish" teacher who expresses regret that she could never understand the Choctaw language that her father spoke (172).

Retrieval of what is lost is a source of frustration, alienation and identity confusion. In an essay titled "Don't Talk, Don't Live," Carol Snow Moon Bachofner (2003) begins her account of being Abenakis by writing, "The story I am about to tell is a harsh one, telling how my family was ashamed to be what they are: Abenakis." The writer acknowledges "this denial was for survival, to keep away insults and disrespect," but on reflection, Bachofner has concluded that "silence is more destructive and deadly than protecting oneself" (141). She explains how her "Nana B." gave her, as a child, an empty basket that she was to fill with the stories and language of her people. The basket became a treasured object, taken to college even after Nana B.'s death. But by the age of forty, she said she still had no language for the basket. An Ojibwe priest, who spoke his own native language, gave her advice on the matter: "Start with the word for the Creator and He will slowly give you the rest" (145). Bachofner has gone on to write a graduate thesis on Native poets of the northeastern United States tribes. In the face of college registrars who insist on changing her ethnicity to Caucasian and official declarations that "there are no Abenakis in Vermont," where she lives, Bachofner is dedicated to filling her basket (145–47).

Neil McKay (2003) (Dakota), is a Dakota language instructor at the University of Minnesota who didn't begin learning his ancestral language until the age of twenty-five. McKay writes of "the spirit of language," the way that language and worldview are inextricably intertwined. He believes "the Dakota language is within the people," and "hearing a speaker and witnessing the spirit of the language" is not the same experience as using books or audio to learn (159–60). An Ojibwe elder tells McKay that when a generation no longer speaks Ojibwe, that generation will be only descendants of Ojibwe. To truly reclaim language, a generation must be raised learning the language from birth, "able to think as our ancestors did" (162). McKay describes feeling a sense of urgency "to gather as much information as possible from (Dakota) speakers, most of whom are elderly" (163).

Nataanii Means (Oglala Sioux) quotes his ninety-year-old grandfather, in the Rebel Music episode dedicated to the rising generation of Native Americans. Means is a hip-hop artist and activist for "Native Lives Matters." His grandfather, who is the last living Omaha to have learned his native language as his first, tells him, "I learned Omaha (language) from people that were born free." Means, the son of American Indian Movement leader

Russell Means,[6] works with Native children and adolescents in school programs to support esteem and Native pride. Means says of his grandmother's words, "That's beautiful." He continues, "I'll never know what that feels like. . . . If we don't reach these kids, we lose our language, we lose our identity, we lose our way of life" (Becker et al. 2015). Means has been active in unarmed protests against the Dakota Access Pipeline project (Blais-Billie 2016). He and others featured in the MTV episode believe in social action as a positive healing action for their people. He states, "Seeing friends drink themselves to death because they're depressed; it's a reality that America doesn't see, and I wanted to portray that in my music and tell them that we're not all just Hollywood Indians on the big screen" (Blais-Billie 2016). Learning their own language is an important piece in the recovery of identity and esteem.

The retrieval and revival of language use is another example of the determination to move forward in a positive process of rebuilding and healing, rather than in destructive anger. As Moore has noted, blaming is best set aside in order to focus on recovery of language and culture (103). This determination to rise above devastation seems as important in indigenous discussions of language as the language itself, when it is recalled that use of tribal language was taken by the colonizer in a manner that was traumatic and violent and that included forced separation of children from family, to boarding schools.

"Attempts at Cultural Genocide Have Failed"

While efforts to reclaim indigenous languages seem insurmountable, young Native American artists are declaring the attempted cultural genocide a failure. Frank Waln (Sicangu Lakota) is an artist, musician, and activist featured on an episode of Music Television's (MTV) "Rebel Music." The episode, already noted, titled "Native America: 7th Generation Rising,"[7] ref-

6. Russell Means (1937–2012) helped form and lead the American Indian Movement during the American Civil Rights era. Along with Clyde Bellecourt, Dennis Banks (1937–2017), Russell Means led a historic seventy-one-day armed siege at Wounded Knee, South Dakota in 1973. *The Atlantic* published an article on Means' role in AIM, in 2012, following the leader's death.

7. The referenced 2015 MTV episode of "Rebel Music" was produced in consultation with an advisory board of indigenous leaders, coordinated by Dr. Melissa Leal (Esselen/Ohlone) who also served as head researcher for the board. Others on the advisory board were Gary "Litefoot" Davis (Cherokee), Klee Benally (Dine), Jarett Martiea (Cree/Dine, Frog Lake First Nation), Dr. Alan Lechusza-Aquallo (Luiseno/Majdu), Dave Kanietakeron Fadden (Wolf Clan Mohawk), Chase Iron Eyes (Lakota, Standing Rock), Simon Moya-Smith (Oglala Lakota Nation). The list includes young academics,

erences an indigenous prophesy that "out of crisis a seventh generation will emerge to restore the balance of the earth" (Becker et al. 2015, 2:15). Waln is one of several artists performing music and discussing their generation's experience and the contributions they are making to their world. Waln performs "My Stone," a song he wrote about the sacrifices his single mother made to raise him well on the Rosebud Reservation in South Dakota (Rebel Music 2014).

On "Rebel Music," Waln evaluates the place of indigenous people in the United States today, in the context of history and concludes that his "long braids are a miracle" (Becker et al. 2015). A participant in the efforts to halt the Dakota Access Pipeline in 2016, and an advocate for social and environmental justice, Waln's works include "AbOriginal," decrying the racism encountered by brown-skinned peoples, pointing to "the plight of the poor" as he raps and dresses for an aboriginal ritual, painting his chest. "If your skin is brown then you're down for the old pain." Dallas Goldtooth of the 1491s—and more recently, a leading role in *Reservation Dogs*—is credited on Waln's video with the "video concept." Youth appear in the video wearing shirts with "self-love" painted across them, as Waln raps about the "reservation blues" (Frank Waln 2013a). Another composition by Waln is titled "Oil 4 Blood," a criticism of the planet-decimating powers building the "Keystone XL, you smell like an atrocity," with lyrics and a hip-hop musical style that condemn colonization and connect the experience of Native Americans to forced "cotton picking" by African American slaves (Frank Waln 2013b). Pointing the way for other indigenous youth, he says, "My ancestors fought and died for me to be alive. I have a responsibility. If we don't pick up that fight (the protection of the earth and water), then who will?" (Becker et al. 2015).

Waln could be called optimistic, as he speaks about these and other issues on the Rebel Music episode and in his own music. But he sees indigenous culture in revival as young Native Americans learn the self-love his video advocates, and refuse hate. The attempted genocide, whether the historic attempt to annihilate whole tribes, or the effort to erase languages and the memory of culture by removing children from tribal homes, has been unsuccessful. Waln says, "It's a miracle that I'm sitting before you with long braids, connected to my culture, because I'm not supposed to be here" (Becker et al. 2015). Repeating the theme in a promotional video seeking funding to publish an anthology titled *Native Voices*, co-editor CMarie

---

authors and storytellers, rap and punk musicians, political activists, an attorney, and a journalist.

Fuhrman introduces the anthology saying, "We've lost so much and yet we are still here" (Fuhrman and Rader 2017).

"The False Historical Narrative Perpetuates Trauma"

Waln and others acknowledge the challenges before them. With a backdrop from Disney's "Peter Pan," Waln raps as the question repeats, "What makes the red man red?" Waln's indignant voice overtalks the Disney track, offering a rap-style indictment of the White man and the Indian blood he has poured out across the violent history of colonization. The 2016 recording interrogates the American narrative, asking why, Waln as a young "red man," knows more about United States history than his teachers? Though determined, Waln finds the false messages hard to escape. He says, "Growing up I internalized a lot of those things colonization taught us. . . . I can't even describe to you the trauma that we're born with. You can't know, unless you live it" (Becker et al. 2015).

As noted in the examples offered, the matter of images in media, drawn from a false, frozen history is mentioned across this data. Those images, though, are only the visible points of the more insidious narrative that many Native writers and artists call out not just as a distortion, but often as a deliberately conceived and propagated lie. A preceding section presented examples at length of the historical record that lies just beneath the American colonizer consciousness. Tribes, post-treaties that ceded land, were left without the economic means of gaining self-sufficiency and so remain in a state of dependency. A 2015 documentary titled *Generation Red Nation* shows how the poorest tribes remain trapped in a situation that leaves places like Pine Ridge, South Dakota, the poorest in the Western Hemisphere, with the exception of Haiti. Director Olga Valanos shows how a history of enticing tribes to give up land in exchange for promised assistance, left once self-sufficient indigenous peoples in a double-bind with no path toward a new self-sufficiency. The film features AIM activist Russell Means and other tribal leaders who discuss the present condition of reservation life with a view to the future, as young Natives move to cities and form Indian communities there. Even as Means, George Tinker, and Oglala Sioux elder Margaret Yankton express hope, they acknowledge ongoing trauma, knowing it must be addressed if anything is to change. Yankton, of Pine Ridge, says she worries about her grandchildren, knowing that 15 percent of high school students on the reservation had attempted suicide in the previous year, and 31 percent said they had considered suicide. The statements of these elder activists are revealing, when placed alongside those of indigenous youth.

The immediately preceding generation, who formed the American Indian Movement, declared a "Trail of Broken Treaties," issuing a "20-point position paper" in 1972 stating, "We want to have a new RELATIONSHIP with you . . . an HONEST one!" (AIM 1972).[8]

As preceding sections makes clear, the very problem taken up here is that too few paid heed to AIM in 1972 or since. Younger Native Americans are insisting the truth be told, again and again, if need be. *Generation Red Nation* opens with a young woman speaking about how Native Americans are ignored by the wider culture. Camille Plumbar says, "They'll put people into four categories: Black, white, Asian, and Hispanic. They don't even mention us anywhere in there" (Valanos 2013). To eliminate a people from a historical narrative is to tell a false story, and to be those who are eliminated is to be dehumanized.

Indian Country Today, now part of non-profit IndiJ Public Media, is important among the data, as it regularly publishes corrective stories that address the false narrative that harms indigenous peoples. Its former publisher, Ray Halbritter, was a Harvard-educated businessman, CEO of the New York Oneida Nation. Halbritter is credited with initiating the anti-Redskins-as-mascot campaign, also. *The Indian Country Today* editorial masthead includes Native American writers, storytellers, and artists whose work disrupts the dominant narrative in a multimedia platform. Political cartoonist Marty Two Bulls offers visual critique of U.S. government policy and American culture (Indian Country Today Media Network 2013). Two Bull's art challenges a deep-seated narrative even while it addresses current events.

One of many films emerging from Native American artists was *Songs My Brothers Taught Me* (2015), which used story to depict the painful difficulties faced by young indigenous people who would leave the reservation. Simply deciding to leave isn't enough for some; family responsibilities, love for their Native culture, and psychological conflict pull against departure, all factors that are arguably the fallout of historical trauma into the present. Just moving off the reservation for urban life is not so simple, the story shows. Filmed using actors from the Pine Ridge reservation, the film offers a complex answer to those who wonder why young Native Americans don't "just leave the Rez." While many are leaving and have left, over the past generation, leaving the reservation means leaving behind vulnerable family members still steeped in the scenario shown in *Generation Red Nation* (2015) and as shown by Mike Cliff in the MTV episode, as he tells a younger

---

8. Capitals appear in the text cited, as does ". . .," which in this instance is not indicating the removal of any text from the original source's quote.

half-sibling that he cares about him, even though he has gone away (Becker et al. 2015).

A significant response to the false narrative that perpetuates trauma is "Native Lives Matter," a protest movement in which elder activist leaders and emerging tribal leaders have worked together. At a rally in Rapid City, South Dakota, the now deceased Dennis Banks walks alongside Nataanii Means, son of Russell Means, and Mike "Witko" Cliff, addressing the narrative that says the Indian can be ignored, or treated as less than the White colonizer (Becker et al. 2015). Cliff expresses exasperation that, "I have to say, 'Native Lives Matter'" (2015). Cliff and the younger Means also participate in an annual march to remember both the infamous Wounded Knee massacre of December 1890 and the uprising and siege of the town by the same name in 1973. Members of AIM occupied the site in an armed standoff with U.S. police forces that lasted seventy-one days, an incident that is referenced as a model for activism and inspiration. The earlier, 1890, Wounded Knee event ended the era of Indian Wars, forcing the last resisting Sioux onto the reservation under the Dawes Act. Today, a seven-mile winter walk from Porcupine to Wounded Knee, South Dakota, recalls both events at once, and urges those enduring a continually unresolved relationship with the United States government to keep speaking out. Recorded at the Wounded Knee Massacre memorial site for the annual march, Cliff speaks to a shivering crowd, "We fought, and we won, and the U.S. was mad enough to come back and shoot unarmed women and children. This is where they pushed us to, and this is where they killed us. . . . We were peaceable, and they murdered us" (Becker et al. 2015). Elder political activist Dennis Banks, also recently deceased, adds insight concerning the passage of time. "Today we face the same enemy" (Becker et al. 2015), Banks tells those too young to remember AIM's efforts. The younger generation grasps the ongoing effects of "Native Lives" not mattering, of trauma continuing. Mike Cliff articulates for those learning from Dennis Banks: "It hasn't changed. They're still killing us. They're just killing us in different ways" (Becker et al. 2015). Functioning in their tradition of community, with no one seeking an inordinate spotlight, Nataanii Means also assesses the situations past and present: "What happened at Wounded Knee, that's our historical trauma. We live with all that. Now we see cops killing our men, just like they hunted us down in the 1800s" (Becker et al. 2015).

To make clear what is being remembered from the more recent Wounded Knee siege in 1973, an account by Mary Crow Dog reveals why "Native Lives Matter" is being asserted still in the twenty-first century, why two living generations, side-by-side, speak of ongoing trauma. *Lakota Woman*, first published in 1990, recounts the story of the AIM uprising as experienced by Native women. Amid flying bullets, Mary Crow Dog gave birth to a son during the 1973 siege at Wounded Knee. The birth was happening while U.S. government militia arrested Indians who'd taken sovereign control of the town. She was arrested and her child taken away. Crow Dog, born Mary Brave Bird and given the name Brave Woman years after the incident, lost her best friend in the fight. Crow Dog writes, "My best friend was Annie Mae Aquash, a young, strong-hearted woman from the Micmac Tribe with beautiful children. It is not always wise for an Indian woman to come on too strong. Annie Mae was found dead in the snow at the bottom of a ravine on the Pine Ridge Reservation. The police said she had died of exposure, but there was a .38-caliber slug in her head. The FBI cut off her hands and sent them to Washington for fingerprint identification, hands that had helped my baby come into the world" (Crow Dogs and Erdoes 2011, 4). For Mary Crow Dog, now in her seventies, both being an Indian and being a woman diminished her value and dignity in the estimation of a colonizing government. That people fifty years younger than Crow Dog are rallying around "Native Lives Matter," is an indicator of trauma perpetuating into the next generation.

The Native Lives Matter march and rally against racism took place in Rapid City, a place reputed for hatred of Indians. Political activist leader Chase Iron Eyes (Standing Rock Sioux) underscored the devaluing of Indian life, noting that in Rapid City, Native people hesitate to call the police out of mistrust and fear. He cites an example of an Indian man who was shot thirty-two times by police. Iron Eyes expresses indignation that there are no prosecutions for cases of police abuse of power. Chase Iron Eyes tells the rally crowd, "A native man was shot and died a day after we organized this first Native Lives Matter rally, and his name is Allen Locke" (Becker et al. 2015). Nataanii Means adds, "He was in his home, a cop went in and shot him five times. . . . This is about changing our future. We need to be able to lay it on the line for that" (Becker et al. 2015).

The theme of ongoing trauma again intersects the matter of being ignored, diminished and devalued. Nataanii Means tells the rally crowd: "If the general population doesn't acknowledge us, how are we supposed to acknowledge us? I could walk out the door right now and get shot. No one knows I have a degree. They just see this," as he holds up his arm and points to tattoos. "It's up to us to continue fighting for what our ancestors died for, to say, no, this is our home. We're here, too" (Becker et al. 2015). Means, as quoted above, extends concern about the ongoing trauma to the youngest members of his nation. He emphasizes, and it is worth repeating, that when Native people are being killed by police, it "shows kids on the reservation that we aren't human. It dehumanizes us" (Becker et al. 2015).

Police misuse of force and urban racism is not the only basis for the need these voices feel to proclaim, "Native Lives Matter." As one more example of ongoing traumatization, Native American land has long and often been the site chosen for disposal of the most toxic waste, putting at risk the health of reservation residents. A story published by National Public Radio tells of a Native mother of ten in Arizona who lost seven children to a disorder called Navajo Neuropathy, a condition "linked to uranium contamination" (Morales 2016). Helen Nez drank from a spring on the reservation now believed to be contaminated from uranium mining and its waste, over the past three generations. Indian reservations are the "somebody else's backyard" that get the waste no one else wants to live near. While mining stopped decades ago, the Environmental Protection Agency has cleaned up only nine of more than 500 mines in the area (Morales 2016). The colonizer government presumes the privilege of addressing waste issues when and how it chooses, while the colonized Native lives at risk and suffers for the colonizers' benefit.

A related example is the arrest and prosecution of tribal members who participated in the protest of the Dakota Access Pipeline in 2016, among them Chase Iron Eyes. Calling themselves "water protectors," indigenous people gathered from across North and South America, in what they insist was a peaceful protest on their part, a resistance to the installation of a section of oil pipeline that would cross under Lake Oahe and the Missouri River en route to a storage site in Illinois, endangering the region's water supply. At Camp Oceti Sakowin, the largest gathering of tribal people in more than a century came together in North Dakota as the summer of 2016 was ending, addressing the effort of Energy Transfer Partners to build its pipeline and to endanger the water supply.

A group called "Stand With Standing Rock" explains its mission as "a battle for survival." Its website says, "In honor of our future generations, we fight this pipeline to protect our water, or sacred places, and all living beings."[9] The fate of the pipeline remained uncertain late in 2023.

"Cultural Appropriation Disrespects Us and the Sacred"

At least two strong indigenous voices are addressing the issue of cultural appropriation, one an academic, another a political journalist. Adrienne Keene, Ph.D. (Cherokee), created the blog site *Native Appropriations*, from which she follows occurrences of appropriation of Native culture and offers commentary. For example, Keene draws attention to fashion designer

---

9. http://standwithstandingrock.net/.

Valentino, whose brand placed a sacred headdress on its price tag. The Brown University post-doctoral fellow writes, "I literally have no more words to talk about the ways these warbonnets have been commodified, separated from the cultures from which they come, and appropriated in advertising, costuming, whatever. I, literally, have been writing about this phenomenon for seven years. SEVEN YEARS! In internet years that's truly forever" (Keene 2017a). Keene's blog site includes a collection of posts pointing out individual non-Native celebrities for wearing tribal headdresses at music festivals and other "hipster" events, inappropriately. In "But Why Can't I Wear a Hipster Headdress?" she breaks down her reasons. Her bullets points are "Headdresses promote stereotyping of Native cultures, Headdresses, feathers, and warbonnets have deep spiritual significance, It's just like wearing blackface . . . pretending to be a race that you are not. . . . There is a history of genocide and colonialism that continues today" (2017a). Keene explains that warbonnets are restricted for highly respected persons within tribal communities, and that to wear one as an undeserving outsider "is an act of utter disrespect for the origins of the practice. . . . It's like running around in a Pope hat and a bikini, or a Sikh turban cause it's 'cute'" (2010). This post goes on to address specific arguments made especially by young people participating in what has been a growing trend at music festivals and other events. Her answer to those who claim they are "honoring" Native Americans when they wear their sacred items, is, "having a drunken girl wearing a headdress and a bikini dancing at an outdoor concert does not honor me" (2010). To those who accuse her of "getting defensive" because "it's just fashion," Keene responds, "It's not 'just' fashion. There is a lot more at play here. This is a matter of power and who has the right to represent my culture" (2010). She notes that imagery that keeps the "collective American consciousness" of Native Americans trapped in the past causes a dismissal of "real issues and challenges in our communities" (2010).

Another strong and respected voice is Simon Moya-Smith (Oglala Lakota) (2014), a journalist who also calls out the headdress trend. He offers an explanation of why so many White people do not understand what the problem is with appropriating indigenous culture. Keene breaks down the issue, and Moya-Smith, in a CNN opinion piece, offers insight as to why this explication is necessary in America, where people seem able to "recognize what's anti-black, anti-gay, anti-Latino" but not to recognize racism and disrespect when it is directed toward Native Americans. He points to Hollywood images; Americans have seen so many Indians with "long hair, bronzed skin and a limited vocabulary," that when Simon Moya-Smith "walk[s] in a room, nobody looks at me and sees a Native American. Why? Because people have been conditioned to think I look, act, and even talk a certain way, and believe playing Indian is OK . . . it's not" (Moya-Smith 2014). Writing in the context of the Washington Redskins mascot issue, Moya-Smith says that the solution is for Native Americans to be seen, as they actually are. "Courtesy of the Web, we are no longer out of sight. We are no longer canceled out of the American conversation. . . . More than 70% of us work, live and thrive in big cities. Native Americans on reservations have smartphones and laptops so geographic isolation is slowly becoming a thing of the past as well. And we use these new technologies to speak out against macro- and micro-aggressions directed at Native Americans" (Moya-Smith 2014). Keene and Moya-Smith serve as exemplary young voices, stating clearly what many of these voices touch upon.

"We Are Part of Our Problem"

The 1491s' logo is an arrow that makes a circle, the point meeting the arrow's end. Team member and filmmaker Sterlin Harjo (Creek/Seminole), also director of *Reservation Dogs* (2022), explains that this is a reminder not to take themselves too seriously (2016). He says the comedy group makes fun of White people, but also takes a critical look at themselves and makes fun in both directions (2016).[10] The group's sketches point to Native Americans as part of their own problem, especially when they play into the very stereotypes they disdain. The group's video, "New Moon Wolf Pack Auditions," shows "Four Hungry Native Actors [who] give it their all to star in the new film in the Twilight series" (2009). The irony and humor are layered as Bobby Wilson attempts a loincloth look, wearing red underwear, and Dallas Goldtooth, also in underwear, doesn't quite get the Native hair right, wearing two ponytails, one on each side of his head. The casting crew asks them to "do their sort of Indian stuff" (sterlz501 2009). The dance they produce is can only be called silly and the audience is made to wonder if these Indians know any more "Indian stuff" than a White person. A little reflection would then raise the question, are the Indians really ignorant of their own culture, or is this an act? Are they being "Indians" as White people want Indians to be on Twilight? (2016). The conundrum is a difficult one for Natives to escape. Wilson, in panel discussion remarks about the Santa Fe art market, says there is pressure for Native Americans to "Indian up"

---

10. Sterlin Harjo is a respected Native American filmmaker, a Sundance Institute Annenberg Fellow, who has directed films. He wrote and directed *Four Sheets to the Wind* (2006), a film nominated for a Grand Jury Prize at the Sundance Film Festival in 2007 and for which Harjo was named Best Director by the American Indian Film Festival.

their work, make their art in the image of the White buyer's Indian art (First Alaskans Institute 2016). This playing to an internalization of stereotypes supports those very stereotypes, making it more difficult for indigenous people to break free and form a healthy identity within a larger culture that does not see them apart from the stereotypes, as noted by Simon Moya-Smith, above. The stereotypes help create and foster Native invisibility.

"We Want to Be Part of Making Our World Better"

The above data, discussed by theme, have revealed an intention among young Native Americans to be part of making their world better, beginning with their own people, but often extending the intention to the larger communities in which they live. The data show that young Native Americans are concerned with the environment and social justice issues, as persons who understand the interconnectedness of life on Earth.

Frank Waln speaks to a group of young activists at the Harvest the Hope concert, a music festival featuring Willie Nelson and Neil Young. The 2014 event aimed to raise awareness of issues around the Keystone XL pipeline project in Nebraska and was billed as "A Concert to Protect the Heartland" (Hefflinger 2014). Waln first laughs that his grandmother is at the concert to see Willie Nelson, even though she has never come to one of her grandson's hip-hop concerts. Then he continues, explaining why he has chosen to be there, saying, "I'm here because I have to be. I'm twenty-five years old. I would rather be doing things a 25-year-old does, but this pipeline forces us into this position. We live in a critical time when we're forced to choose between oil and water. These artists, the people, these human beings, we're here to let you know that we choose water" (Hefflinger 2014). While not every Native American twenty-five-year-old is Frank Waln, Waln is recognized and admired, serving as a model along with Mike Cliff and Nataanii Means and Inez Jasper, encouraging their own generation and those even younger to follow this path of restorative activism. Their vision is one of community, working together. Jasper states, "We need everybody . . . Not one person can do it alone. We need our voices to come together as one" (Becker et al. 2015).

6

Theological Reflection
Turning Their Messages at Ourselves

CAN "OTHER SHEEP" LEAD US?

The chapters preceding have addressed the social situation of Native Americans, touching on questions of the relationship of a colonizer culture with indigenous people of the United States. This relationship was shown in a review of history and in the themes that emerged from the data. That data included examples of political action by young Native American leaders, in relation to the dominant, non-Indian culture, and in relations to their own tribal members, especially vulnerable youth. This chapter's theological reflection, part of the larger social analysis, will look toward the spiritual condition of the wider culture, in response to the messages of these young Native leaders, artists, and writers. This consideration will use reflection, as required by social analysis, toward understanding why and how we in the United States of America have arrived where we are, and then, how we can take action toward justice (Holland and Henriot 1980, 7, 12).

First, this chapter will reflect upon how the problematic matter of Indian identity is connected to the White sense of superiority present and functioning broadly in a dominant American culture. This presumption of superiority arises from the complexity of the European colonizing culture, including from a misuse of Christian truth-claims deeply entangled with the sense of being a superior civilization, with both features feeding opposition to cultural and religious pluralism.

Second, this chapter considers young Native Americans' concerns for the environment, which brings attention to an insistence from Native Americans that they have always known the Creator, the very God whom European missionaries presumed to teach them about. Native writers claim that tribes even had a covenant relationship with the one creator God that involved a responsibility to live in harmonious relation to the rest of creation (Charleston 2015a, 162). The White sense of superiority is related to the problem of non-listening in that this attitude may prevent the church in the Americas from receiving theological truth from its indigenous sisters and brothers.

Third, and related to the consideration of an indigenous peoples' covenant relationship with the Creator, this reflection will look to that indigenous worldview, whose insights speak to matters that Pope Francis (2015) calls "urgent" for the protection of life on Earth (13). It will conclude with a reflection on the praxis of young Native Americans, and their pursuit of justice through political action and efforts at community healing.

This reflection, then, will first delve into the presumption that God's unfolding salvific work in history was not present in the Americas prior to its delivery by Europeans. The presumption will be examined in light of Jesus' claim that he has sheep other than the Hebrew nation, mysterious sheep whom the Good Shepherd does not specifically identify (John 10:14). This theological reflection will consider newly published works from a Christian indigenous spiritual leader who puts forth a claim that God indeed was speaking to indigenous peoples, pre-colonial encounter, and that the creator God even made a covenant with these peoples to live in harmony with the land and the creation. The reflection will then turn respectfully to the testimony of the emergent generation of Native Americans, who bear fruit compatible with the Christian call to social and environmental justice.

White Sense of Superiority and Native Identity Issues

The themes distilled from the data and presented in this work are a summary representation of contemporary expressions of young Native Americans. Together, the data would point us to reflect theologically on the problem of the White European Christian culture's deeply imbedded sense of superiority, as this problem is noted contiguously to the identity issues described across the data. This is not necessarily to speak identically of an ideology of white supremacy, which may be a closely related symptom or outgrowth, a systematization of the attitude. Nor is this reflection merely a matter of defining racism, though the presumption of White superiority is, of course, racism. Whiteness, as skin tone, is part of the superiority complex, in the psychological sense of that term, but this is a complex on a social scale, a pattern of behaviors arising from conscious and unconscious assumptions related to power and identity. White skin occurred in Europe, the culture whose colonizing members presumed themselves and their Christian culture superior. The data point to an arrogance so endemic and overbearing that even the victims of it internalize a sense of inferiority in its face. The European colonizer culture, from earliest history of invasion to the present, has believed his own commercial, so to speak, on a level so astonishing that generation after generation has taken for granted the superiority of White European Christian culture, even amid its own claims it does not want to be racist. The European Christian sense of superiority and the accompanying privilege of Euro-descended persons within American culture is so profound that the colonizer culture finds no need to even listen to the nonwhite other,[1] and hence the problem at hand.

Historically, belief in White cultural superiority has served to support justification for the killing of whole peoples who by their existence were in some way obstructing the White race's progress. Further, this sense of superiority also facilitated the presumed privilege of creating a historical narrative that disguised the killings, and the attempted genocide. Deadly arrogance continues to blind and deafen White American culture to the ongoing repercussions of the American past, the fallout being that Native American peoples are left traumatized in the wake of colonization, and when they speak out, their assertions have been further ignored. Theologically speaking, the presumption of White superiority is a great social sin. The command to love one's neighbor as one's self is made a mockery of in the face of the malignant distortion of Christianity's core teaching that is embedded in this sense of superiority.

Academics in the twenty-first century can no longer distance themselves from culpability in colonization and cultural genocide. To recognize that a label, Manifest Destiny (Tinker 1993, 10), served as a semantic cloak for colonizer atrocities is an insufficient response, after hearing what the newest generation of indigenous leaders is saying. Nor can Christians point to settlers, entrepreneurs, and government as the agents of White superiority. Christianity's function as co-power of European nation-states may be many centuries in the past, but the fallout of colonization is profound, and

1. This reflection will italicize *other* when used in the sense of a group marginalized by a dominant group and set apart, usually labeled in some way, colonized, and oppressed by the dominant cultural group.

ongoing, traceable to the institutions of church, state, and commerce. The legacy of Manifest Destiny lingers. Europe's historic power struggle between popes and kings looked different in the New World (Deloria 2003, 206). White colonizing Europeans rushed to make land claims, but as the new nation emerged, the indigenous peoples became the outsider; things White-and-European blended, formed in contrast to those viewed as uncivilized non-Christian natives. George E. Tinker (1993) identifies a Euro-American Christian theology mistakenly rooted in White superiority. In *Missionary Conquest*, Tinker shows that the cultural genocide of the indigenous peoples of the Americas arose amid the "confusion of virtually every missionary between the gospel he, or occasionally she, proclaimed to Indian people and the missionary's own European or Euroamerican culture" (4). The political, the economic, and the religious are inextricably intertwined in Tinker's historical analysis. From these conclusions, he points from the past into the present and calls for an awakening out of this false sense of superiority. Tinker writes:

> If we concede good intentions to the missionaries in general, we also must be careful to recognize them as people of their own times, incapable of the hindsight of critical analysis with which we are more likely to be blessed. That they confused their spiritual proclamation of the gospel of Jesus Christ with the imposition of new and strange cultural models for daily life is today inexcusable. But a century or more ago, the distinction between gospel and Euroamerican[2] culture was far less clear. Add to that the apparent cultural superiority, in the European mind at least, of wearing clothes, using a fork, and other seeming technological wonders. Moreover, the missionaries most often came to an Indian nation after the effects of conquest had already become visible, increasing the missionaries' sense of cultural superiority. (9, 10)

Tinker (1993) notes that one missionary's observation of how the Potawatomis lived in "squalor" is completely absent any consideration of their recent conquest and the accompanying trauma (10). A feeling of superiority arose, with little account of context. Christianity and civilization were equated, with scant examination, in the writings of missionaries as well as that of government agents (102). Tinker's equating error demonstrates the blind assumption of White superiority at work. Tinker, as a

---

2. The usage of Tinker's term "Euroamerican" is used beyond direct quotation of Tinker because of its appropriateness for the material being discussed, and its accuracy in meaning.

former professor of American Indian Cultures and Religious Traditions, and a Christian minister, shows the deep entanglement of belief in White superiority with the Christian gospel, as understood during the settlement of the Americas by Europeans. White superiority, in action, represents disturbing and destructive behavior in the human family, and especially so, as it manifested in United States history. Young Native Americans heard in the data, expressed their identity struggles, their sense of learned inferiority, and their frustration at being ignored in a culture that presumes White superiority to indigenous Americans and non-white persons. A White sense of superiority represents division and separation as opposed to unity and equality; it expresses an especially insidious form of division, one based on a distorted image of other human beings, and creating the Other.

Distorted Images of God, Other, Self

The presumption of White superiority represents a distortion of reality, and of the teaching of Jesus and the prophets. This reflection builds on the assumption that all human beings are made in the image of God and are therefore equally valued and equally worthy of dignity (Holland and Henriot 1980, 9). This theological assumption is partner to a pursuit of social justice. Within Christian theology, the acceptance of all human beings as created in the image of God suggests an acceptance of all others. It also implies an inclusive stance, rooted in a sense of the connectedness of all humans as opposed to one focused on difference as adversarial. This has been a historical problematic for Christians, even within their own communities, and more so across faith traditions and ethnicities. Jesus' prayer for the unity of all his believers (John 17:22–23) points to a desire for a similar dissolving of separation in humanity. Jesus points out that all people will know that his disciples belong to him, and his father, because of how his disciples love one another.

For Jesus, humanity as a whole is never forgotten, as his salvific mission aims to restore. Paul's epistle reiterates this, reminding the church that God wills the salvation of all persons (1 Tim 2:4). This is demonstrated in the Gospels every time Jesus disrupts social norms by his interactions with the marginalized, his crossing of culturally constructed barriers that would keep people from experiencing God's presence. His was a pluralism of the prophets, whose vision of peace on Earth did not wipe out social difference—even concerning religious practice—but rather, pointed to the possibility of peace and justice without a forced homogeneity. The prophet Micah's vision makes room for the possibility that each person may worship their god, while the Hebrews worshipped their God, and that this may be an acceptable and desirable state (Mic 4:3–7). The reign of God proclaimed by Jesus was good news for the poor and outcast, if not for Pharisees, and other holders of power, protecting traditional religious purity. The Christianity delivered to the Americas five centuries ago, though, was absent Micah's generous vision. In addition, it is this theological absence—this blind spot— which allowed for the diminishment of indigenous peoples, and the failure to see them as fully embodying the image of the living God. A people whose God is not inclusive will not imagine outsiders as equal before that God.

To reflect theologically, recognizing and remembering that any given group of persons, collectively or as individuals, represents the image of God, precludes defining that group as Other. This capitalization is used to indicate the concept beyond the usual usage of other, and to speak of the conception of another human being as something other than one's own human self. To make them other than the human being that you are is to create the Other. To create any Other represents a failure to uphold the image of God in the Other. This move is arguably a root of the arrogance that is White superiority, a cultural distortion rooted in White Christian Europe. The dismissal or refusal to acknowledge the image of God in the designated Other is a falsehood, a lie necessary for colonization in the name of religion. This process is well described in Steven Charleston's (2015b) chapter on the dehumanization of the indigenous woman, creating an Other with the label "squaw" (148–50). Even seeing an ugly historical example does not explain how a blind spot of the magnitude of White superiority manages not just to exist, but also, and especially, to have flourished among those who claim to be the disciples of Jesus Christ.

The Mystery of a Culture's Blind Spots

This reflection suggests that if any blind spot of White culture is to be revealed to White persons—it is already recognizable to non-white persons— White people will need to see themselves from outside themselves. Both Christian thinkers and academics across history have in some degree fallen into the culture's error, marking the way for the wider culture to follow. Both might ask themselves the questions Pierre Bourdieu (1980) did. Bourdieu echoes elements of Tinker's observation of missionaries' work, and Deloria's (2003) critique of Western academic methodology.[3] In his introduction to

---

3. Vine Deloria Jr.'s *God Is Red* (2003) is a seminal work by the late Native scholar, one addressed to academics and theologians. Its criticism includes the problem of Christianity's "inability to respect or tolerate those who are different" (viii). It is

The Logic of Practice, Bourdieu (1980) describes the experience of seeing himself and other social scientists from outside himself, then points out his own failure and that of his fellow social scientists, in wording similar to Tinker's consideration of the intentions of missionaries. Bourdieu writes:

> Those who nowadays set themselves up as judges and distribute praise and blame among the sociologists and ethnologists of the colonial past would be better occupied in trying to understand what it was that prevented the most lucid and the best intentioned of those (sociologists and ethnologists) they condemn from understanding things which are now self-evident for even the least lucid and sometimes the least well-intentioned observers: in what is unthinkable at a given time, there is not only everything that cannot be thought for lack of the ethical or political dispositions which tend to bring it into consideration, but also everything that cannot be thought for lack of instruments of thought such as problematics, concepts, methods and techniques. (5)

A consideration of what Bourdieu finds "cannot be thought" would point to language theory, particularly toward understanding how Euro-American culture developed its two-way identity blindness, blindness to the full humanity of non-white persons in its midst, and blindness to its own place in humanity, one of an inflated self-perception. It behooves Christian and academic alike to consider how our very language imbeds the assumptions that continue to produce social tension and violence in American society.

Tinker (1993) shows how Christian tradition is deeply entangled in assumptions of White superiority formed by equating the Christian gospel with European civilization. Christian teaching, Scripture, creed, and liturgy, could have come to the Americas ready to be received by indigenous cultures, able to engender local Christian theologies that were also uniquely Native American. The confusion of the Christian faith with one cultural performance of that faith—the European cultural model—brought about the situation Tinker describes.

One might conceive, in the functions of language, the dynamics that gave rise to this distortion of a dominant culture's self-image. Robert Schreiter (1985) uses language theory in a way that might help in conceiving how a cultural narrative can drive distortion as it is lived out, or performed, in a given context. Schreiter builds a "linguistic model for communication" by

---

recommended reading as a starting point for any scholarly understanding of contemporary Native American perspectives.

drawing a comparison of Noam Chomsky's model for language acquisition to the "problem of Christian tradition" (114–15). To understand Schreiter's model, consider that Chomsky posits competence in language as part of the human condition, but distinguishes this innate competence from what he calls "performance" (114). Grammar, meaning the formal rules of a given language, stands separate from competence and performance, for Chomsky, and grammar can only offer critique of performance as incorrect. Grammar furnishes rules, while competence allows performances, or creative usage, of language which grammar cannot anticipate (114).

Schreiter's construct draws a parallel of grammar with orthodoxy or creeds, and of innate competence with faith. Performance, in Christian tradition, is visible in liturgy and ritual; religious practice is drawn from faith, and like language usage, it is inexhaustibly generative and creative. Creeds can critique practices as they arise, but practices will arise which orthodoxy has not anticipated, just as occurs in language usage. Schreiter sees tradition as the larger system that includes a triad model of *faith* (Chomsky's innate competence), *performance* (or practice), and *orthodoxy* (grammar) (116). With this model in mind, it is possible to overlay Schreiter's application of Chomsky's language model onto the cultural system of interaction between Euro-American colonizing culture and its relations with indigenous peoples. Faith and the performance of it as European Christian culture were so welded that it left little room for indigenous expressions or performances of faith, and few new local theologies to be examined for their orthodoxy. The competency of the indigenous was smothered in this model, and continues to be so, as demonstrated by the existence of the problem this work addresses; a dominant culture that doesn't listen to its Others. The Other becomes less human in the view of the Christian missionary when their faith is dismissed as inferior; this is dismissing Chomsky's innate competence and hence the creation of someone who is placed in an inferior category.

The category of competence, which Schreiter parallels to faith, within Christian tradition, can be equated with Indian identity. This is to speak of Indian identity as innate, meaning who Native Americans are as human beings existing in their place and time. This is an identity about which the indigenous are not confused, for which they do not strive. It is what it is to be Indian, that not-easily-defined matter which Sherman Alexie (2000) continually asked and re-answered: "What is an Indian?" (217–38). This is not to say that the Native American is deliberately conscious of it herself or himself, any more than a speaker of language thinks through the rules of grammar when he or she speaks her native language competently at age five. Like faith, and Chomsky's theorized wiring for language acquisition, Indian identity exists. This connection of identity to language was recognized, in the data, by the grandmother who told her granddaughter to "start with the word for the Creator and He will slowly give you the rest" (Bachofner 2003, 145). Bachofner's Nana understood this generative aspect of Indian identity, tied to the language and functioning in the same manner as faith and language acquisition do. She knew her granddaughter was competent.

Schreiter's (1985) comparison of language performance with liturgical and theological expressions can be distilled as practical wisdom (85; 115), and can be overlaid upon Native American performance. This includes the practical actions indigenous people perform as well as the performances, in the usual sense of the word, that constitute the data being reflected upon, such as the 1491s videos, and the essays written. These performances arise from Indian identity as it is, not as the colonizer culture defines it, nor even as the Native American child has internalized it from that culture's definition. This parallel of functional performance arising from an innate knowledge of identity is arguably Leslie Marmon Silko's (1977) thesis in *Ceremony*. It is in the performance of ceremony that the protagonist Tayo finds healing and self-understanding; he must reject the White definition of himself in order to harmonize this faith-competence level of identity with action. When they act based on an internalized White definition of "Indian," the Native American person is at war with this inner competence, the creative heart of his or her being.

This example, in turn, points to Chomsky's placement of grammar as merely an apophatic definer of performance. Grammar cannot give rise to performance, it can only say when a performance of language usage is incorrect in terms of established rules. Schreiter's (1985) application of grammar in Chomsky's model parallels creeds in Christian tradition. "Creedal formulas set boundaries on belief but do not attempt to describe all possible combinations within those boundaries," writes Schreiter (116). Schreiter shows that orthodoxy does not create a community's theology just as grammar does not create language usage. Rather, these flow from the creative center of the human person. Chomsky called this competence, Schreiter compares it to the role of faith in tradition. Here, it can be compared to the image of God in the human person, the spiritual competence of the Indian.

The role of grammar-orthodoxy in this comparison can be extended to dominant narratives in Euro-American culture. This, then, is the loci of White superiority. The Christian narrative, as understood and insisted upon, sets a boundary that only the creative, faith-competence center of the person can transcend. However, if that very center is distorted in the Other, by the very narrative, that Other can be held captive. The same apophatic definitive action that grammar applies to language performance, and that creeds assert toward the performances of Christian communities, occurred in the colonization process; because of the erroneous equating of the gospel message with European culture, indigenous cultures were conceived as "ungrammatical," clearly outside the boundaries of Christian orthodoxy, and likewise uncivilized. The creation of the indigenous Other begins here, and the process of creating the Other, of undermining in traumatized populations the very competence that would show their creative competence, initiated a dehumanizing cycle of oppression. Psychologists might liken it to emotional abuse, on a grand scale.

This unseen function of fused cultural and religious orthodoxy proved insidious in the conquest of indigenous peoples. The orthodoxy of White Christian European superiority said that the indigenous inhabitant of North America was not practicing a recognizably orthodox religion, therefore it was a false religion, and it was negated along with its adherents. The Doctrine of Discovery (Canadian Conference of Catholic Bishops 2016) used this presumption in justification of colonial conquest and U.S. Justice John Marshall applied it legally, as shown in the above review of history (Morris 2003, 111). Chomsky's model, and Schreiter's application, use the three loci of competence, performance, and grammar as points of a larger system, respectively, language as that larger system and, in parallel, Christian tradition as embodying faith, praxis, and orthodoxy. The process of colonization, likewise, functioned on all three levels, not merely showing up with a set of creeds to be presented to the indigenous heathen. The truth claim of Christianity and its entanglement with European culture arguably created a doctrine of White superiority that swallowed up indigenous performance and then eroded competence, leaving the Native American a few generations later asking, "What is an Indian?" (Alexie 2000, 230). This process, clarified here by its comparison with Chomsky's language acquisition model, is revealed and confirmed in the data studied and in the voices heard. Tinker (1993) identified equating of the Christian gospel with European civilization as the seed of the White sense of superiority, a seed implanted in the new American culture that would form in the centuries following.

Even as creeds provide boundaries for communities, they also furnish a basis for negatively defining the non-member, the Other. Unless the community formed is aware that the community is itself part of a larger human community, there is the danger of defining all outsiders, all Others, as enemies. There is a further danger when the community in question exerts power over the outsider. The power to define one's own community does not include the privilege of defining the Other. This, of course, was pointed out by Deloria in the twentieth century. It will be shown further that the arrogant act of defining the Other is a historical failure closely tied to presumptions of White superiority, and that horrific and ongoing harm are its fallout.

Christian Identity, Native Identity

Despite an arguably distorted misadventure of evangelism in the Americas, indigenous peoples converted to Christianity. This work, while reflecting upon contemporary Native voices, acknowledges questions about the authenticity of conversions in the context of conquest. Whatever the motivation and experience of indigenous persons upon initial receipt of the Christian gospel message, the testimony of Native Christian communities in the United States today is that they are Christians, believers who have received the faith of Jesus Christ. Works that verify and explicate this are cited below, in the context of this reflection.[4]

Robert Schreiter (1985) would have Christians apply the aforementioned theory of tradition (113) in the struggle for "faithfulness to the gospel in its theology" particularly in local communities, as theology arises out of local contexts (117). Schreiter offers five questions, formed from applying Chomsky's language acquisition theory, that are useful in considering Tinker's (1993) criticism of missionary endeavor in the so-called New World. Tinker might arguably find that the Christian missionary to the Americas fails Schreiter's Criteria for Christian Identity (Schreiter 1985, 117). It is worth attending once more to how Tinker (1993) explains the objective of his work *Missionary Conquest*, and summarizes his thesis. He writes,

> The primary objectives of the study are to demonstrate the inevitable confusion of virtually every missionary between the gospel he, or occasionally she, proclaimed to Indian people and the missionary's own European or Euroamerican culture, and to trace the resulting devastation of Indian peoples and their cultures. The motivation and the theoretical basis for the missionary endeavor, apparent both from the actual practice of the missionaries and from their writings, will demonstrate that they not only *preached a new gospel of salvation*, but also just as energetically imposed a new cultural model for existence on Indian people. The evidence will show that these two tasks became nearly indistinguishable in practice. (4)[5]

---

4. Achiel Peelman's *Christ Is a Native American* (1995) provides extensive interviews with indigenous Christians, documenting their experiences of being "Amerindian" and Christian, and arguing for an inclusive Christology that allows the Amerindian to contribute an eco-theology to interreligious dialogue (203).

5. Italics added.

While bearing in mind the hermeneutic of time elapsed since missionary contact, and the accompanying evolution of understanding both in theology and social sciences as described by Bordieu (1980), it remains valuable to comprehend explicitly any manner in which the Christian tradition failed in its encounter with the indigenous peoples of the Americas. As shown by the data, the harm is ongoing and emerging Native leaders are urging the descendants of the colonizer to encounter their own history. This work, this writer, joins those who are urging the wider European-descended American culture to reconsider our understanding of our own history and of our related presumptions.

Now, a consideration of Schreiter's criteria for Christian identity, arising from local communities, points to Tinker's bold assertion that: So distorted was the message of Christian missionaries—both Protestant and Catholic, per his samples—that the gospel they preached had even become a "new gospel" (Tinker 1993, 4). Tinker's assertion points to the surrounding issues of tension between syncretism and orthodoxy, perhaps of unschooled faith failing the tests of orthodoxy. It also points to arrogance of the type satirized by the 1491s sketches and delineated by Tinker and Deloria. Schreiter's (1985) "First Criterion: The Cohesiveness of Christian Performance"[6] calls for a recognition of "a hierarchy of truth" noting that "some truths of the Christian faith are more central to belief than others" (118). The thesis of *Missionary Conquest* points to a failure to meet this first criterion. European civilization held as equal to Christian truth created an incoherent message, and even, as Tinker insists, a new gospel. Tinker writes of the endemic confusion of the gospel proclaimed with "the missionary's own European or Euroamerican culture" (4) and he insists that the preaching of the gospel and the imposition of a "new cultural model for existence" had for the Christian missionary, become "nearly indistinguishable in practice" (4).

Schreiter's (1985) "Criteria for Christian Identity" address the problem of identifying whether local theologies, as they arise, are in fact Christian. He notes that failing to meet even one of the five criterion might mean a negative judgement against a developing local theology (117). Tinker's (1993) above described failure shows that despite good intentions, mission

---

6. The First Criterion emphasizes coherence of doctrines and symbol systems, showing the interplay of the two, and that logical consistency alone is not the measure, but cohesiveness. Schreiter offers the example of Arianism, which was more philosophically consistent but undermined "Jesus' role as the definitive revelations of God's salvific presence in history, and in doing so, wreaked havoc with any theology of grace and sacrament" (1985, 118). While the *homoousious* as establish at Nicaea is not a perfectly logical concept, it is coherent with the whole of Christian doctrine and symbol.

venture in the Americas may have been guilty of a form of cultural-economic-political syncretism that turns the tables of Schreiter's criterion. It can be conceived that the Christian "local theology" of Europe had been distorted by the Church's historic relationship with nation-states, in a form of syncretism that formed the distorted gospel that Tinker insists was delivered.

Schreiter's (1985) tools for listening to a culture may offer a way of further understanding how the false narrative of White cultural superiority came into colonizer consciousness. Schreiter suggests the semiotic study of a culture, treating a "culture as a vast communication network" (49) that uses mutually understood signs. Defining "sign" simply, Schreiter notes, "The bearer of the message is seen to stand for the message" (49). Within Western Christian culture, this confusion of message and message-bearer emerges. Christianity became the *habitus* of European culture, an "embodied history, internalized as a second nature and so forgotten as history" operating in a dialectic of institution and the *habitus*, the church and the culture functioning with what Bourdieu (1980) calls "regulated improvisations" (55–57). The encounter with indigenous peoples radically disrupted this dialectic. The bloody conflict and attempted genocide are the symptoms of this disruption. The failure of a culture to navigate its own signs and those of the culture it encountered resulted in confused false narratives, most notable Manifest Destiny, but less obviously, an insidious presumption that European civilization, as the *bearer* of the gospel, is superior and even the savior of non-Christian cultures. The culture's sign system, in part, served as a basis for colonization. European culture *is* Christianity—the sign of one is sign for the other—and the missionary brings its signified truth.

Tinker's (1993) well-argued thesis that missionaries equated and confused the gospel with European civilization would interrogate those who claimed to deliver the gospel of Jesus Christ, and points next to another of Schreiter's (1985) five criteria, "The Praxis of the Community" (119). This evaluation based upon the "fruits" (Matt 7:16) of a given local theology, when functioning as the measure of mission endeavor, shows that while seeds of the Christian gospel surely took root among the indigenous peoples of America, the seed planted also apparently brought forth trauma and death. To extend the metaphor, the error of equating Christianity with European culture produced a hybrid seed, and that hybrid seed grew into a near-genocide, with religion providing license, as needed, to economic colonizers. The interests of the missionary and the interest of political and commercial enterprise both grew into a mission of civilizing the indigenous, and hence a cultural-economic-political syncretism arose, in which Christian mission became unrecognizably intermingled with conquest (Tinker 1993, 10). It is to be expected that such a local theology arose in the Americas, if one accepts that a similar syncretism took place for pre-Christian Europe. The seed grew its own kind. The colonizer's confused message arguably represented a hybrid gospel, yet one that bore the name of Jesus Christ, and wrought conversion among the indigenous. One does not gather grapes from a thorn tree, Jesus taught in a parable. The missionary in the Americas largely failed to recognize a good vine in the culture of Native Americans, and instead worked to harvest from his own corrupted vine, one that had thorns grafted in (John 7:16; 15:1).

Two-Way Theological Evaluation

Native American Christian communities today clearly constitute orthodox, creedal Christian communities, and thus the Christian church of the twenty-first century in the United States should submit itself to inquiry of the type noted in Schreiter's fourth criteria, "The Judgement of Other Churches." Schreiter (1985) notes that established hierarchies must not apply critical judgement of local theological developments in a one-way fashion, but must allow themselves to be challenged by "younger churches" and must "respond to the challenges of the poor churches to their wealth and their complicity in oppression" or, Schreiter warns, the established church structure may "find themselves lacking in Christian identity" (119–20). Here Schreiter underscores and validates the core of this work, but with one assumption needing clarification, that being, in what sense or to what extent the young Native Americans comprising this research data are Christian. This stands as a complexity of the Indian identity issue being explicated here and informs how Christians hear the contemporary indigenous person. Further, the question points to Schreiter's fifth criteria, that of "The Challenge to Other Churches" arising from local Christian communities (120). If American Indians speaking, writing, and creating today are Christian, and if their messages are to constitute valid criticism of older church structures, their praxis should bear fruit worthy of the gospel of Jesus Christ.

To answer, in a word, the data are not explicitly Christian. Some among the data spoke explicitly of their Christian faith, others spoke of it implicitly. The situation is best described, perhaps, by saying young Native Americans have inherited Christianity as a presence in their communities. The actions and words of leaders like Frank Waln and Inez Jaspers (Becker et al. 2015), along with many others heard, would ask us to consider the fruit of these communities, and how to explain it. Jesus connected fruit with a tree's identity, saying, "You will know them by their fruits" (John 7:16). Schreiter (1985) calls for an examination of the older Christian community by the newer. Presuming Christian community identity in some, and the image of God in all, and scanning for "fruit" that evidences Christian values and concerns, the data should be received as recommended. Schreiter's warning that it is possible the older churches find themselves lacking in Christian identity (120) must be taken seriously if these communities bear the fruits of which Jesus speaks. Steven Charleston, in his co-edited work with Elaine A. Robinson (2015b), *Coming Full Circle: Constructing Native Christian Theology*, offers an example of Native Americans applying these very criteria to the European-descended Christians and their gospel. In 1805, a Seneca nation leader tells a missionary how his people will respond to the sacred book the Christians embrace as truth, saying, "We will wait a little while and see what effect your preaching has upon (the European settlers who were the Seneca's neighbors). If we find it does them good, makes them honest and less disposed to cheat Indians, we will then consider again what you have said" (Charleston and Robinson 2015, 9).

Achiel Peelman's (1995) work, *Christ Is a Native American*, shows how the Christian gospel was accepted by the indigenous peoples of the Americas, and in large numbers. Peelman argues, though, that the Christians delivering the good news need to detach from expectations of how the living word will look in a very different culture. Peelman asks:

> What about those unexpected fruits which the gospel also produces in the cultures of the peoples to whom it is proclaimed, the new fruits which do not necessarily correspond to our western [sic] theology and structures? We are dealing here with a theological and pastoral issue that the universal church cannot avoid: *the capacity and the courage to welcome responses to the gospel which, to the missionary who has sown its seeds in a foreign soil, are creative, unique, original, and properly unheard of.* The mystery of inculturation is nothing other than the extraordinary power of the gospel (the living word of a living God) acting upon a culture from within and producing with that culture responses of faith which often exceed our expectations and predictions. (92)[7]

Both Peelman and Schreiter challenge Christian endeavor to make room for the living word of God. Though the data, as discussed, do not expressly identify as Christian, some do speak of Jesus.

---

7. Italics original.

"One Good Man" (Alexie 2000)

Jesus does appear explicitly in the work of one of the writers constituting the data for this work. The young Native voices speak of Christianity as intermingled with their Native identity, often coexisting, present in a grandparent who was Christian, a mother who brought them to church and taught them Christian songs. Jesus is a backdrop, believed in, unquestioned. Sherman Alexie's (2000) essay sample, "One Good Man," cited earlier for its repeated question "What is an Indian?" (218), begins with a discussion between two Indian carpenters, Sweetwater and Wonder Horse. Sweetwater, not given to chat, is stuck on a single thought he repeats to anyone listening: "Jesus was a carpenter" (209). The discussion that follows presumes a recognition of the Christian Jesus, as Sweetwater insists, "He was the Son of God. I think he could multitask" (213). Alexie's writing often describes this backdrop of Christianity as embedded in the Indian consciousness. In fact, a thoughtful read of "One Good Man," with its introductory discussion of Jesus as carpenter—stated once in the Spokane language by Sweetwater—the chapter then moving into Alexie's repetitious query, "What is an Indian?" leaves the attentive reader wondering if Jesus is, in fact, the "One Good Man." The varied answers offered to the question, "What is an Indian?" harken back to the chapter's opening conversation, which the narrator notes, "reeked of theology" (210). Alexie suggests, between the lines, that to be an Indian, and a good Indian, is to be like Jesus, whom Sweetwater insists, was a "real carpenter," and a good carpenter (212). And yet, when Wonder Horse tells Sweetwater, "Now you sound like a Christian," Sweetwater responds with, "Hey, that's dirty," and Wonder Horse apologizes (212). The two Spokane carpenters have this discussion while building a wheelchair ramp for the terminally ill father of the story's narrator. Alexie shows that Native American Christian identity is nearly as complex as Indian identity. While whole works are dedicated to the question, clearly Native Americans in large numbers identify as Christian, and if not, still find Jesus worthy of imitation.

Steven Charleston's (2015a) work informs this question. A citizen of the Choctaw Nation, Charleston is bishop of Alaska for the Episcopal Church and has held teaching posts at three Protestant seminaries, including that of Systematic Theology at Luther Seminary. Because of his elder status, he was not constituted in the data here, yet two recently published works speak to the question reflected on here. In a work he calls "a personal theology," Charleston tells the story of his own experience as both Native American and Christian" and the "struggle to reconcile these two halves of who I am": (1). *The Four Vision Quests of Jesus* speaks to Schreiter's third criteria, the local community's praxis (119), speaking out of the struggle of the colonized indigenous Christian to embrace Christian belief in the face of the arguably poisonous fruit borne by missionary conquest. Charleston's work offers a Native Christology formed in the struggle to reconcile his Choctaw ancestry with his Christianity (1).

Tinker (1993) is also a Protestant minister, one whose sharp critique of missionary endeavor identifies what he argues are failures in practice, stemming from a failed practical theology. Yet, both Tinker and Charleston (2015) look toward practical theological reconciliation. Charleston offers "a Christian theology that is based in Native tradition" (2). In *Coming Full Circle*, Charleston constructs a Native theory of practice that points to story as core, asserting that "Native theology . . . is story" (Charleston and Robinson 2015, 7). Charleston identifies three criteria for Native communications that serve to maintain indigenous practice, absent strict hierarchal structures, and arising around story. The three, accessibility, adaptability, and accountability, have their loci in story, and offer approaches to theology that could serve as correctives for older Christian practice, as prescribed by Schreiter. The practical power of story lies in its being a medium managed by the community, kept as "a core value" (Charleston and Robinson 2015, 4). Briefly, story serves Native theology by allowing every person to participate in an intimate form of human interaction, by being open to narratives that may confirm, challenge, or even apparently contradict tradition, and by providing a communal evaluation of the story communicated (Charleston and Robinson 2015, 5–6). It is not difficult to imagine Charleston's Native theology offering correction. The narrative of White superiority, tied to a historic confusion of gospel and White culture, could be considered a story unevaluated, without accountability, one that resists challenges, rather than a story accountable, accessible, and adaptable.

A Call for Academic Honesty

Post-Indian Wars, Post-Assimilation, and Post-Relocation Act, Deloria (1969) decried the blindness of twentieth-century anthropologists, and their imbedded sense of superiority. He points to an attitude among academics that ignored the intelligence of Native American epistemologies, objectified and thereby dehumanized Natives being studied, invalidated indigenous knowledge, even instilling self-doubt and a self-devaluation that made "Indian people begin to feel they were merely shadows of a mythical super-Indian. Many anthros [sic] spare no expense to reinforce this sense of inadequacy in order to further support their influence over Indian people" Deloria writes (86). The presumption of superiority among social scientists may have been rooted in the pride of rationalism, a subtle attitude of superiority, if not racism, that made the academic a different kind of savior. Deloria's critical insights arose alongside breaking insights in anthropology and sociology, as theorists began to question their own approaches. Pierre Bourdieu (1980) explains in detail his lost faith in academic approaches that dismissed the study of certain categories such as ritual traditions as too primitive to be "legitimate objects" of study (3). In an introduction cited earlier, which reads like a confession, Bourdieu describes in *The Logic of Practice* his process of realization, from 1958 forward. He writes that he had, in his rationality, not only been dismissive of all works that included that study of ritual traditions, but that he needed to "retrieve (the study of ritual) from the false solicitude of primitivism and to challenge the racist contempt which, through the self-contempt it produces in its victims, helps to deny them knowledge and recognition of their own tradition" (3). A sociologist's work in postcolonial contexts in Algeria would have found many indigenous informants for whom their own traditions were not fully known to themselves, due to colonization by the French (3). Bourdieu calls it all "a particularly scandalous form of ethnocentrism . . . tending to justify the colonial order" (3).

Bourdieu's confession, noted earlier, also speaks to Tinker's (1993) complaint of the good intentions of missionaries, with both sociologists and Christians operating in what today appears as an astonishing blindness. Bourdieu (1980) describes the postcolonial criticisms of ethnography arising particularly around the matter of concern to him, ritual traditions, pointing to a methodological hypocrisy that dismissed ritual's importance while claiming to approach the study of cultures objectively (1980, 5). Bourdieu's attention to the objectivity that runs through our subjectivity (21) can assist more broadly. Bourdieu calls for a "learned ignorance" to lead us. Speaking primarily to practitioners in his field, he nonetheless offers insight into the problem of embedded blindness in understanding a social situation, and local theologies. That situation, today, is a White-dominated American culture that exists in varied degrees of blindness to its own sense of superiority to its indigenous peoples, to the descendants of African American people it imported as slaves, and to every immigrant group that falls short of White European-ness. In the search for concepts that might help a culture "think the unthinkable," Bourdieu advises:

"One has quite simply to bring into scientific work and into the theory of practices that it seeks to produce, a theory—which cannot be found through theoretical experiences alone—of what it is to be 'native,' that is, to be in that relationship of 'learned ignorance,' of immediate unselfconscious understanding which defines the practical relationship to the world" (19).

Charleston provides such a theory to address our learned ignorance and perhaps to help White Euro-American Christians think the unthinkable (Charleston and Robinson 2015, 10–15).

The Scriptures and Pluralism: Other Sheep

Charleston (2015b) opens *Coming Full Circle* with a bold assertion: "There is a complementary theology to the testimony of ancient Israel, an ancient theology that arises out of another promised land. There is a story of the indigenous nations chosen by God to dwell here, in North America" (2). He makes this statement after describing an early experience in a Christian seminary, in which he was told that the awareness of a monotheistic God was unique to the tribal nation of Israel and resulted in a covenant relationship between the Israelites and God. Charleston tells how he thought, "I have heard this story before. . . . It is the story of my own ancestors" (2). Charleston's introductory chapter states that the Native theory he describes as necessary to forming a Native Christian theology "reminds us that the teachings of Christ were not imported to America: they were rediscovered here" (26). This seemingly radical statement echoes the voices of Native Americans younger than Charleston speaking the same truth, which Charleston names Native theory.

The truth claim of Christianity creates a theological problematic that demands to be addressed in the context of the matter at hand. If Native Americans of past generations and of today are telling the White, Christian, American world that they find our stance toward other peoples and other religions arrogant, that our theology is intertwined with an odious White sense of superiority, then *if we are listening*, we are obliged to identify and detangle the Euro-Christian assumption of superiority that Tinker shows confused European culture with the gospel of Jesus Christ and resulted in near cultural genocide among the indigenous peoples of North America. To quote Tinker (1993) again, the work of cultural and theological detangling is "part of America's unfinished business" (5).

What would a theologically plural, peaceful United States of America look like? While Christian Scripture offers examples, at least one vision of a peaceful kingdom, ruled by a just messiah, is regularly truncated when quoted. The minor prophet Micah writes, "And he shall judge between many peoples, and shall arbitrate between strong nations far away; and they shall beat their swords into plowshares, and their spears into pruning hooks; nation shall not lift up sword against nation, neither shall they learn war any more; but they shall sit under their own vines and under their own fig trees;

and no one shall make them afraid: for the mouth of the LORD of hosts hath spoken" (Mic 4:3–4 NRSV).

The next verse demands to be included in considering a response to the problem of Christian truth claims and pluralism, as the passage is interpreted widely in Christian understanding to refer to the fulfillment of the messianic kingdom, a reign of Jesus Christ, whom the angel Gabriel announced would be given "the throne of his ancestor David. And he will reign over the house of Jacob forever; and of his kingdom there will be no end" (Luke 1:32–33 NRSV). The prophet Micah continues: *"For all the peoples walk, each in the name of its god, and we will walk in the name of the LORD our God forever and ever"* (Mic 4:5 NRSV). [8]

Charleston (2015b) was surprised to hear, as a new seminarian, that the Hebrews were a uniquely covenanted people of God. His Choctaw heritage taught him that many indigenous tribes considered themselves to have a special relationship with the one Creator God, and were "chosen to inhabit a special land and to be in covenant relationship with their Creator" (1–2).[9] Charleston insists God was speaking and develops a Native Christian theology around this covenant relationship. The question of God speaking to indigenous peoples anywhere should not be a difficult matter for Christians. The Psalmist declared that the work of creation itself speaks to human beings, without language, declaring the glory of God (Ps 19:1–4). Pope Francis (2015) notes the teaching of Saint Francis, who drew from the Book of Wisdom, that nature is a "magnificent book in which God speaks to us" (13). Pope Francis includes in *Laudato Si* a chapter and section that addresses "Educating for the Covenant Between Humanity and the Environment" (136).

For many non-Native Christians, construing nature's revelation as covenant-making between the Creator God and non-Abrahamic peoples may sound preposterous upon first hearing. Yet Jesus told his disciples, "I have other sheep" (John 10:16 NRSV). This statement must be considered as meaning more than that Jesus would have followers outside Judaism, based on the Gospel passages that declare him as having come for all people. Jesus not only tells his disciples he has other sheep, but he says that he (Jesus) will bring them into the sheepfold. He does commission his followers to go and evangelize, and he also says that he, himself, will bring in the other sheep and that these sheep will hear his voice. The commonly accepted

---

8. Italics added.

9. *Coming Full Circle* (2015) lists Steven Charleston and Elaine A. Robinson as co-editors. Charleston, however, is the author of chapter 1, "Theory—Articulating a Native American Theological Theory," in which he makes the claim of a covenant between the Creator and indigenous tribes of the Americas.

interpretation that Jesus referred to the gentile church, the body of persons who would believe and become God's people without being born Jewish, does not preclude Charleston's described covenant tradition. These words of the Christian gospel are not inconsistent with the insistence of Native Americans who claim not merely a pre-evangelism preparedness, but a knowledge of Jesus, having heard his voice, proclaiming, "Christ regenerates us to a new life. Our ancestors knew him already, but they preferred to speak of God instead" (Peelman 1995, 101). A Native theological interpretation of the healing of the Canaanite woman's son by Jesus shows a "transformation of Jesus' mind and heart" concerning the will of his Father. In Matthew's and Mark's Gospels, Jesus insists he is sent to "the lost sheep of the house of Israel," yet the woman's argument convinces Jesus that the Father's gifts should extend to the Canaanite (Matt 5:21–28) (Peelman 1995, 186). Peelman suggests that even Jesus experienced a broadening of understanding in the face of the Canaanite woman's faith, that the house of Israel are not God's only sheep (186).

As Robert Allen Warrior's (2006) essay, "Canaanites, Cowboys, and Indians" points out, the indigenous person shares the experience of the Canaanite in the Exodus story, more so than that of the Israelite escaping slavery in Egypt (235). Jesus demonstrates that the boundaries of God's favor extend beyond what God's people can imagine. Yet, the notion that the Native American had a relationship with the God of Creation—the God of Abraham, Isaac and Jacob, and the Father in the Christian Trinity—before the White Christian evangelist-missionary arrived is at the least, a surprising consideration. It is even unsettling to begin to think that God was up to something other than managing the nation of Israel and planning the salvation of humankind, working out a great mystery, throughout Israel's history, unfolding it all under the Roman Empire. At last, the messiah's time to appear arrived, and then began another great mystery unfolding, that of the church. However, even Jesus, across Gospel accounts, must break out of the historical, theological, national narrative into which he was born, to proclaim and demonstrate that God, his Father, has other peoples. He calls them other sheep, and himself their shepherd.

The people-in-the-making, the church, is visible between the lines of the Gospel narratives, as Christ reveals himself over a brief three-year public ministry, then leaves behind a group of confused followers. As a new tradition emerged from the old, what we know as the Christian church took shape. The gospel of Jesus Christ spread throughout the Mediterranean region and then east, south and north, even as doctrine was determined by the earliest church councils. But an ocean prevented this gospel from moving west for a millennium and a half. The Christian narrative places the indigenous peoples of the Americas—and elsewhere—in the path of the church's onward march through history. At last, they receive the good news. Except, there are accounts that say those living on the land across the ocean had already heard.

Linear Time and First-Hearer as Truth-Dispenser

Tinker (2005) offers an insight that speaks both to the problematic history of evangelization of the Americas and to the deep sources of the White sense of superiority questioned here. In *Spirit and Resistance: Political Theology and American Indian Liberation*, Tinker locates areas of misunderstanding that stem from differing cognitive structures and presuppositions; Western consciousness being linear and time-based, indigenous understanding being spatial, place-oriented. While this insight is ubiquitous in social sciences and theology, Tinker applies it interpreting liberation theology for Native Americans. He begins by challenging the opening assertion of Gustavo Gutierrez (1984) in *The Power of the Poor in History*, that "God reveals himself in history" (5). Tinker (2004) responds, "American Indian theology must argue out of American Indian spiritual experience and praxis that Creator ("God"?) is revealed in creation, in space and place, and not in time" (104). He continues by saying the Western conception of a linear history created a linear hierarchy of knowledge dispersion. He explains, "Those who heard the gospel first have maintained and always maintain a critical advantage over those of us who hear it later and have to rely on those who heard it first to give us a full interpretation. In a historical structure of existence, certain people carry the message and, most importantly, hold all the wisdom" (104). Tinker's insight extends easily to speak to the problem of a White, American culture's deep-seated presumption of superiority to Others, nuancing this attitude's roots. The European Christian colonizer reasons: We had the gospel first, therefore we have a superior position in relation to God. We knew his truth before the Other.

In an earlier work, Tinker (1993) asserts the confusion of equating the gospel of Jesus Christ with Western, White-European civilization. In the outtake from *Spirit and Resistance* (2004) above, he shows how the historically informed orientation of Western thinking provides a platform for the presumption of White superiority, and for the confusion of gospel and civilization that he shows as devastating to the indigenous of the Americas. His later work shows how a cosmological conception of God working across a linear history helps create the problem.

Together with Tinker's insight, Charleston's insistence on an indigenous covenant with the Creator dissolves the basis for this sense of superiority. Together they challenge the Christian to imagine a God who is revealed in history, as transcending history to function in spatiality, God as not limited to a progressive march of truth proclaimed *only* through time, but existing and being revealed in places, all possible places, beyond time. Tinker points to the problematic of Christianity's entanglement with Western linear thought as a factor limiting the Euro-American understanding of God, contributing to the ongoing failure to hear Native American theologies that arise from an indigenous sense of space and place (2004, 104).

Tinker's explication of a non-linear experience of God, in or out of history, is not exactly the same as the Christian theological distinction of the triune God as both immanent and transcendent. Tinker describes spatial versus linear conceptions of how God works and reveals God's self. The historical-linear conception, Tinker argues, traps God in time. This conceptual trap prevents the Christian believer from easily conceiving the possibility of Charleston's claim that many indigenous tribes and peoples preserve a "memory of themselves as a People, chosen by the one God to inhabit a special land and to be in covenant relationship with their Creator," a people with the responsibility of living in harmony with the creation (Charleston and Robinson, 2015, 2). It is possible to imagine Christians and academics alike, upon first exposure to Charleston's story, rending their garments in the manner of Caiaphas (Matt 26:65). It is unsettling, especially to those with a stake in structures of power, to imagine God acting radically outside those presumed structures.

Charleston (2015b) calls his claim "the other half of the story of monotheism" and insists there is a "complementary theology to the testimony of ancient Israel, an ancient theology that arises out of another promised land" (2). Charleston goes on to explicate that disruptive, complementary theology. A serious consideration of Tinker's identified error in evangelism, and Charleston's insistence on a Native covenant, require an answer to related theological issues, Christological in nature. Were the indigenous tribes implicit Christians, knowing, without knowing, Christ? An answer would need to begin with the universal will of God to save all peoples, and with Karl Rahner's proposal that there exists implicit faith in Christ (Wong 1995, 613). Charleston's (2015b) insistence upon a covenant that existed between the one Creator God and many indigenous tribes in the pre-colonization Americas differs from Rahner's conception, though, in that Charleston speaks of a whole people relating to God, whereas Rahner's anonymous Christian arguably describes individual faith relationship becoming aware of an implicit faith. Yet Charleston's and others' descriptions of indigenous ontology as one open to the spiritual mysterious, and accepting of ambiguity, explain how a whole people could find and function in a covenant relationship with the Creator (15). As Native writers repeatedly point out, their people function in a communal mindset. It would follow that their sense of relationship with the Creator would be communal, as well. The loss of this communal way of being to the individualism that defines the dominant American culture is an important aspect of the cultural genocide described in the data, and something many Native leaders resist. While the vision quest and other indigenous rituals do bring an individual aspect to spirituality within a tribal community, the goal is always to find how one will serve the community (5). Did whole Native communities who lived in covenant relationship with the Creator prior to missionary contact, function as Rahnerian "anonymous Christian" communities, with implicit faith in Christ which became explicit upon pronouncement of the gospel? Pope Paul VI (1965) declares that salvation is by communities, that humans are chosen "not just as individuals, but as members of a certain community" (32). These questions may prompt the American Christian, trapped in an individualistic mindset beyond his or her individual faith, to reflect on the communal aspect of their own salvation experience. Charleston's work reveals loci at which the Christian church could respond to an "inner dynamism" that alters the anonymous state (Wong 1995, 614) and that may place it more communally. The existence of indigenous people as communities of faith responding to their creator God reveals the social in the salvific, the element of God's work that the church too often deemphasizes. To speak in terms of individual conversion to any people whose identity is communal is, perhaps, to ask the wrong question, and even to bring the wrong good news.

Conversion was problematic for indigenous communities, who experienced individual conversions as division, or what the church would call schism. And even today, Native Americans born into Christian homes, or who, like George Tinker, have both an Indian and a Christian parent, must sort through the situation (2004, Dedication). If Tinker is correct that the gospel presented was one confused with culture, his assertion would explain why a Rahnerian movement from implicit to explicit knowledge of Christ was problematic for indigenous communities. To accept that pre-colonial Indians were anonymous Christians, one must also ask what happens when the messenger brings a confused gospel, a civilized, European Jesus. Further, to think of those among the indigenous community who do not identify as Christian as anonymous Christians, today, sounds like continued colonizing, the same White sense of superiority at work. Joseph Wong (1994), though, underscores in a discussion of the anonymous Christian thesis, that Rahner wrote instead with the intention of "broadening" the pre-Vatican II "outlook of the Catholic Church on the followers of extra-Christian religions" (615).

The issues noted in this chapter, that supported the White sense of superiority, continued in full influential force into the twentieth century and Rahner was among those leading the way toward a more inclusive theology. Conceiving anonymous Christianity was a first step for Catholic theology. Rahner's insights toward pluralism inform the question of whether God may have been co-covenanting with people an ocean away from Christianity's reach. Yet, a pre-incarnate Logos, a Spirit of Christ at work prior to the incarnation of Jesus Christ, is not an idea new to Christian theology. The same "was in the beginning with God" (John 1:2 NRSV). Wong (1995) cites Clement of Alexandria, who believed that the Holy Spirit had, prior to the incarnation, inspired not only the ancient Hebrew prophets but even the Greek philosophers (628). The Vatican II "Declaration on the Relationship of the Church to Non-Christian Religions" states that "The Catholic Church does not reject anything that is true and holy in any of these religions and, in fact, looks upon them with sincere respect" (Huebsch 1997, 88). It should be noted, that "these religions" does not expressly include indigenous traditions; they are left out of the Declaration. It can be argued the spirit of the Declaration would include them.

If it is acknowledged that the Holy Spirit is and was at work, universally, across time *and* place, then Christian theology is obliged to acknowledge the possibility that God made a pre-Christian covenant with the indigenous peoples of the Americas. And if this is accepted, it implies that the theologian, the Christian community in the United States and worldwide, as well as the public that comprises the dominant culture, should listen for what is "true and holy" (Huebsch, Vatican II In Plain English: The Decrees and Declarations 1997, 88) from these religious traditions, and especially, per Schreiter's (1985) criteria, listen to the Christians among them. Yet, as the data show over and over, American Indians are regularly overlooked or ignored. Indigenous peoples are rarely included in considerations of transcendent human thought.

The evidence exists that the Creator God was present with indigenous peoples in the Americas, speaking, revealing, sustaining. Their covenant for living on the land included caring for the land, respecting their place in the cosmos, honoring all of creation as dignified, all beings as bearing the image of their creator. Achiel Peelman's (1995) *Christ Is a Native American* presents a Christological response to Native Christianity, looking for "signs of the mysterious presence and action of Christ among Amerindian peoples" (15). Peelman's interviews show indigenous Christians who envision Christ as "a community builder," as "an abused person," as "a very concrete being," and as "the Son of God" (107-110). One man answers the question of who Jesus is for him, in part, by saying, "I am convinced that Jesus would have been a good Indian! He prayed and fasted. Love was his central message" (109). It is incredulous to think that it took millennia for the Christian world to begin to even consider that God had been at work in other places, and that the peoples encountered might have truth to teach the Christian. It is, perhaps, more humbling to find that it is young people today who may be prophets speaking to the church. Peelman's work finds that American Indians, by their very survival in the face of an attempted genocide, carry and are inspired by a "conviction that the Indians have won a moral victory in their long confrontation with western [sic] civilization" (57). As seen in the data, young indigenous leaders deliberately choose forgiveness and non-violence in their confrontation with the culture that need to hear them (Becker et al. 2015).

By Their Fruits

A final consideration remains, in an argument for accepting that indigenous communities have been given insights to which the rest of the world must attend, and that those insights come from the Creator, the same Spirit that swept over the darkness and void in the Genesis account of creation (Gen 1:2), the Spirit that spoke through the prophets of Israel, calling for justice and a holy life. That consideration is that the data represented here, the expressive work of young Native Americans, evidences the work of the Holy Spirit, and arguably stands up to the test offered by Jesus, that you will know them by their fruits (Matt 7:16–20).

The New Testament, including the epistles, suggests that being a covenanted people of God is and always has been a spiritual matter. Bearing fruit is a metaphorical reference to the concrete manifestation of what is in the heart. The Jewish prophets, especially Jeremiah, point to the heart as the seat of faith, the place of knowing God's law. Jeremiah foretells a new covenant "with the house of Israel," but one must ask exactly with whom God will "make a new covenant," since the Christian church is not the "house of Israel" nor the "house of Judah" (Jer 31:31). The prophets repeatedly suggest that compassion and justice are the evidence of this law being written on one's heart. Jeremiah delivers the promise of his God, proclaiming:

> But this is the covenant that I will make with the house of Israel after those days, says the LORD: I will put my law within them, and I will write it on their hearts; I will be their God, and they shall be my people. No longer will they teach one another, or say

to each other, 'Know the LORD,' for they shall all know me. (Jer 31:33–34 NRSV)

The Pauline Epistles likewise echo this truth (Rom 2:15). This work of respectful listening and reflection finds that the indigenous insistence upon the connectedness of all life is a demonstration of God's law in their hearts, an insight the church has carried for centuries, especially in the life of its great saint, Francis of Assisi. Pope Francis (2015) revived his namesake saint's insight, as the pope wrote *Laudato Si*. The encyclical letter calls for protecting and caring for the home all created beings share, echoing the vision of indigenous peoples. In response to the unquantifiable question of whether the Creator made a covenant with indigenous tribes of the Americas prior to European contact, the test that Jesus gave can be applied. The young Native Americans whose individual and collective voice constitute the data, show evidence of fruit that is compatible with the Christian call to social and environmental justice.[10] It is as though Pope Francis had been listening to these young people speaking, or, perhaps, as if these young people had previewed *Laudato Si* before Pope Francis published his letter; both voices are asking all people to care for our common home, Earth. Whether anonymous Christians, the descendants of Christian converts, or whether holding an exclusively indigenous identity, these young people are concerned with caring for the earth, with creating a just world where all people can live. They are respectful of human life and refuse to dwell in anger toward the colonizer. In these actions and attitudes, they *are* living out the social teaching of the Catholic Church and the essence of the teachings of Jesus Christ in the Christian Gospels. This living praxis renders believable the claim that the indigenous knew the same God who made a covenant with Abraham in the desert, the God who incarnated through a descendant of Abraham and of David. The data reveal fruit-bearing that is identifiable as compatible with what is Christian.

Is it colonizing to make this statement, something this work has shunned expressly? The statement is not *assigning* Christian identity to any of the voices heard; to evaluate and identify the actions and the "fruit" of a group as being of the same spirit as Christian action is not to force a Christian identity on them. It is to say: The fruit they are bearing is good fruit, even as they emerge from attempted genocide, and cultural devastation.

---

10. *Laudato Si* is part of the social teaching of the Catholic Church, a body of writing that addresses the social situation of the modern world, recommending what the response of the church should be. Pope Francis address the Encyclical Letter not only to Catholics or to Christians, but to all people, due to the urgency of the environmental concerns he raises.

These young Native Americans may be better Christians than the Christians they eschew.

White European culture, particularly in twenty-first-century America, bears a mixed basket of fruit, to extend the test of Jesus and its metaphor. Racism, or more specifically here, the presumption of White superiority to other peoples, is unconsciously embedded in the minds of both White Americans and often the minds of Native Americans, Blacks, Hispanics, and other minority and immigrant groups who find themselves pressed into a system that would make them less than the full human beings God created them as. This mental and spiritual infestation is well described in Leslie Marmon Silko's (1977) novel *Ceremony*, which Tinker (1993) chose to open his work, *Missionary Conquest* (1-2). The novel's protagonist has an awakening moment in which he recognizes that he has internalized White superiority. As Tayo "steals" back his own cattle from the White rancher who stole them, he grapples with even calling the cattle stolen, because a White person has taken them. Silko (1977) describes his transformational moment:

> He knew he had learned the lie by heart—the lie which they had wanted him to learn: only brown-skinned people were thieves; white people didn't steal, because they always had the money to buy whatever they wanted. The lie. . . . The liars had fooled everyone, white people and Indians alike; as long as people believed the lies, they would never be able to see what had been done to them or what they were doing to each other. (190–91)

A new generation of Native Americans has awakened to the lie. Leaders from their own communities have pointed the way. The younger voices emerging point out that they are being ignored, that the images of the Indian are caricatures, that the wider culture finds them invisible at best, but finds their spirituality worthy of appropriation. And yet, these young indigenous people are speaking. They have decided that the heritage they are painstakingly reclaiming is needed, now. They are determined to save themselves, and the rest of us, collaterally. This is Christlike.

It is possible that hearing the Native American, in the sense defined at the beginning of this work, can save the White man from himself by helping us see ourselves. The faith of the young indigenous people whose voices have been attended to for this work is a faith and spirituality of action. To refuse to listen is to choose death, rather than choosing life so that all people may live, as Israel was instructed by Moses (Deut 30:19). Christians in the United States need to submit themselves to the "fruit" test of Matthew's Gospel (Matt 7:16). As some of the best-educated among

Christians, missionaries had access to the Scriptures. The "black robes" were holy men, ordained, priests. Others were Protestant preachers, respected spiritual leaders, sent as evangelists to carry the Word of God to indigenous peoples. Centuries later we can acknowledge that missionary endeavor was, in varying degrees, misled. There is little question that Tinker is correct in his assessment that their great mistake was equating the Christian gospel with Western European civilization. Yet it leaves Christians within a White-dominated America to ask: How can we stop being so arrogant? The truth claims of the Christian gospel present problems not only for believing Christians, but also for people of goodwill wishing to live in pluralistic society. The problem, for the believing, of holding to Christian doctrine as unchangeable truth, and yet acknowledging truth-value in other religions is one that is not yet resolved. It continues to energize a sense of superiority for the Christian unless examined.

Johnson's Generous God of the Religions

Elizabeth Johnson (2007) in *Quest for the Living God: Mapping Frontiers in the Theology of God* points to the "Generous God of the Religions," noting that the world's religions are no longer tied to the geography of their origins (153). Johnson suggests that the global community arising along with the technology that enables it forces Christian communities to ask the question: "What has God been up to outside our tribe?" (155). She shows how the Catholic Church has acknowledged the work of the Holy Spirit "in a manner known only to God," in situations that make God known, but not explicitly (156).[11]

The Christian can speak of humility as a virtue, but if they believe their faith is right and their neighbor's faith is wrong, untrue, misleading, leading that neighbor to hell, such belief places them in a category apart, and even above, that neighbor. The neighbor is now Other. Fear of collapsing the integrity of doctrinal truth claims can leave Christianity a shell. The church must discover how it will retain a Christology of integrity, true to the Pauline insistence that God wills all people to know God, to come to knowledge of the truth, *and* that Jesus Christ is claimed as the one mediator between God and human beings (1 Tim. 2:4,5). And Christians must do this while remaining humble before their global, or indigenous, neighbor. Can we negotiate and embrace a faith that believes itself to be uniquely true, yet remains humble in the face of the Other, whose faith practice appears so

---

11. Johnson's 2007 discussion of religious pluralism quotes *Lumen Gentium 16* and *Gaudium et Spes 22*.

different from our own? Johnson points to the use of dialogue and suggests we experience its "powerful effect" (Johnson 2007, 163). Unfortunately, the "amicable relationships" Johnson argues are necessary for effectual dialogue between people of different faiths" are often weak, if not absent, in relations between indigenous peoples and the wider culture (163). Indigenous religion is not directly named in most discussions of pluralism, from Vatican II to Johnson; "the religions" being Hinduism, Buddhism, Judaism, Islam, and varied other faiths whose teaching and practices are written down, in some form available for discussion. A passing reference to "pagans" and 'others'" is hardly an invitation to an amicable discussion (169). This omission explains, in part, why the existing relationship of twenty-first-century Christianity is not conducive to promoting dialogue with indigenous peoples. As Winona LaDuke (2017) wrote in her opinion piece, quoted earlier, Native Americans are "tired of being invisible to you all." When even the most earnest advocates of pluralism and interreligious dialogue forget to mention the indigenous, it is a wake-up call. It points to the need for action that begins with the humble listening that began this work.

7

Listening

Saying Yes to Being Changed

OUR OWN ERRORS, SOMETIMES SECRETS TO OURSELVES

This book begins with three references to listening chosen from the sacred texts of Judaism and Christianity. The first command of Israel's God to the nation is "hear." Jesus of Nazareth addresses the commandment to whomever is paying attention. "If you have ears to hear, then listen." This statement appears again in the Gospels as "Let anyone with ears listen." How is this rhetoric working? Who does not have ears? Jesus is teaching about a spiritual reign of God to which not all are attentive, that not all may notice, or to which not all will say *yes*.

We have spiritual blind spots, and truth we do not hear. The Psalmist and King of Israel David offers a prayer pertinent to this later question of listening "with ears to hear" and with a heart to understand. In Psalm 19, David praises the God of creation, pointing to the witness of the heavens and the earth to God's glory. The Psalmist asks, in a reflective tone, "Who can understand his errors?" He continues in a prayer, "Cleanse thou me from secret faults. Keep back thy servant also from presumptuous sins; let them not have dominion over me." He explains why he makes this petition. "Then shall I be upright, and I shall be innocent from the great transgression" (Ps 19:12, 13 KJV). David, the mighty warrior king, the adulterer, the beautiful musician and psalmist, the young shepherd, expresses a final desire before his God. "Let the words of my mouth, and the meditation of my heart, be acceptable in your sight, O Lord, my strength, and my redeemer" (Ps 19:14 KJV). David's psalm as translated here suggests there are "errors" that are secrets, and in the context of his prayer, he recognizes that these may not even be recognizable to himself. He asks to be freed from such errors. The psalmist is asking to be kept free from spiritual error blindness.

All three scriptures speak of "hearing" and point to this kind of listening beyond the sensory meaning, and even beyond mental understanding. Clearly, there is a listening that is done with the heart, that could be called spiritual, and that as such may have a transformative effect on those who hear. Yet, it is possible that we must desire the hearing, and that this is what it means to have ears to hear.

The Mystery That Listening Is

Years before I completed my work of listening respectfully to what Native Americans have been telling White America, I suspected that listening was perhaps the most important aspect of inner growth in life. As that suspicion grew, I found that, like many of my peers, I did not know in any deeper way what it meant to listen. It was unsettling: I realized that I carried little more than a shallow presumption of what listening was.

What does it mean to listen in this deeper manner? This is a question arising more and more frequently in a politically and economically polarized twenty-first-century America. It is a question pertinent to all matters concerning justice, peace, and the well-being of an increasingly interconnected humanity. The status quo of listening has proven inadequate to the call of our times. Our century and our times are a time to listen. But listening never happens from a stance of refusal to allow what is heard to change us; listening means saying *yes* to being changed. It may not change us, but these pages aim to show that this openness—this *yes*—is a qualifier, a necessary aspect of what we call listening, and particularly to what listening means in the cultural context addressed here, an inner listening for change.

I will repeat this working definition: Listening means saying *yes* to being changed.

We are accustomed to listening for what comes from without, that is, to hearing what we hear as data from outside of ourselves. Listening is perceiving, with the perceived sensory information taken in, heard as vibration in our ears, sorted with our mental faculties. We are pretty good practitioners of scientific method, of observation. We are not as good at feeling and empathy and of attending to our own heart perceptions.

Listening with the heart is an exercise that can be cultivated. Meditation, prayer, time in natural surroundings, and even deliberate focus on the beauty of fellow humans are ways to grow our capacity for this kind of listening. It is clear that prayerful, heartful listening is something different than listening for outside information. It does not require auditory perception. It may even be argued that the term "listening" is a metaphor for how we perceive something wholly interior that may or may not manifest as a sound or as vision. We may just as possibly listen to a bodily ache or stirring, a taste, a thought or a vision, or a sense of disturbance.

Privileged Ones Who Listened

This work sets out to examine the listening relationship, or failure thereof, between the power-holders across American history and the peoples who inhabited the land that is today the United States of America. It is no accident that it begins by citing texts from the Christian tradition. These texts have informed and misinformed their adherents, sometimes disastrously. Yet from those trapped in "presumptuous errors" or perpetrators of "secret faults" may emerge the very freed captives Jesus came for. A version of the Jewish tradition was morphed into a Christian worldview that served to support a European sense of superiority to a world lost without its Christ; it is from within this very tradition that White voices, powerful male voices, traditional voices from palaces and monasteries, offer remedies for the distortions of their own flock. Before we attend to Native American voices, consider two twentieth-century teachers, a Jesuit theologian and a Trappist monk. These Catholic men of European descent were observant of their own times and turmoil, and from there notice there is a need for listening.

The Trappist Thomas Merton and Karl Rahner S.J. offer instruction in this strange act of inner listening that is sometimes called contemplation. Rahner points, first, to the state of "unhearing" in which we find ourselves, post-Enlightenment. In *The Need and the Blessing of Prayer*, Rahner describes an artificial gap within, a separation of ourselves from a part of ourselves, by the "Enlightenment's philistine" (1997, 20), a worldview which drew a line parting reason and matters of faith. Enlightenment thinking bracketed out that which could not be perceived by the body's reasoning capacities, placing such experiences in the category of the unknowable or the irrational. Any perception of the voice of God within us, especially, fell into this category, and educated persons came to doubt they hear such a voice at all. Rahner asserts that failure to notice the voice of God's Spirit within ourselves is a mark of how abstracted our inner listening has become. He finds this "non-listener" who says "I don't notice any of (the Spirit of God speaking within me)," to be a non-existent I" (1997, 20). The non-listener is a person divided from themself, at best. Rahner's description of unhearing is a starting place to consider why and how the nation and culture I was formed in—an America of European descendants as the standard citizen and of Christian presumptions as the prevailing ethos with an undercoating of Enlightenment—fails so audaciously and catastrophically to hear its own critics.

Merton, in *New Seeds of Contemplation*, also expresses concern with this non-listening condition, warning that it results in a false self, and in our not being what we truly are, but rather a "shadow" of our true selves (2007, 34). As Merton addresses the individual contemplative soul, he provides insight into a means for cultural reconciliation that has long eluded would-be peacemakers. Merton's insight suggests it is possible that White America is a culture with a false self, and if that is the case, the resolving of divisions, conflicts, and tensions between cultures within the wider American culture would be stalled, at best. We, as a culture, might be functioning as shadows of the ethos-selves we would like to imagine we are, divided from ourself and ourselves. Reconciliation arises in truth. A culture alienated from its own true self would likely not be listening for messages about that self from outside voices. It would remain in its own shadows, blindly insulated and thickened with privilege, perhaps resenting the disruptors of that settled self. This state could become even more insular if the only voices it heard were its own. A false self could solidify and harden. Merton's words suggest it would take a work of Spirit—already trapped inside the fortress—to soften the hardness of such a cultural self-identity. Only then could an inner voice hear what is true for those outside the self-satisfied haven.

How does this, or any, inner listening happen? How might one individual—much less a wider society—begin to hear and perceive something that they have tuned out and turned off? The great listeners Rahner and Merton tell us that listening happens by an action of God in us, and by action you or I take to allow ourself to hear. In his chapter titled "The Helper-Spirit," Rahner repeats many times—as though we might be hard of hearing—that it is the Holy Spirit who "prays in us" (1997, 21, 23). He reminds us that our own prayer matters, too. Rahner writes, "I must not want to hear his word while being silent, but rather I must say my word so that I hear his word" (1997, 21). We must say *yes*. We must pray as David did, desiring to be cleansed from secret faults.

Merton likewise emphasizes that it is God who "utters Himself in you." That is, we hear and discover this inner voice because God, in mercy, finds us (2007, 39). And like Rahner, Merton recognizes a response, a *yes*, on our part. "Our inner self awakens, with a momentary flash, in the instant of recognition when we say 'Yes!'" This new hearing happens as "I consent to the will of God" and as we begin to see the mercy of God in the "events of life" (2007, 42, 41).

Both teachers remind us that listening brings us into a life that was unimaginable before we started paying attention. Merton says this awakening of faith by our consent brings us into "the presence of hidden majesty" that is not "outside myself" (2007, 41). It is the key to our living the life that is truly unique to us, that we were created to live, that is ours and no one else's, as opposed to living a self-deceptive life in which we cloak our falseness with "pleasures and glory" and live a life that is hollow, in which "I am my own mistake" (2007, 35, 36). For Merton, this is a tragedy which leads to division, a "disease" based on spiritual pride that inhibits this true living (2007, 47). Merton's application can extend to a collective self with shared cultural assumptions—conscious and unconscious. A culture, like an individual, may live a self-deceptive version of itself and become its own mistake. It is remarkable that these two contemplatives, White men who by definition are embedded in all the mistakenness that has been and is the American nation, its religious heritage and its cultural arrogance, each identify this phenomenon of ourselves as our own mistake. And they do this through inner listening.

Merton and Rahner each find that listening is powerful. It will change us and it is possibly the only thing that can. Our consent to listen will turn loose God's consuming fire and will leave us broken, warns Merton. But he gives us a vision of the gain that comes of saying *yes* to the sacrifice of "being broken": We become the instruments of healing of the divisions, or reunion (2007, 70–72).

Rahner finds that God "loves squanderingly" and pours his spirit "torrentially into us" (1997, 20). It should not surprise those listening that this Spirit would respond to our *yes* by urging the listener into the same "squandering" love for God's other creatures. Rahner shows that the Spirit helps us pray this generous, torrential prayer that can only come from God in us. When we begin to listen, we hear this spirit speaking in us, singing in us, though we don't know for what we should pray. Rahner instructs, "(The Spirit of God), however, knows, and that is enough. The shout of our heart seems to die away in the deathly stillness of the God who is silent, unheard. (The Spirit of God) however, shouts safely and perceptibly over the abysses of the nothing that separate us from the Eternal" (1997, 22). The power of this prayerful listening lies in its dissolution of fear. When we experience the Spirit speaking, says Rahner, "then we are not afraid." We find that when the spirit prays in us, with "the unshakable certainty of the eternal God," that a transformation begins to happen to our own prayer. Our fear, as Rahner describes, dissolves as "(the Holy Spirit) prays in us," and "we repeat his word to him. We pray" (1997, 22–24).

Both Merton and Rahner show how listening is able to transform us as it teaches us to pray. Merton, throughout his writing, emphasizes the power of this attentiveness and consent to God's voice to lead us to authentic lives, to the joyful fulfillment of being who we truly are, doing what we were truly meant to do. Rahner also speaks of this transformative power to overcome the divided inner condition, when we listen. "One can't practice polytheism before the altars of the heart," says Rahner (1997, 18). It is the healing of this division within that transforms us; when we single-heartedly attend to what we hear inside of us, the Spirit takes our inner "noise" and begins, like a grade school music teacher, to bring it all into concert, into true prayer. When the division within is healed, we become able to heal division without.

This, my reflection concluded, is listening. It is a spiritual work that ends in healing and reconciliation, first with ourselves, then moving outward. We are still full of noise and squeaking and flatness. But these teachers tell me that we need not be virtuosos to come or to join the choir. We simply need to come, and listen to the song, until we find ourselves joining in the singing (1997, 22). The singing, this sound from within, is the chamber of change. It is the presence of that squandering love that wants us to listen, to say *yes*, to hear singing and to join in. If we can hear it, and if we say *yes* and join it, we are changed. It is a sound that comes through a place within us that knows who we really are, to whom we belong, and that we, in fact, belong to each other. The next chapter will turn toward a hoped-for transformation. It will ask how we can start saying *yes* in broader ways, if we have been able to listen with our hearts. What action can be taken as we are listening?

To dismiss this inner listening is an act of presumed privilege to avoid, leaving us where we have always been. Where there remains the problem of a culturally embedded White sense of superiority, it can exist for each of David Tracy's (1981) three publics. We must ask how each—the academy, the church, and the wider society—might become free of, respectively, intellectual, theological, and cultural distortion tethered to narratives and practices from the past (6). It will recommend action in each case, in response to the beautiful data and these reflections on what Native American voices have been telling us.

8

Hearing, then Healing
Recommended Action

FORSAKING THE PRIVILEGE OF AVOIDANCE

The United Nations Declaration on the Rights of Indigenous Peoples affirms "that all doctrines, policies and practices based on or advocating superiority of peoples or individuals on the basis of national origin, racial, religious, ethnic or cultural differences are racist, scientifically false, legally invalid, morally condemnable and socially unjust" (United Nations 2008). Native Americans have been and are speaking, but as has been shown, the wider culture has not been listening. This is the problem this work has addressed, and its very existence within American culture points to an odious sense of the superiority of White persons and White culture that pervades the consciousness of United States society. To ignore, to dismiss, to define another is a form of arrogance, morally condemnable.

To presume to define, and then ignore the Other, in whole groups, whole populations and communities, is a "morally condemnable" privilege (United Nations 2008). The slave cannot choose to ignore the master, and so it is with power structures. The White sense of superiority that exists both unconsciously and expressly within the United States, in minds, played out in interactions, in public media, in legal and educational settings, represents a failure of equality at best, flagrant oppression at worst. Once an awareness of this sense of superiority is awakened at all in those who possess it, the process of dismantling it might begin. But that process has been elusive throughout twentieth-century United States history, and continues to elude in the twenty-first century due to a very old chicken-and-egg type quandary. It is difficult to identify a point of entry when it is unclear if the attitude creates the culture or if the reinforcing culture is creating the attitude. Answers are needed to the question, How can we bring about structural change, real social transformation, as called for by the method of social analysis? (Holland and Henriot 1980, 37). Change will require a recognition that listening to Native Americans will mean putting an end to the privilege of selective listening, on both an individual and cultural level. White persons must give up the privilege of avoidance.

The work of listening to those who have been historically ignored, rendered invisible and inaudible by the dominant power-holders surrounding them, has revealed a surprising response from young Native Americans. In the same manner that White, Euro-American culture has for centuries ignored the voices of indigenous peoples, there is a sense in which that same dismissive White culture is being ignored. Even as young Native Americans express indignation, pride, encouragement, or humor, they speak first to their own people. They are not asking the White culture's permission to speak, nor do they seek approval or validation. Rather, when the broader culture notices what they are saying, those speaking tend to minimize the attention (the1491s 2016). For example, as the 1491s gathered as a panel, they note that there are academics studying what they are doing. The panel members make it very clear that their intent in creating videos is not to be studied or examined; they are not addressing the academy, the Christian community, or White culture expressly. The presentation's title speaks of addressing stereotypes, but this is directed first at the internalized stereotypes from which indigenous people themselves seek freedom (the1491s 2016). If the wider culture hears, it will be incidental, the artists imply. As noted in chapter 1, this work has deliberately shunned the study of Native Americans, in favor of respectful, reflective listening. To presume that Native Americans are always addressing the wider culture in desperate hope of being heard or understood is demeaning and dehumanizing to those who speak. Further, such a presumption also represents a privileged self-importance so odious that it almost seems some of these young Native Americans comprising the data might ignore it altogether, but for the power still exerted by that wider culture upon non-whites in general, and Indians in particular. Ryan Red Corn's "Wounded White Warrior Savior Photographer" is an example of this disdain of White self-importance; the comments on this 1491s video support the impression that many indigenous persons find the attitude of privileged White people disrespectful and even laughable (2016).

As will be seen shortly, Steven Charleston (2015b) speaks of Native theology as carrying three "memories" from a past that the European colonizer nearly destroyed. One is "an acceptance of ambiguity as a value not a problem" (15). Charleston is a tenured professor of theology, a Harvard-educated seminarian, and an Episcopal bishop, expertly aware of scholarship surrounding the ideas of which he writes. Yet, his work on the themes of ambiguity and plurality as related to Native theology never make mention of the work of David Tracy, a theologian of Charleston's generation whose work on these themes is arguably seminal, known to theologians. To write of ambiguity in theology and not mention Tracy is comparable to writing a work on liberation theology and not mentioning Gustavo Gutierrez. Charleston has nothing to prove, nothing to be approved. His works stand, and perhaps implicitly, by omission, make the point that Tracy's (1981) ambiguity, even an analogical imagination, were present in indigenous cultures long before the White colonist erased them, and then found the concepts needful as Western enlightenment and "pure reason" reached its limits (30). Whatever one concludes about Charleston's work, or Tracy's, it is clear that the American Indian community is not waiting for an invitation to speak. It is a moral responsibility, called for by the requirements of social justice, that the privilege of not listening be laid down by those who have clung to it. The sole purpose of listening is that action might be taken toward justice and peace.

The remainder of this chapter will consider how each of Tracy's (1981) identified "publics" within society (6) might accomplish the so-far elusive task of setting aside the privilege of avoidance, and how each might respond to what this work has heard from twenty-first-century indigenous voices.

The Academy: Confront the Narrative

What action can academics take, in response to what young Native Americans are saying today? Academics may contribute by confronting the culturally embedded narrative. The White sense of superiority and the truth-claims shown to be tied to it, may be thought of as resistance to pluralism. Together they have built and reinforced among European-descended Americans an unspoken sense of being set apart, and an impulse to create Others who are not our equals, whole peoples who are not "Thous," in Buber's (1970) sense (53). This sense of superiority and the fixation on dogma also represent a failed relationship with ambiguity. Academics who wish to help build a pluralistic society might more deliberately teach ambiguity. Many may respond by insisting that they already are taking this action, but as will be considered, social conditions in the United States suggest inadequacy of action. The Southern Poverty Law Center's annual report on hate groups in the United States surveyed 10,000 educators, 90 percent of whom said "the climate of their schools had been negatively affected" by the 2016 presidential campaign rhetoric (Southern Poverty Law Center 2017). Hate and division abound.

The narrative that supports a White sense of superiority, while often functioning unconsciously, is surely more conscious to academics. This narrative is false on many levels, but in part it is false by being simplistic. Academics, especially theologians, must engage in truth-telling against a culture that arguably wants to be deceived, *mundus vult decipi* (Buber 1970). Academics' truth-telling is a truth by explication, and it is this task that can continue the work of interrogating our own cultural narratives. While Native American scholars like Dunbar-Ortiz, Tinker, and Deloria resist the narrative, the non-Native academic must do the honest work of examining their own internalization of the narrative, and from there move outward toward structures colonized by the insidious narrative. Academics know this; what they ignore is that decolonization is a work of the intra-personal, as described previously. The work requires interior awareness that can move outward into the many campus-wide programs that address issues related to cultural narratives. These initiatives can be more effective if supported by instructors who have deeply examined their own ongoing relationship to the cultural narratives.

The primary structure in need of transformation is the narrative itself. As Holland and Henriot (1980) point out, there are not necessarily models and precedents for transforming "advanced industrial capitalist societies," nor may there be precedents for the transformation of the most deeply imbedded narratives in a given society (40). The American narrative as it exists is a false one, one that ignores the indigenous, that glorifies the settling of the West and leaves out of expansion the accompanying genocidal acts of the United States military with the cooperation of Christians and business enterprise in cultural genocide. It is a convenient lie. The truth, the reforming and restructuring of the narrative, has the power to change society. Yet, as Holland and Henriot predict, there may be no map to follow. Recasting the narrative will require a continuing response from across society, and it is academics whose work can pull apart layers of falsehood in a manner that is necessary and possibly adequate to its undoing. That exposing by explication is and must be a public work if it is to have a part in social transformation. As Tracy (1981) argues, the work of the theologian must be public discourse that can "aid the cause of clarity" (28). Each of the "publics" identified by Tracy as those to whom the theologian intends to speak in a pluralistic society, has a role (7). Inasmuch as Jesus insists knowing the truth sets people free (John 8:32), the false American narrative concerning the relationship with its indigenous peoples is a theological problem, one that requires public discourse for truthful correction to set free all who are entrapped in its falsehoods, and who will be free.

Further, the role of the academic can hardly be underestimated in the world of digital communication, as the need for explication appears increasingly urgent with each new venue of instantaneous communication. While the academic theologian's work may seem too complex to be communicated to a society consuming abbreviated ideas, Tracy would underscore the "commitment to authentic publicness" that the theologian makes; the nature of the theologian's work is to address "fundamental existential questions" and these are social questions (5–6). America's White superiority problem, the narratives that gave rise to it and that sustain it, along with questions of where it is manifesting now, why and how, are matters that academics, Christians, and every American should better understand. Academics need life-giving passion about their work, bearing in mind always that a society structured on falsehood cannot thrive.

If creating and dissipating a corrected narrative were an easy fix, though, surely it would have happened already. If distorted narratives did not contain some particle of truth, it would be easier to expose them as false. This is where the need to embrace ambiguity arises. Tracy in 1987 suggested the value of an interruption of our false historical narratives, even naming the narrative surrounding Native Americans (68). Tracy writes, "To be an American, for example, is to live with pride by participating in a noble experiment of freedom and plurality. But to be a white American is also to belong to a history that encompasses the near destruction of one people (the North American Indians, the true native Americans) and the enslavement of another people (the blacks)" (68). Of course, Tracy's *Plurality and Ambiguity* is addressed primarily to a "public" of academics, though this shorter work on the problem of pluralism is arguably more accessible than *The Analogical Imagination*. Tracy's advocacy for ambiguity would have academics accept the complexity of the American narrative while acknowledging the "skeletons in the Western closet" (68). The situation in United States society, decades after the publication of *Plurality and Ambiguity*, suggests that Tracy's insights influenced the academy, but reached other publics in a degree too small to have effectually transformed the historical narrative. America in the twenty-first century is witness to a rise in White supremacist movements and race-driven hate incidents not witnessed since the Civil Rights era (Southern Poverty Law Center 2017). Tracy (1987) looks to the role of academics in "interrupting" history, in the way feminist historians have done over the last century, "retrieving and writing the history of women" that was repressed by a male-dominated narrative; he praises historians who have labored in the "archeology of the other," that is, digging up the histories of peoples who "suffered the fate of often being ignored" (71). If the hard work of academic theologians, historians, linguists, and anthropologists speaks only to the academy, or even to academy and church, but has limited influence in the wider society, then challenges to the wider society's narrative can be insular and ineffectual.

American Indians began the task of retrieving their own history, of retelling their own story, and of developing an indigenous scholarship tradition that is not waiting for the White American academic to do so, just as academic women since the 1970s have taken responsibility for the archeology of women in history. How can the academic theologian, especially, speak across publics in a way that will alter an insidious and harmful narrative and possibly transform society? Briefly, it will mean taking more risks. Tracy (1981) reminds the theologian that "no thinker, not least the theologian, dwells in some privileged place from which to view what is happening 'out there'" (339). He calls for a "radical risk of self-exposure to the other that any attempt to analyze the present culture must involve" (339). It is risky to "confront and denounce" (339) one's culture, but this is the assistance that the academic, especially the theologian, can lend to the problem. Denouncing is high on the list of ways to assist.

Confrontation with a false narrative might happen in the pages of scholarly journals, and even in books that reach into retail markets, but there is another venue in which the theologian has influence and can challenge false cultural narratives; that is, the classroom. Pope Francis (2018) issued directives to Catholic universities that speak to this difficulty. Both academic theologians and those in other disciplines have an opportunity to bring scholarship to the public via the classroom. Every academic who stands in front of a classroom must take her or his role of teacher as seriously as he or she takes the role of scholar. The classroom stands as the borderland between the academic world where ambiguity and pluralism are givens, and the non-academic public. Students are the public, discovering the world of study. While many undergraduates will not go on to graduate study, and fewer will become career scholars, every person in a classroom situation represents someone who can carry away, with his or her degree in hand, an appreciation for critical thinking and with it, an exposure to ambiguity and pluralism. It is possible that academics minimize this opportunity and thereby diminish the possibility of public dialogue. Surely most teaching professors intend to instill in their students an open-mindedness and a value for critique of assumed narratives, but it is too easy to focus on the few who are already thinking critically. Academics need to value the classroom as possibly their most valuable point of influence, as a place of proclamation and a seedbed of transformative dialogue.

This recommendation may seem so obvious as not to be worthy of mention. It is worth stating, though, because there are obstacles to this kind of influence, hindrances that did not exist a generation ago. While university administration urges multi-cultural awareness everywhere, the digital world and especially social media have created a student body unlike any previous one. The generation commonly called "digital natives" is instantaneously connected as well as accustomed to obtaining information easily. As of this writing, all young students are digital natives. This generation has been served bullet-pointed lists of "hacks" to solve problems and is inundated with pop wisdom in slogan form. The classroom, including the online classroom, is an opportunity to interrupt, explicate, and deconstruct; or at least to show students that these are possibilities. The theologian and philosopher, especially, because they deal with questions of meaning and existence, have a unique opportunity to engender the open-mindedness that can question the erroneous logic of clever internet memes, as well as dominant cultural narratives. The classroom space is liminal in its locus between the academic and the wider social world where students dwell. Tracy's (1981) insistence on the theologian's public role (29) suggests that students in a university classroom should be treated as a unique "public," part of society, part of academia, to whom instruction rendered represents "articulation of fundamental questions and answers which any attentive, intelligent, reasonable, and responsible person can understand and judge in keeping with fully public criteria for argument" (69). This point is again, crucial, as some academics may find before them students who barely seem to possess Tracy's presumed qualities. This is no excuse to reserve complexities for fellow academics, nor a reason to lower standards for undergraduates. Rather, if there is a perceived inattentiveness, lack of reasoning abilities or responsibility in students, this is more reason to focus effort there. If the light of learning and critical thought goes out, the opportunity to influence in a university classroom may be lost. Francis' (2018) Apostolic Constitution *Veritatis Gaudium* calls for theologians who work with open minds and "on their knees" (Calvarese 2018). Any academic, not only the Roman Catholic, might benefit the society outside his or her university campus by heeding Francis' admonishment against mediocrity, toward dialogue, and interdisciplinary awareness. More importantly, Francis exhorts the theologian to remember the joy in his or her work, as the truth of the theologian is "not an abstract idea, but is Jesus himself, the Word of God in whom is the Life that is the Light of man" (2018).

Another perhaps less obvious hindrance to the academic's public mission has been the slow-rising phenomenon of the university as business, alongside or even replacing in varying degrees, the model of university as public institution established to serve the common good. This alteration of mission or mode may or may not represent a conflict of interest; its effects upon the academic can be disheartening and may impinge the joy of which Francis speaks. It is recommended here that university leadership consider, and study as needed, the effects of the business model of operation upon the fulfillment of their mission statements. It becomes difficult to take the risks Tracy advocates if employed in an environment where the nobler academic goals and ideals are undermined by fiscal concerns. In such an environment, Tracy's (1981) call for the "prophetic passion of a Jeremiah, an Isaiah, an Amos" may be unappreciated at best (339). This is not a matter far afield from the problem of a cultural mega-narrative that is feeding inequality and racism, and that has kept indigenous peoples oppressed and marginalized for centuries. The academy's freedom to confront is tied to social justice and peace, and academics must take up the challenge, even at personal risk. University administration, as part of the academic community, has a moral responsibility to serve the public good in its own way, and to support the efforts of scholars whose work challenges accepted narratives both outside and inside the institution.

There are related practical actions that the academic can take in response to the problem. In many humanities and social science fields, it makes sense to expose students to indigenous voices. Directives toward multicultural campus communities are the standard, and yet in many places of learning, the Native American is nearly invisible. An instructor might use videos of the 1491s as a course text. Inclusion might take the form of reading an essay of Vine Deloria Jr., who is widely recognized as speaking for Native Americans, if anyone is. The stereotypes decried by so many of the voices comprising the data can be dispelled when students see young indigenous people on YouTube, when they laugh with those young people, and when they encounter Native scholarship. Just as importantly, students can be asked to become aware of their own responses to the material. A first step in the disruption of a sense of White superiority is for White people to notice that they have internalized certain attitudes, that they make certain subtle assumptions, despite mental dissent from racism. Such a holistic approach to instruction would move beyond thinking about the problem to understanding oneself, the student, as a possible part of the problem. Reflective work can take many forms, and can be as simple as discussion, as complex as keeping a semester-long journal. Thinking about an attitude of White superiority is insufficient to changing it; these thoughtful discussions have been taking place for decades. Encounters with Native voices and explorations of personal responses to their messages are a missing piece for social transformation. The classroom opportunity is a singular one, and the academic may be remiss who does not use it toward the ends of peace and justice in their own culture. In every confrontation, that academic's work should include or encourage dialogue. It should not assign terms or names for marginalized peoples, even if one's intent is respect. Rather, the academic should ask how persons or a people name themselves. Not to do so risks making the academic guilty of the very sense of superiority they may intend to confront and dispel.

Beyond the classroom, academics do well to heed Bourdieu's (1980) insight into methodological approaches to social science, and to examine their own methodologies, watching, if not for flagrant "racist contempt," for subtler prejudices that might prevent early twenty-first-century academics from seeing what will possibly be "self-evident" by mid-century (3; 5). Any academic whose field possibly touches on indigenous issues should be familiar with Vine Deloria Jr.'s (2003) criticisms of Western academics' approaches, and his arguments for the presence of blind spots in Western academic methodology, as presented in *God Is Red*. Last, the academic, and the theologian especially, must examine their own responses to Deloria, Tinker, and the Native academics like those collected in *Native Voices: American Indian Identity and Resistance* and other anthologies. This kind of reflective approach represents allowing oneself to be confronted by the voices of the indigenous, and it is from that confrontation that one can move outward in whatever context is available and then confront the distorted images of Native Americans and the narrative that upholds oppressive structures.

Dialogue with Native Christian Theology

Pope Francis calls for the "systematic study of the living Tradition of the church in dialogue with all people of our time, listening attentively to their concerns, their sufferings and their needs" (2018).

Steven Charleston's Native Christian theology demands its place in discourse. As a theologian, he has spoken explicitly out of his situation as Christian and Choctaw to academics, to the church, and to the urgent social situation in the United States. Charleston's works represent the values of plurality and ambiguity at work. Charleston (2015b) identifies "three cardinal memories" embedded in the Native theory of which he writes. These are vehicles of memory, which "carries the Native story" and which he says have stood the test of time as "foundational" to Native theological "truth-claims" as they arise in dialogue within Native communities (15). Charleston lists these cardinal memories as: "a sense of human anthropology centered in the communal as opposed to the individual, an understanding of reality as an integrated whole rather than a compartmentalized subject, [and] an acceptance of ambiguity as a value and not a problem" (15). While it can be argued that all of these exist within Christian theology, if not in Christian practice, it is also arguable that these values have been deemphasized, where not wholly forgotten, in Christian practice.

The consideration of a Native Christian theology can no longer be dismissed as syncretic. The Christian community can no longer exist in an unspoken policy of theological assimilation, in which the Native American Christian is expected to become an American Christian, one who leaves indigenousness at the church door. The indigenous community brings the church insights from its history and context, theological insights to which European-imported Christianity must listen. Charleston's *Four Vision Quests of Jesus* (2015a) presents both a Christology and a soteriology arising from his identified Native "cardinal memories," serving to enrich Christian tradition while remaining faithful to its core doctrines (2015b, 15). Imagining John the Baptist through the archetype of the clown (2015a, 78), or reading the Gospel through a lens of what "wilderness" or "mountain" means for the indigenous Christian is an exercise in openness to pluralism (2015a, 92, 113). Archiel Peelman's (1995) work, likewise, offers Christological insights from indigenous Christians whose understanding broadens and deepens traditional understanding of Christ, imagining Christ as "the most powerful medicine" (120), and challenging the dualism that invaded Western theology (197).

Not only does much Christian theology discount indigenous contributions, but it has dismissed indigenous spiritualities for inclusion as religions. From Vatican II to Elizabeth Johnson's (2007) chapter on "the religions," Christian discourse on other religions too often renders the indigenous invisible (157). Indigenous practices are often discounted among the world's religions, possibly because tribal practices vary, are not systematized, and are not written in books. While it is true that many indigenous people do not like to have their practices referred to as "religions" because they shun Western systemizing and scripturalizing, this should not allow discussions of world religions to render them invisible. This dismissal privileges written or systematized religion. Those discussing world religions can make a distinction, explicate the differences that the indigenous find important, and show how and where the practices have commonality with traditionally recognized religions despite a different relationship to time and history. An apparent invisibility of indigenous spiritual practices in considerations of world religions is difficult to explain. It may be that they do not fit established definitions of religion, lacking a well-defined deity, explicated doctrines, or clear requirements for membership. While indigenous ceremonies are often kept within the community, this is no reason to leave them out; most of the world's religions have a level of ritual practice that is known only to inner circles, including Catholicism. Whatever the cause of the omission, it is disrespectful and represents the kind of oversight that indigenous voices call out (Tinker 2004, 104). After indigenous spiritual practices are considered worthy of consideration alongside other religions, the academy and the church might begin to listen to indigenous Christian theologians.

The Church in America: Show Up as Communities

What can the church do, in response to what young Native Americans have pointed out? This work has limited itself to hearing and responding to what young indigenous people are saying primarily in the United States. That research choice was made, in part, because the experience of Native Americans arises from interaction with and influence of the United States government and military, as well as within a uniquely American culture. While the situation in Central and South America, or in Canada, bears similarities in that indigenous communities in these places were likewise colonized and traumatized by Europeans, American Indians and the wider American culture have a singular relationship. Awareness of indigenous rights and of the horrors and trauma of colonization has grown in recent decades in all of these situations, but the United States does not lead in reconciliation efforts.

The church in the United States might, again, look to Canada for a model of where to begin. The Canadian Conference of Catholic Bishops, the Canadian Religious Conference, the Canadian Catholic Aboriginal Council, and the Canadian Catholic Organization for Development and Peace, together formed a coalition to plan for action. Reconciliation is a long process, and the Catholic Church in Canada has not formally issued an apology, though individual religious orders who operated residential schools have, including the Jesuits (Dettloff 2017). Canada's First Nations have asked for an apology from Pope Francis, who has offered a general apology, and has asked forgiveness for the Catholic Church's role in colonization; Pope Benedict XVI, though, expressed "sorrow" over the church's historic role in indigenous trauma in Canada (Dettloff 2017). None of the responses are adequate in the face of the magnitude of the offense.

Information is only as helpful as are those who handle it. As theologians listen for what and how Native American voices speak to faith, the community that claims itself disciples of Jesus Christ must also determine its response. The church in America—meaning Christians in leadership, denominational leaders, pastors and teachers, and just as importantly, lay persons in local communities and parishes—must begin with the problem of indigenous invisibility. Churches involved in social justice action often focus locally, which means reconciliation with tribal nations is not a pressing concern because there are no Native Americans in view. Again, it is often forgotten that more than three-quarters of American Indians live in cities (Martinez et al. 2016, xi). Concerned leaders, whether ordained or lay persons, can do the work of finding Native communities within the larger community and inviting Native Americans to make themselves and their truth known in local church settings. Universities often provide venues for Native American students to connect; this is a space where the urban Indian is visible. Students might be open to a respectful invitation to educate non-Natives about their identity, history, and hopes for the future. If this kind of connection is not a possibility, there is nothing preventing the promotion of shared viewing of Native-produced films, videos, and books. This is appropriate for small groups in parishes, youth groups, and adults concerned with social justice. Larger cities may have indigenous community centers, and this should be investigated locally. Every church should know if there is an American Indian community within the wider community they serve, and the church community must make that community visible within their own.

If concern and interest are not already present in a local body, efforts to raise concern by bringing indigenous peoples' truth before a group, are likely to fail. People are busy and stressed and tend not to want to be burdened with what they may view as one more problem. As will be shown shortly, the remedy for this perspective is seeing our indigenous neighbors as a gift to our own communities, as carriers of truth and beauty that we, the church need. Films and books cannot substitute for the work of the Holy Spirit, but the Spirit may accompany these works. The church must begin wherever the Spirit begins; that is to say, with whomever the Spirit has given concern. The model of small communities is a valid one for this purpose. A group gathered out of concern for justice, healing, and reconciliation with indigenous peoples clearly constitutes "a form of apostolic mission to the wider society" (Sowing Seeds 2008, 10). This work recommends the small community model as it exists in varied Christian traditions, as a guide to lead from concerned faith toward action. Native Christian writers like Charleston, Tinker, and Clara Sue Kidwell, and many others can serve as conversation partners present to small communities through their writing, where concern has already moved a few to gather in the name of Jesus and ask, "what shall (we) do?" (Acts 22:10 NRSV).

As seeds of concern take root in a community, awareness then must become public. It will be recommend here beginning with the church, but also for the wider public, that every possible form of public apology be made to tribal communities. For an example, the church in America might look to Australia, where Christian leaders called for a national apology in 2001, and that apology was offered by Prime Minister Kevin Rudd in 2008, followed by public parades and demonstrations. The National Council of Churches in Australia in 2001 "committed itself to educating the churches on their involvement in the history of child removal, making church and agency records available and addressing allegations of abuse in church-related institutions" (Simons 2001). Indian Country Today Media Network documents seven public apologies made to American Indians (Lee 2015), some from government, some from ecclesial bodies, but the media network notes elsewhere that these apologies come with inadequate attention (Capriccioso 2010). Australia's example demonstrates that the church can lead in reconciliation, but it must be ready to move from awareness and sorrow to proclaimed apology; yet even its 2001 apology came a few years after legislation that addressed the "Stolen Generation" of indigenous children and establishment of a "National Sorry Day" every May 26 (Reconciliation Australia 2023). For this to ever be a reality in the United States, a shift toward concern and a sense of being "sorry" must take place, and the disciples of Jesus Christ may not wait for government action. We need a few voices crying in the wilderness for repentance; apologies ought to be arising first from Christian communities. American's tribal nations have been violently rendered vulnerable, and as they reclaim their dignity, Christians must take to heart the example of Jesus in relating to groups that his own people, the Jews of the Roman era, had marginalized; women, Samaritans, lepers, the poor, gentiles. Small communities can begin with meditation on these stories, and imagine what a healed America might look like, and what action the Gospels would recommend toward that. The church's awareness and repentance could follow with a ritual demonstration of repentance, forgiveness, and reconciliation in a larger memorial gathering.

Wounded Knee Massacre as Anamnesis

One could envision gatherings at Wounded Knee, in South Dakota, or locally, across the United States, on December 29 each year, as anamnesis for Native Americans, a eucharistic event and place that crosses from

1890 into the present, a marker of memory, resistance, and preservation of identity. When indigenous people gather for the memorial of the massacre and remember the short-lived taking back of sovereignty in 1973, they walk (Becker et al. 2015). The march is a long walk, timeless, especially if those present believe they are in the presence of the ancestors and lost loved ones, as was promised by the prophet Wovoka at the inception of the Ghost Dance (Brown 1971, 390). The young generation at Wounded Knee walk with the invisible community, a Ghost Dance for today that evokes the dangerous memory of which Johann Baptist Metz wrote, post-twentieth-century holocaust, a memory that represents a "form of eschatological hope" (Metz 2007, 169). One can imagine uncanny parallels to Catholic teaching on Eucharist, "uncanny" in the usual sense of the word and not necessarily as David Tracy uses it; yet both usages apply. Does one have a place at this table without first confessing complicity in the deaths being remembered? The White descendants of European immigrants may experience an existential "not-at-homeness" when confronted with the attempted genocide that provided the homes and lifestyle they now enjoy, an experience that explains the privileged avoidance described above, and the continued rendering of Indian peoples as invisible (Tracy 1981, 356). It's uncomfortable to remember. Wounded Knee, both as historic event in the 1890 massacre and as sacred place in what is now the state of South Dakota, serves as holder of memory; for the Sioux Nation, for tribes who suffered similar losses, and for White Americans willing to look, and to remember.[1] To gather at Wounded Knee is to remember death, and to remember deliberately. The church needs to show up at this remembrance, and for remembrances across the land that it helped colonize. This need not mean a pilgrimage to South Dakota; local demonstrations can be transformative, also, and it is not assumed that the Lakota or other nations want such a trail of visitors. Nevertheless, a physical sign of solidarity is called for, a memorial that involves moving, standing, facing, remembering.

---

1. Historian Dee Brown's *Bury My Heart at Wounded Knee: An Indian History of the American West* (1971) offers a seminal account of the events leading up to the Wounded Knee massacre. The 2007 film by the same name, directed by Yves Simoneau, offers a less rigorous account, yet for many Americans may serve as an introduction to the relationship between Indian tribes and those settling the western United States territories. The murders on December 29, 1890, of more than 300 people, including women and children, many Minneconjous led by their Chief Big Foot, is considered to have ended indigenous resistance by war. The U.S. Army 7th Cavalry left dead bodies in the snow, because a snowstorm was impending (Brown 1971, 414-16). Those bodies remained there through that winter, and photos taken when a removal party arrived have been widely published.

The Ghost Dance prophet Wovoka promised a renewal of the land, a return of the buffalo, and a reconciliation with the dead ancestors. The ritual dance Wovoka taught is for the Indian peoples; the renewal promised might be shared with White people who survive Wovoka's prophesy of White people drowning in massive flooding (Brown 1971, 390). A gathering at Wounded Knee could not be to partake presumptuously in tribal ritual; it would have to be done as an act of repentance, an offering, a sign.

Tribal motorcyclists set an example for the church. A motorcycle event, the Lakota-sponsored Wounded Knee Memorial Run, states its mission as aiming to "preserve the memory of the Lakota people who suffered and died at the Wounded Knee Massacre on December 29, 1890. There will be prayer and ceremony, and honoring of the Ancestors by remembering their suffering and paying respects" (Wounded Knee Memorial Motorcycle Run 202+ n.d.). This annual event invites riders by registration every August. The summer event is not as arduous as the December gathering of indigenous youth and elders at the Wounded Knee cemetery, the site of the infamous massacre of nearly three hundred people that left corpses in the snow, and that ended the era of Indian resistance in open warfare. The walk to the cemetery and the Wounded Knee Memorial Run represent remembering, in place. The gathering of the church community, whether at Wounded Knee, or from wherever a Christian community is located, could bring about an outward growth of awareness and repentance. Christian communities would do best to go in person, in December; respect would require contacting tribal leaders, asking if a group might come as a demonstration of repentance and solidarity. The long trip to South Dakota from the population centers where many White people live, can serve as remembrance of the long walks that indigenous tribes endured, the Trail of Tears and other marches that removed them forever from their homes. Apologies should be offered, along with an articulation of the intention to remember, alongside the indigenous survivors. When the church, members of the military, privileged White Americans, and the descendants of murdered Indians stand together, at the site of Wounded Knee, the remembrance has the possibility of evoking hope, what Metz called "a solidarity looking back" in which "the dead and the vanquished" are present also, breaking "the spell of history as a history of victors" (Metz 2007, 169). The presence of the "victors," remembering suffering their own ancestors caused, making confession that Wounded Knee was not a victory, can disrupt the false narrative. This may be the first dose of the healing medicine America needs.

Steven Charleston (2015b) in presenting his Native and Christian theological insights argues, "Identity . . . originates in memory" (10). It follows that the erasure of stories of Native American trauma correlates with confused identity. Charleston points to the loss of language as the primary tool of erasure; he asserts that the "Native collective consciousness" exists in pre-Columbian memories and post-conquest memories (11). Charleston insists that this erasure is not unique to the suffering and identity loss of Native Americans but is a "strategy of oppression" and an "insidious form of domination (which) has been practiced around the world" (11). Like Tinker, Charleston is a Native scholar looking for restoration. This work asserts that restoration of indigenous memory and Charleston's prescribed "truth-telling" is needed to restore both indigenous communities and a Euro-American dominant culture comprised of persons benefitting from the historic trauma of Indians, but without truthful memory of historical realities (12). Charleston's theological theory shows how Native memory holds valuable content for the "concerns of global society" (18). But how can the descendants of European colonists, institutions of White power built on "the tragic myth of the Doctrine of Discovery" (18) possibly awaken their memory, and find motivation toward a restoration that, for them, means a loss of power? What might shake the White sense of superiority at its core, in order to drive transformation for the oppressor, who needs it in a very different way?

This careful work of listening to young Native American voices points to the need for a work of active listening on the part of Euro-descended Americans. It points to ceremony, to a creative work of liturgy. Americans should go to Wounded Knee and join Native Americans who gather to remember the mass killing that ended an era in United States history, and which represents the wall on the present side of the chasm in memory to which Charleston refers. The end of the Indian Wars was the end of hope of returning to the pre-Columbian memory of Native life. It is the place where two cultures fought and both lost. It is a place where painful memory can be resurrected, a place White Americans need to look at. Wounded Knee should become a Mecca, a Jerusalem, a place of weeping to which every Christian, every citizen who has inherited any form of privilege at the expense of the indigenous inhabitants of the Americas, should journey for the purpose of remembering. Those who cannot journey in person should view the 2007 film *Bury My Heart at Wounded Knee*, or read Dee Brown's seminal book by the same name (1971) or any of the other important works cited here by indigenous authors. While these works are surely no substitute for human encounter, or for the power of experiencing place as a marker of history, the scholarly work of a dedicated historian can trigger change. Further, these experiences represent actions that respect the primacy of storytelling, honoring indigenous ways of communicating knowledge about themselves.

It is difficult to imagine the meaning of Wounded Knee, as place, for America's tribal nations. As part of a PBS film project, *The West* gathered varied perspectives of the American frontier. Rick Williams (Oglala Lakota) is featured on the project's website. He writes,

> Wounded Knee happened yesterday. For Lakota people, Wounded Knee is today. Wounded Knee represents all the frustrations of those years and years and years on the reservation. Even though it happened in 1890, it's fresh in Lakota peoples' minds and in their hearts. That tragedy, that destruction, that devastating thing that happened to them, it exists today. It exists in our hearts and our minds, the way we think when we see about, when we talk about Indian-White relations, that's the first thing that comes to mind. We'll never forget Wounded Knee. (Ives 1996)

What if Christians led the way by coming out to recognize Wounded Knee, joining in the annual remembrance, by showing up, with visible signs of repentance? Are we able to "share the table" with Native Americans at the place they remember as a place of crucifixion of their people? Tracy (1987), in his chapter on "The Question of History," discusses the self-deceptive optimism that is sin, that "inauthentic existence" in which "the self keeps turning in upon itself . . . in an ever-subtler dialectic of self-delusion" (74). Tracy continues by pointing out a dual action of grace working in history, showing how "Grace comes as both gift and threat" (75). It is possible to conceive the voices of young Native Americans as deliverers of grace to a White American culture, a grace as threat, which, writes Tracy,

> Yet grace also comes as a threat by casting a harsh light upon what we have done to ourselves and our willingness to destroy any reality, even Ultimate Reality, if we cannot master it. Grace is a word Christians use to name this extraordinary process: a power erupting in one's life as a gift revealing that Ultimate Reality can be trusted as the God who is Pure, Unbounded Love; a power interrupting our constant temptations to delude ourselves at a level more fundamental than any conscious error; a power gradually but really transforming old habits. No interrupter can understand what Christians mean without using the language of power: a power that comes as both gift and threat to judge and heal, not fundamentally moral transgressions or sins, not errors, not mistakes, but that ultimate systemic distortion, sin itself (75).

Can we thank Native Americans who are writing, publishing themselves on video, singing, and rapping, for being the grace that threatens us? Can we receive this grace? This may be the most important work of the American Church.

Participation in a memorial gathering at Wounded Knee, deliberately remembering this massacre and horror in our history, could represent the kind of memory that imagines as Tinker (2004) notes, not bound in history, but as spatial, related to place (104). Tinker points out that a Native American understanding of *basileia*, especially as used in the Gospels, is related to place, though this has been disallowed in favor of questions of when the "kingdom" of God might appear (93). While such disallowance may have been a corrective to otherworldly conceptions that situated the *basileia* in heaven as opposed to Earth, Tinker argues for moving out of a narrow and sexist conception that represents a "transcultural blind spot" (93–94). If the *basileia* is not a place out there somewhere, but neither is it only the reign of God, present in the hearts of human beings, it might be more generously conceived as manifesting out of sacred places, as hearts come together in those places. Tinker argues that this is no "aberrant cultural reading" of the *basileia*, but rather that Mark's Gospel especially points to usages of "the way," comparing this to a Native American conception of the Good Red Road, which points to a spiritual way of life lived out in material space (96). A gathering at Wounded Knee presumes the presence of those who died in that place, the ancestors themselves. To place ourselves, as descendants of those who helped destroy the dead, in that circle, and at that table, could represent ceremony of the kind needed to begin cultural healing.

To recommend a concrete action, Christians, then, might show up to remember Wounded Knee as a physical sign of repentance and solidarity, but it may be almost equally effectual to establish December 29 as a National Wounded Knee Memorial Day, dedicated to Americans partaking in the resistance that tribal nations continue to stand in, into the present moment. This may take the form of local public gatherings or even showing up in South Dakota, though again it is noted that there is no standing invitation from the indigenous. The substantial component to action is a public expression that responds to what Native Americans are saying: a recognition and admission of harm done, the asking of forgiveness, and the willingness to stand in solidarity with indigenous communities for their dignity, even if that stance is unpopular and costs us something.

Paying attention to efforts at healing and reconciliation, as contiguous to the data, it becomes apparent that there are groups within the wider society who are arguably more assertive for reconciliation than the church. A group of United States military veterans offered an exemplary action during the winter of 2016 when they traveled to join the Dakota Access Pipeline protests with indigenous peoples who call themselves Water Protectors. Lead by Wesley Clark Jr., the son of NATO Supreme Commander Wesley Clark Sr., the veterans came before Sioux tribal leaders and knelt down, apologizing for the actions of the United States Army in a formal ceremony, asking forgiveness for genocide committed against their people by the U.S. Army. Many of the veterans were members of the still-existing Army units who carried out the orders that killed whole Native communities in the same location.

While Christian denominations have offered official apologies, the veterans' apology was especially meaningful to the indigenous gathering for several reasons. First, the apology was very specific and named crimes against the tribes. Wesley Clark Jr. says,

> Many of us, me particularly, are from the units that have hurt you over the many years. We came. We fought you. We took your land. We signed treaties that we broke. We stole minerals from your sacred hills. We blasted the faces of our presidents onto your sacred mountain. When we took still more land and then we took your children and then we tried to take your language and we tried to eliminate your language that God gave you, and the Creator gave you. We didn't respect you, we polluted your Earth, we've hurt you in so many ways but we've come to say that we are sorry. We are at your service and we beg for your forgiveness. (Dickinson 2016)

To be present at a protest that was protecting the earth and particularly, its water, was meaningful. To be present alongside Native peoples in a situation that meant risking arrest was even more meaningful, along with the fact that the veterans had to make a long and arduous winter trip to be with the tribes in tribal space. This constitutes a full act of solidarity, standing alongside, sharing the risk of confronting a danger to the earth. It was, arguably, fruit worthy of repentance (Luke 3:8). The 2016 gathering at Standing Rock, in resistance to a pipeline planned to pass under the Missouri River, around the city of Bismark, North Dakota, and along the edge of the Pine Ridge Reservation, included clergy, who made the same long trip and took similar risks.

Chief Leonard Crow Dog (Sicangu Lakota) accepted the apology formally, as tribal voices in the gathering made sounds of excitement, and members of the military contingent wept (Dickinson 2016). Crow Dog, from a wheelchair, reminded the gathering that while the Lakota are a sovereign nation, saying, "We do not own the land; the land owned us." He told the veterans, "One of these countries has to tell the truth, that we are human beings." Crow Dog cites a series of treaties that allowed the Lakota to be a sovereign nation (Oceti Sakowin Camp 2017). The ceremony is powerful and exemplifies the grace that the Native communities offer the culture that colonizes them.

News reports on the Standing Rock protests confirm the presence of faith leaders to join the pipeline protest. Their presence was reported as motivated by concern for environmental justice as well as other concerns and represented risk of arrest. Around 500 clergy showed up at Standing Rock; Methodist, United Church of Christ, Episcopalian, Mennonite, Presbyterian, Baptist, Catholic, Unitarian, and others from around the world came out after the protest had drawn out a heavily armed police presence. Though reports of numbers varied, veterans came in greater numbers than clergy, by about four times. Unitarian minister Rev. Kelli Clement (2016) explained the clergy's presence, saying that water is not merely a Native issue, and that the clergy were also present "to say that whites were wrong, that the Doctrine of Discovery was wrong, that churches were wrong." Clement (2016) says that she is there as a "middle-class, middle-aged white woman" to take back to her congregation of "middle-class white people" her understanding of what is happening at Standing Rock, and to ask, "What can we do to help?"

Of course, the hope would be that Americans of many affiliations and identities would follow the example of Christian clergy and U.S. Army veterans. The church needs to show up with fruits worthy of repentance, that is, at personal cost. When it is impossible to be physically present, solidarity can be symbolic, but the most powerful symbolic presence is the sign of one's own body. As discussed above, small communities who begin to find a vision of the need to address indigenous peoples and be part of reconciliation, should plan demonstrations of their intentions, whether this means presence at protests or through published letters, digital expressions, or giving money to the legal funds set up for Native Americans who were arrested at Standing Rock, whose cases are in courts.

American Society: Remember December 29, 1890

What actions can non-Native Americans take, in response to what young Native Americans are saying today? First, many Americans have to answer questions surrounding responsibility. They need to resolve for themselves the issue of how they are culpable in the present situation, when their personal history does not appear to intersect with Native Americans. In a word, and as previously noted, one need not have personally participated in harm—even across time—to be the beneficiary of that harm. And to benefit from a harm done puts individuals in the place of asking what is their responsibility to those harmed persons, those who have been called "crucified peoples?" (Sobrino 2008, 3). The Christian is obligated out of Gospel commands, but the citizen who cares for justice and peace is obliged to answer as well. Those persons are obliged to ask: What does it mean that I have benefitted from violence and destruction to whole peoples?

The directives here parallel those for the academy and the church in that privileged White Americans must see and hear Native Americans and their story. Film is an effective communicator and has been used well recently, in works praised by Native American sources for being respectful and honest. Indian Country Today called *The Revenant* (2016) "a game-changer" for its move out of stereotypical depiction of Indians (Killsback 2016). This stands in contrast to reviews a decade earlier of *Bury My Heart at Wounded Knee* (2007), which Indian Country Media reminded readers was not a documentary, but fiction based on historical fact (Melmer 2007). By 2018, the same media outlet was more hopeful of respectful portrayal of American Indians, as a review of *Hostiles* (2017) called it "a gut punch of reality," and praised its "profound respect for Native culture" (Schilling 2018). More recently, *Killers of the Flower Moon* (2023) was released late in 2023 to acclaim for its account of oppression and trauma in American history. Those who are unlikely to read Dee Brown's work, or to research the history of treaties, might begin with these and other films that increasingly are Native-created. If individuals begin the processes of becoming informed, and of self-examination, asking questions about their own responsibility in the present social situation, those individuals may become motivated to urge their government to act more justly.

Canada's civic response serves as an example in some ways. Its commission gathered input, collected extensive data, and issues calls to action, a model that can be followed (Truth and Reconciliation Commission of Canada, 2015). It is difficult even to imagine a "truth and reconciliation commission" formed out of the federal government of the United States, regardless of administration or party. Yet, Canada formed this commission in response particularly to the harm done in the era of boarding schools, when First Nations children were taken from their parents in efforts to assimilate the children to Canada's own version of White European culture. The commission determined that the residential schools, and the policies that created them, amounted to "cultural genocide" (Smith 2015). A report in the *Ottawa Star* newspaper summed up well the commission's findings, calling the final report "a heart-wrenching and damning 381-page summary . . .

detailing the history and legacy of residential schools—largely operated by churches and funded by the Canadian government—that saw 150,000 First Nations . . . children come through their doors for more than a century" (Smith 2015). The commission's Royal Proclamation of Reconciliation calls for "a complete overhaul of the relationship between Aboriginal Peoples, the Crown, and other Canadians" (Smith 2015). Most importantly, Canada has officially and very openly apologized for the harm and trauma its policies and actions caused its indigenous people. And while United States presidents have issued apologies to Native Americans in the past, their actions were paid such scant attention that Native Americans responded with feelings of being insulted and ignored. Indian Country Media called the 2010 apology event, a signing by President Barack Obama, "a sorry saga" because so little attention was given to it (Capriccioso 2010). The United States government can look to the example of the Truth and Reconciliation Commission of Canada, and its effort to heal relations between Canada's indigenous peoples and its non-indigenous population, and a very public reconciliation effort that named the harm as cultural genocide.

Listening as Deference

A societal move toward an honest "shared memory" (Charleston 2015b, 13) must proceed in a manner similar to that recommended above for the church, informed by deference. Those who share a history with indigenous peoples of the Americas need to listen to their story, be willing to correct the narrative that is serving the colonizer, and out of that encounter, accompanied by apology, form a shared memory. If the memory is an honest one, it can heal.

The situation calls for deference at every step, in every action. There is little hope for change until privileged persons looks at their own attitude, see themselves as the indigenous person sees them, and set aside the privilege of presumption, deferring to the voice of the Other. This deference creates a new listening to what the indigenous person is saying, initiating a beginning point for self-examination. It is not clear, even, what questions a White American might ask, so embedded is our identity as the standard by which the Other is measured. That is what this work's listening offers; the insights gathered by listening as academic, as Christian, as American, and transcending all of these public roles, as human being. Young Native Americans have told spoken to White society's deeply embedded sense of superiority, to its distorted identity, which in turns distorts the identity of Others, and to the need to see the harm this is causing those Others.

Sources from this research, including several 1491s videos and Adrienne Keene's blog on Native Appropriations, point to an immediately accessible respectful action. Americans can surrender their use of indigenous spiritualities, practices, and symbols. Suzanne Owen (2008) traces the American appropriation of Native American practices, noting that the most widely appropriated has been Lakota spirituality, beginning with John G. Neihardt's rendering of the vision of Oglala Lakota elder and holy man, Nicholas Black Elk (40). Neihardt's *Black Elk Speaks*, first published in 1932, became widely read and was received as representative of indigenous religions, in general. Black Elk[2] became an Indian for public consumption, via Neihardt's story, and the appropriation has never waned.

Americans participate in appropriation of Native American spirituality when they purchase manufactured, imitation items, from dream catchers to war bonnets, that borrow from tribal cultures things that are sacred to those tribes. More insidious, perhaps, are appropriation by non-Natives claiming to teach indigenous spirituality to Americans willing to pay. Ward Churchill (Keetowah Band of Cherokees) Native American Studies professor and AIM activist, has written of "spiritual hucksterism" and has offered examples of "plastic medicine" practitioners (Owen 2008, 92). The White sense of superiority identified resists even being questioned about the use of Native American symbols, practices, or culture imagery of any kind. To feel entitled to such use, dismissing the clear messages of the people to whose cultures these things belong, is an odious stance, at best. After Americans expose themselves to indigenous history of the United States, and to Native voices as they exist presently, as prescribed above, it is recommended that they also listen to what the Native American says about why appropriation of their culture is so offensive to them. Adrienne Keene articulates the matter very well, in the context of cultural situations such as Valentino designer labels (2017a) and "hipster" war bonnets (2010). Indian Country Today regularly publishes articles on related topics. It is not, in the digital age, difficult to find the voices speaking out about cultural appropriation. Those who don't listen are guilty of the ignoring and the rendering invisible of which Native writers speak. To listen is to begin to defer. It is difficult to move out of the privileged habit of answering questions for the marginalized. The habit may look like this: A news video or media post says Native Americans want White people to stop appropriating their culture. White people think about it momentarily, and then decide that no one owns spirituality, or a

---

2. The cause for the sainthood of Nicolas Black Elk was introduced in October 2017. In addition to his position as an Oglala Lakota Holy Man, Black Elk was a faithful Catholic convert who served as a catechist and is credited with converting about 400 people to Jesus Christ.

particular art form, or comes to some other conclusion, and then dismiss the question without having ever listened to, read, or spoken to a Native American about it.

A process of disruption of the colonizer's self-supporting narrative can begin with individuals hearing what the Other thinks of White America, of its narrative, of its self-identity in relation to Native Americans. No matter a person's role and function in social life, she or he can facilitate listening to Native Americans by making a decision to pay attention, not to dismiss. Heeding Winona LaDuke's (2017) assertion, satisfied White Americans can stop ignoring indigenous communities, can make them visible by listening and then talking about what they heard. Yet, the member of a privileged social group always must be mindful that it is an act of privilege to choose who can be made visible, who will be heard. Self-examination should include the painful awareness that White persons are not doing Native Americans a generous favor by finally listening; they are correcting a shameful wrong of which they have been partakers. It is a difficult matter to disrupt those who have, so to speak, believed their own commercial.

The wider American public has absorbed, in varying degrees, the Christian narrative of Manifest Destiny, even if a secularized or post-Christian public is not consciously aware of an internalized self-concept of being a city set on a hill or the light of the world (Matt 5:14). The formal civic structural foundations of the United States of America were not explicitly Christian, yet American culture, even in the twenty-first century, is surely a Christian-informed culture. An American self-concept as exceptional in relation to a global community, is easily conceived as formed from the early biblical narratives contributing to a national myth of Manifest Destiny. This situation calls for the action of Christians, as members of the society to which they belong, in disruption of the mythical narratives that have used the Christian tradition for purposes contrary to the gospel of Jesus Christ, as Tinker's (1993) *Missionary Conquest* so aptly argues. Academics have for decades pointed to this false narrative, but their critical work is often not read by the wider public who still function as if the myth were true, with little if any conscious examination of it. Surely some responsibility lies with Christians within a diverse American society to speak out more widely and continually against any misappropriation of their tradition. America's distorted pseudo-theological self-talk continues its harm in that it can allow no standard by which the self-appointed righteous may be judged. If the White American insists on judging themselves as the good and the chosen, dismissing any evidence to the contrary, they must lie when truth confronts this. It is especially difficult to uphold a cultural lie when that confrontation comes in the form of the Other, a face, a story, a poignant image. This closed mindedness toward self-examination is harmful to hold to; the descendants of Christian European immigrants need to confront the false narrative bravely and put to it rest.

The healing that American society needs requires this turn from avoidance to face the horrible truth that our ancestors committed genocide in order to create the nation we enjoy, and that those acts of murder are repugnant and shameful, that they created a legacy of trauma in which whole peoples still struggle. Christians carry an important measure of responsibility in correction. While the wider society of European immigrants, generations removed from Wounded Knee, may not see how the American Indian is their problem, the Christian is always her brother's and his sister's keeper. In this sense, the Christian community can act as preserving salt and light (Matt 5:13–14) by demonstrating deference to the Other and the concern that must begin somewhere, with someone. And, they can surrender any perceived right to appropriation.

All persons of goodwill can respond in the manner described for Christian communities; by listening, by showing up in apology, and by working creatively toward reconciliation. Holland and Henriot's (1980) radical model for bringing about social change "requires direct input from communities of ordinary people into the key decisions of our society—those in the political, economic, and cultural arenas. The 'common good' is the consequence of cooperative participation by the people affected" (38).

As shown in previous chapters, Native identity is formed around community, and the response of the wider non-Native society should not be the response of individuals only. To be effective toward social transformation, communities must respond, and this is arguably why healing has eluded American society's relations with its own indigenous communities. There is little sense of community responding to community. Catherine Nerney and Hal Taussig (2002) describe an "American disaster" of lost community in the wake of an ethic of individualism (137–39). Nerney and Taussig find that the building of community can be "re-imagined" in America, but they know it will "not just appear" (223). It must be imagined, and chosen.

Any sense of United States citizens as community *with* tribal nations is almost non-existent. The White American needs to realize that individual awareness of what Native Americans are saying now, of a problematic false historical narrative, of continuing trauma, is not sufficient to healing a deeply divided society. Individually concerned citizens need to seek out communities, and together see and feel deeply that it is themselves, the White, dominant Euro-American society of privilege, the descendants of the colonizer, the beneficiaries of colonization, who stand in need of correction and healing. Nerney and Taussig point to the church, Christian communities, as models from which the wider American society might again learn what community looks like (226).

Yet, any action toward reconciliation has the potential to improve relationship and facilitate social change. Americans could join in a symbolic recognition of the horror that is Wounded Knee, which is indigenous history in the United States. To date, concern over the state of America's tribal nations is low because visibility is low. As indigenous voices have repeatedly pointed out, Native Americans are ignored. If this is to change, visibility must increase in education, in media, and in face-to-face encounter. Solidarity as action, for the privileged, means giving something up, losing. The loss may be status, safety, or privilege. Merely to say you agree is insufficient.

The recommended National Wounded Knee Memorial Day would need to be established under the advisement of those tribal nations most directly affected, and in deference to the voices of all indigenous peoples in the United States. If the radical model of action described by Holland and Henriot proves too difficult to implement due to conditions in "the political, economic, and cultural arenas," there is nothing to stop "ordinary people," theologians, clergy, academics, teachers, small Christian communities, neighbors, civic leaders, and every citizen concerned for the common good, from participating in an undeclared Wounded Knee Memorial Day. Healing need not wait for official declarations; Americans can create and act in their own form of Australia's Sorry Day. Social media has proven effective and powerful in dispersing news of social movements and this need be no different. It's an action that rightly should be implemented by White Americans, as the only parties who can take responsibility for this past; no one else can possibly carry a sufficient apology to the indigenous peoples of the United States. Ojibwe journalist Mary Annette Pember (Red Cliff of Wisconsin Ojibwe) recommends that Whites decolonize their minds:

> To decolonize is not only an act of humility and acceptance; it requires the courage to take responsibility for our role in this great, relentless process that is our life on Earth. In decolonizing our minds, we embrace the notion that we are a part of rather than apart from the Earth. Whether or not we enjoy camping or prefer to dwell in high-rise apartments without our feet ever leaving pavement, we are all subject to the same natural processes. There is no escape; there is only community and responsibility. (Pember 2020)

The Native voices of this new generation have called on American culture to question its lie. They serve as a reminder of a dangerous memory, the memory of what really occurred in the forming of the United States of America. Any remedy for estrangement within society must include responsible truth-telling. Jesus' statement, "You will know the truth and the truth will set you free" is not merely true in a spiritual or existential sense. It surely encompasses the truth of factual history, when lies about that history hold peoples and a society in divisive gridlock (John 8:32).

Americans can no longer propagate or participate in a public, cultural narrative that is a harmful, pernicious lie. Christians can no longer do so and consider themselves the people of God proclaiming truth—and love. Those who participate in the lie are the ones in need of a prophetic voice proclaiming truth. This is what Native American voices are to the church, the dominant culture, the privileged, and even the academy. These young Native Americans that have comprised this data are prophetic voices bringing correctives. Americans who wish to continue to see themselves as people of good will seeking justice and peace must hear these prophets from the margins, proclaiming, "There is no peace" (Jer 6:14 NRSV). If we have no peace, as a society, perhaps it is because we continue, as Metz reminds us, to function in a world built on the suffering of those rendered non-persons, voiceless (Chopp 1986, 64). Unless we remember the suffering from which we still benefit, disrupt our lives to make the memory known, and pay the price for doing so, we are not the enlightened beings we'd told ourselves we were. It is time to remember, and to demonstrate that remembering in a public way, to be willing to take risks to make known that memory of the suffering of Native Americans, past and present.

Weeping as Sign

A sign that blindness is under correction, and that suffering has been in any sufficient way remembered, is weeping. Tears will signify that White Americans have set upon the path to their own healing. Only after individuals and communities weep over the suffering of Others by which they have received their good lives, will those persons be prepared to move toward reconciling themselves with the past. Those persons must confront the privilege that they enjoy, and hear that it was bought with the crucifixion of a people estranged from them because of violence, cultural genocide, and trauma to families, and that the trauma continues into the present. One can only weep because they feel the deep horror of the pain Native Americans have suffered at the hands of ancestors whom living, twenty-first-century White Americans did not know, but who passed on to them the benefits of the horror inflicted. Tears of the kind described represent not just self-examination, but self-judgment that can open the way to "creative transformation of our civilization" (Holland and Henriot 1980, xv).

Finally, and not of lesser importance, it should be noted that the research, reflection, and recommendations presented in this work do not overlook the other historical traumatization of a people that has benefitted White European immigrants of the United States. The enslavement of captive Africans is a horror yet to be fully revealed, fully looked upon by Americans in its stark truth. While the indigenous of the United States suffered a different experience in their near-genocide, both American Indians and African-Americans in the twenty-first century continue to suffer trauma and to be dehumanized by the false narrative of White superiority.

The vigorous truth-telling necessary to begin social transformation of a wider American society that includes indigenous peoples, is likewise called for in the face of continued marginalization and even flagrant violence against African-American communities. This is a subject too complex to examine alongside the problem addressed here, but one which the author hopes her conclusions may also speak to. Every continued injustice against another human being is sufficient cause for weeping, and for action.

9

Sitting in the History Until Avoidance Breaks

HAS GOD RECORDED MY TEARS?

This work continues with an account of the author and researcher's experience, as it began and unfolded. I began with an account of the psalmist asking to be cleansed from his own secret faults, and I find more fodder in the Psalms. Psalm 56 finds the human crying out to God, certain his tears are kept in God's flask, recorded in heaven (Ps 56:8).

While writing the chapter of this book that gathered its historical context, I found myself blocked while reading the accounts of removal of indigenous peoples, the death and suffering along the Trail of Tears, allotment and legislative theft of their land, the cultural genocide by means of kidnapping their children, erasing their language, outlawing their spiritual practices. It was a loathsome and sad trod through the facts. Each time I sat before my computer, amid piles of books and papers that described this history, this American holocaust, I was frozen. I felt sick to my stomach and my aversion to writing an academic account of it was so great I repeatedly got up and walked away from it. Or I sat and stared. For weeks I accomplished almost nothing. It was summer and I needed to get the work done.

I had read all of these books. I had seen films showing the story. I had walked on Indian Reservations. I knew at least some of the horrific truth. Now I was faced with writing about it, reflecting on it, and I had no words. Something in me was refusing. I struggled through a discernment process. It was intense and would not be ignored. What is blocking me? What in me is resisting? Am I pushing my soul into something it opposes? Am I not listening? What is this resistance to writing telling me? I prayed. Why the fight with my own inner self? I am not often a soul at war with myself, or with God. I love and reverence both, and at personal cost. What is the problem here?

As I discussed the matter with a spiritual companion, she asked a question many have asked me over the years I have been engaged in this writing project: "How can you stand to be immersed in that subject? It's so horrible." This person is herself very bold, not someone who shies away from hard truth. "I could not even finish reading *Bury My Heart at Wounded Knee*," she said. I recalled I also had stalled somewhere in the last half of Dee Brown's book (1970). The sadness of history was overwhelming and I could not sit long in it. Maybe, as a scholar, I'd learned to respond like a trauma nurse, steeling myself against the corporal horror in order to accomplish a necessary task. I'd become accustomed to the traumatic content in front of me. Peter Nabokov (1999) opens a chapter on the formation of Indian reservations with an account of the spring of 1865, when the bodies left frozen in Sand Creek were thawing. He writes, "A United States senator visited Sand Creek in the Colorado Territory and picked up the jawbone of an Indian child 'whose milk teeth had not been shed.' The youngster was among two hundred Cheyenne Indians whose camp was flying an American flag when they were killed the previous autumn by U.S. soldiers" (187). Grim stories filled the books and papers piled on my desk and I had to pause in reverent memory of that one Cheyenne child who died with baby teeth intact, and all the others I was capable of comprehending. Their spirit was demanding it of me. Until I did, I was frozen with them.

I reflected on another time when I had been frozen at my writing desk, as a journalist, after I had witnessed painful injustice in a courtroom.[1] I was standing at the foot of the cross that day, witnessing the social crucifixion of African Americans, their men, their children, their women, a community crushed. After witnessing a father sentenced to eight years in prison for selling drugs, seeing a wailing mother escorted from the courtroom with her two small sons, I was livid. I went back to the news desk and stared at my screen for a long time before I could write the short report on a murder sentencing I had been assigned to cover that day.

How did I tolerate being immersed in the suffering of a people, an attempted genocide, a violent cultural erasure of their memory? I had not

---

1. "A Day in Court" was published in 2008 by the *Daily Southtown*. It is my account of seeing a parade of men of color file into court for sentencing and witnessing a mother of two small boys cry out, "Eight years is too much," when the boys' father was sentence for repeat drug offenses. She was escorted out of the courtroom, one child on her hip, the other looking back at the judge's bench, where his father stood, head hung.

asked myself this question ahead of the task, but now the question was asking me; the work in front of me was not advancing until I answered it. The stalled effort and the inner resistance, the sick stomach and headaches, were all speaking now. How could I envision a work that I hoped would bring healing of my own White culture's spiritual sickness, and not anticipate that I would have to endure a close-up, sickening encounter with the very horrors that had established the present condition? The grisly details of human history and the sickness with which my body responded were a block, a dam that would have to be broken. In my aversion, when my human resistance to looking on slain infants seemed impenetrable, as a great wall that could not be scaled, I prayed, and I began to cry.

That is when the dam broke and I realized that weeping and tears were necessary to both the immediate question of why I was blocked, and the larger questions of healing and reconciliation that had led me into this work. I had to weep to continue writing, once I had read, heard, seen, and deeply felt what had happened. Truly listening to what Native Americans are saying leads to weeping. If I did not weep myself, as an academic, as a White American, as a Christian, as a person with a presumed Native grandfather, and as a human being, I could not continue and form any recommendation for action by others. The conclusion that arose was this: I recommend tears.

What does any person do when he or she begins to see how deeply sick the White colonizing culture is, and worse, that she has a stake in it, as a White person? I asked this, and the terrible realization that came was that the sickness is in me. It is as if the low esteem that White Americans have put on the indigenous needs to be thrown back on ourselves. And when we feel it, it feels terrible. And we want to cry out and vilify the Other when confronted, because: the truth about myself scares me. That is what I, and every privileged American has to feel and must sit with. There are other things White people do out of shame, ways of avoiding their shame. But the more the Native American people just do their thing, be what and who they are, stop trying to prove anything, yet resist and stand with dignity, the more we have only ourselves to look at. And, ouch. We have to feel our shame. We must own it.

After the writing was finished and this book had been accepted for publication, I revisited my work for a final edit. During a re-read of my grapple with dark history and what I had written about it some years earlier, I remembered a dream I'd had during that time. I am giving an account of that dream because it seems important. I'd recorded it in a journal at the time. It was one of those dreams that don't just evaporate in the morning, but that you feel you will always remember. I was sitting on a floor in a house with gray walls that were not really walls, they were just vague partitions out around me, and they had no tops. It was a room without a roof and the sky was gray like the walls so it all blended together. There were people about but no one in the strange room with me as a woman approached me from behind me, on my right. I saw her coming without turning my head. She walked slowly and steadily, almost like she was floating. She had long, dark hair like mine and she didn't speak. She was not young or old. She was maybe middle-aged, and beautiful. Her beauty was in her calm deliberateness. She knew exactly what was.

As the woman approached on my right side, she sat next to me on my right and put her left arm around me, cradling me like a child. I felt her goodness and care for me, so I rested as she let my head fall back into her arm. Then, to my great surprise, she bent forward over me. She quietly released a long exhaling breath, and then she put her mouth over mine and pulled the air out from my lungs. She sat up and so did I, and I watched as she exhaled and blew upward a cloud of brown smoke with specks in it. I was in shock and I said, "That came out of me?" She looked at me and nodded. I wasn't sure it was a good thing that my lungs had been full of brown smoke. Her look assured me that it was as it should be. Then, she stood up and left the same way she had come. I sat in the center of the floor, in wonder.

10

The Beautiful Breakthrough Moment that is *Reservation Dogs*

FINALLY, REAL INDIANS BROUGHT TO US BY REAL INDIANS

Grace. Native Americans are being who they are and saying what they have to say and in doing so, the wider American culture is blessed. *Reservation Dogs* is bestowed up White America and everyone else. Members of the 1491s comedy troupe who provided the data for this research just a few years ago, have created an FX series about the lives of teenagers coming of age on a reservation. Director Sterlin Harjo and series co-creator Taika Waititi launched what would be three seasons of *Reservation Dogs* (Harjo, 2021) an event in indigenous self-representation that is nothing less than momentous. As a person who determines to listen respectfully to what young Native Americans were saying to the wide American culture, and as someone who was dismayed at the failure of generations of White Americans to listen to indigenous America, the work feels like a triumph. The triumph is not that the wider culture determined it would at last listen; it is that Native Americans, as the only persons qualified to show America who and what they are, did so. The rest of us do not deserve this gracious rendering of twenty-first-century Native American youth coming of age, in all its painful beauty. We have been treated to this. It is a grace.

Since the series' appearance on Hulu in 2021, the media and academics alike have been talking about *Reservation Dogs*. This chapter won't cite the multitude of articles discussing the importance of the series, of Native representation by Native Americans, the show's completely original approach to, well, everything it is doing. A Google search will turn up those articles, for those who are listening. Each accolade and analysis represents increased listening by the wider culture.

Across three seasons, *Reservations Dogs* showed indigenous life as uniquely Indian and as American; its central characters are teenagers, its lens from that of youth. The characters come of age in the shadow of a friend's suicide and in their own process of grieving and healing as a group, they trudge through tragic history, twenty-first-century reservation life, and Native spirituality that is present with them in the form of ancestral and other spirit visits. It's jam-packed with goodness and heart. The series finale featured forgiveness driven by young Native Americans who pointed their elders toward reconciliation. It was about healing happening for and from the community. The whole series is about healing community, ending with a funeral and old people laughing about death while young people figure out how to carry on.

Native Americans continue to speak, to create, to gain agency. An indigenous woman, Deb Haaland (Laguna Pueblo), became secretary of the interior in 2021. As secretary of the interior, Haaland oversees the Bureau of Indian Affairs and other federal agencies with direct impact on indigenous communities. Native American voices, stories, self-representation seems to be exploding. On the heels of *Reservation Dogs* series finale came the release of *Killers of the Flower Moon* (2023), the telling of an oil-and-land grab from the Osage Nation in Oklahoma in the 1920s, directed by Martin Scorsese. Indian Country Today Media Network is a growing non-profit media hub that puts Native American news, faces, and stories online, available to anyone online who wants to listen. Artist and activist Frank Waln travels, is taking his music and activism cross country and encouraging young Native Americans to pursue scholarship. Adriene Keene published a book titled *Notable Native People: 50 Indigenous Leaders, Dreamers, and Changemakers from Past and Present*.

What do all of these voices, and especially the presence of *Reservation Dogs* mean for White Americans who have not been listening to Native Americans, who've been only marginally aware of history or of what Indians look like, act like or live like in the twenty-first century? It means, the Indians have spoken, and Hulu and FX are the means of translation for those of us not good at hearing. The brilliant creators who began with YouTube comedy sketches for an audience made possible by the internet, expanded their creative expression in a work that is being recognized as groundbreaking. Native Americans have created the opportunity for non-Natives to listen in a new venue. Americans who are unlikely to read Vine Deloria Jr. or George Tinker's work can stream *Reservation Dogs* on Hulu. It is momentous, but what is especially notable is that White culture is incidental to what is happening with this series, its appearance and availability. The healing begins with the Indian community creating and expressing with seemingly little self-consciousness. Native Americans are showing us who they are and they don't seem to care what we think because they are having fun doing it. The Native voices are there for those who have ears to hear. And they are not the voices of a White professor or an anthropologist interpreting Indian culture or history for you. These actors, writers, producers, directors, and storytellers are Native Americans telling their own story of how healing can come. They care not for we White people, they are not really talking to us. *Reservation Dogs* is a story for every American. It is the indigenous who are being inclusive and generous, who are dignified with or without permission. They may or may not be talking to us, but they can be, if we choose to listen.

References

1863. "Winona Daily Republican." Darrell W. Krueger Library Archive, September 25. Accessed October 15, 2017. https://digital.olivesoftware.com/olive/apa/winona/sharedview.article.aspx?href=TWR%2F1863%2F09%2F25&id=Ar00212&sk=378595C8.

1989. *The HarperCollins Study Bible: New Revised Standard Version*. San Francisco: HarperOne.

2017. "About Project 562." Accessed October 30, 2017. https://www.project562.com/about.

AIM (American Indian Movement). 1972. "Trail of Broken Treaties." Accessed November 11, 2017. https://www.aimovement.org/archives/index.html.

Alan Eichler. 2016. "Patti Page, I'm an Indian, Too, Annie Get Your Gun." *YouTube*, January 14. https://www.youtube.com/watch?v=RP5JBUpa3Ag.

Aldred, Lisa. 2000. "Plastic Shamans and Astroturf Sun Dances: New Age Commercialization of Native American Spirituality." *The American Indian Quarterly* 24 (Summer) 329–52. http://muse.jhu.edu/article/193.

Alexie, Sherman. 1998. "Superman and Me." *Los Angeles Times*, April 19. http://www.teach4real.com/wp-content/uploads/2014/08/The-Joy-of-Reading-and-Writing.pdf.

———. 2000. *The Toughest Indian in the World*. New York: Atlantic Monthly.

———. 2016. *Thunder Boy Jr*. New York: Little, Brown.

Aljazeera Stream Team. 2014. "The 1491s." *Aljazeera America*, March 21. http://america.aljazeera.com/watch/shows/the-stream/the-latest/2014/3/21/-the-1491s-.html.

Allen, Lee. 2013. "Edward S. Curtis, Whose Photos Defined a Race of People, 'Reframed.'" *Indian County Today*, November 6. https://indiancountrymedianetwork.com/culture/arts-entertainment/edward-s-curtis-whose-photos-defined-a-race-of-people-reframed/.

Allen, Paula Gunn. 2003. "Indians, Solipsisms, and Archetypal Holocausts." In *Genocide of the Mind: New Native American Writing*, edited by MariJo Moore, 305–15. New York: Nation.

———, ed. 1989. *Spider Woman's Granddaughters: Traditional Tales and Contemporary Writing by Native American Women*. Boston: Beacon.

Asenap, Jason. 2016. "Six Great Native Artworks from 'As We See It' Exhibit." *Indian County Today*, August 13. https://indiancountrymedianetwork.com/culture/arts-entertainment/six-great-native-artworks-from-the-as-we-see-it-exhibit/.

REFERENCES

Associated Press. 2013. "How Many Native Americans Think 'Redskins' Is a Slur?" *CBS Local*, October 8. http://washington.cbslocal.com/2013/10/08/how-many-native-americans-think-redskins-is-a-slur/.

Bachofner, Carol Snow Moon. 2003. "Don't Talk, Don't Live." In *Genocide of the Mind: New Native American Writing*, edited by MariJo Moore, 141–47. New York: Nation.

Baudrillard, Jean. 1975. *The Mirror of Production*. St. Louis: Telos.

Becker, Eric, et al., dirs. 2015. "7th Generation Rises." *Rebel Music*, Season 2, Episode 3. Aired on May 7. http://www.mtv.com/news/2154171/rebel-music-native-america-7th-generation-rises/.

Bevans, Stephen B. 2002. *Models of Contextual Theology: Revised and Expanded Edition*. Maryknoll, NY: Orbis.

Blais-Billie, Braudie. 2016. "'We've Done This Totally Unarmed': Hip-Hop Artist/Activist Nataanii Means on the Front Lines of #NoDAPL." *Billboard*, December 5. http://www.billboard.com/articles/columns/hip-hop/7597548/hip-hop-artist-nataanii-means-no-dapl-exclusive-interview.

Bordewich, Fergus M. 1996. *Killing the White Man's Indian: Reinventing Native Americans at the End of the Twentieth Century*. New York: Anchor.

Bourdieu, Pierre. 1980. *The Logic of Practice*. Stanford: Stanford University.

Brown, Dee. 1971. *Bury My Heart at Wounded Knee: An Indian History of the American West*. New York: Bantam.

Buber, Martin. 1970. *I And Thou*. Translated by Walter Kaufmann. New York: Touchstone.

Calvarese, di Marco. 2018. "Pope Francis: 'Veritatis Gaudium,' 'the Theologian Who Is Satisfied with His Complete and Conclusive Thought Is Mediocre.'" January 29. https://agensir.it/quotidiano/2018/1/29/pope-francis-veritatis-gaudium-the-theologian-who-is-satisfied-with-his-complete-and-conclusive-thought-is-mediocre/.

Canadian Conference of Catholic Bishops. 2016. *The "Doctrine of Discovery" and Terra Nullius: A Catholic Response*. https://www.cccb.ca/wp-content/uploads/2017/11/catholic-response-to-doctrine-of-discovery-and-tn.pdf.

Capriccioso, Rob. 2010. "A Sorry Saga: Obama Signs Native American Apology." *Indian Country Media Network*, January 21. https://indiancountrymedianetwork.com/news/a-sorry-saga-obama-signs-native-american-apology/.

Charleston, Steven. 2015a. *The Four Vision Quests of Jesus*. New York: Morehouse.

———. 2015b. "Theory-Articulating a Native American Theological Theory." In *Coming Full Circle: Constructing Native Christian Theology*, edited by Steven Charleston and Elaine A. Robinson, 1–26. Minneapolis: Fortress.

Charleston, Steven, and Elaine A. Robinson, eds. 2015. *Coming Full Circle: Constructing Native Christian Theology*. Minneapolis: Fortress.

Cone, James H. 2011. *The Cross and the Lynching Tree*. Maryknoll, NY: Orbis.

Cook-Lynn, Elizabeth. 2011. "The Lewis and Clark Story, the Captive Narrative, and the Pitfalls of Indian History." In *Native Historians Write Back: Decolonizing American Indian History*, edited by Susan A. Miller and James Riding In, 41–51. Lubbock: Texas Tech University Press.

Crow Dog, Mary, and Richard Erdoes. 2011. *Lakota Woman*. 1990. Reprint, New York: HarperCollins.

REFERENCES

Decoded. 2015. "White People Whitesplain Whitesplaing." *MTV*, November 4. https://www.mtv.com/episodes/w0b23r/decoded-white-people-whitesplain-whitesplaining-season-2-ep-6.

Deloria, Vine, Jr. 1969. *Custer Died for Your Sins*. New York: Avon.

———. 2003. *God Is Red: A Native View of Religion*. 30th Anniversary Edition. Golden, CO: Fulcrum.

Dettloff, Dean. 2017. "Why Indigenous Leaders and Canadian Catholics Still Want an Apology from Pope Francis." *America Magazine*, June 5. https://www.americamagazine.org/politics-society/2017/06/05/why-indigenous-leaders-and-canadian-catholics-still-want-apology-pope.

Dickinson, Natalie. 2016. "Watch Standing Rock Tribes Cheer as Vets Apologize on Behalf of U.S. Government." *Occupy Democrats*, December 6. http://occupydemocrats.com/2016/12/05/watch-vets-just-offered-powerful-apology-standing-rock-tribes-centuries-mistreatment-us-government/.

Dube, Musa W. 2006. "Reading for Decolonization (John 4.1–42)." In *Voices from the Margin: Interpreting the Bible in the Third World*, edited by R. S. Sugirtharajah, 297–318. Maryknoll, NY: Orbis.

Dunbar-Ortiz, Roxanne. 2014. *An Indigenous Peoples' History of the United States*. Boston: Beacon.

Eastman, Charles Alexander (Ohiyesa). 2003. *The Soul of the Indian*. Mineola, NY: Dover.

Elbein, Saul. 2017. "The Youth Group That Launched a Movement at Standing Rock." *New York Times*, January 31. https://www.nytimes.com/2017/01/31/magazine/the-youth-group-that-launched-a-movement-at-standing-rock.html.

First Alaskans Institute. 2016. "#ANDORE2016: Day 1—1491's 'Using Digital Media and Comedy to Address [and laugh at] Stereotypes.'" *YouTube*, February 29. https://www.youtube.com/watch?v=2VkYw7kAk_Y.

Fixico, Donald L. 2000. *The Urban Indian Experience in America*. Albuquerque, NM: University of New Mexico.

Fraher, Diane. 2003. "About American Indian Artists, Inc." In *Genocide of the Mind: New Native American Writing*, edited by MariJo Moore, 337–39. New York: Nation.

Francis, Pope. 2015. Laudato Si': *On Care for Our Common Home*, Encyclical Letter. Vatican City: Our Sunday Visitor.

———. 2018. "Apostolic Constitution *Veritatis Gaudium*: On Eccelsiastical Universities and Faculties." https://www.vatican.va/content/francesco/en/apost_constitutions/documents/papa-francesco_costituzione-ap_20171208_veritatis-gaudium.html.

Fuhrman, CMarie, and Dan Rader, eds. 2017. *Native Voices: A New Anthology*. Accessed November 17, 2017. https://www.kickstarter.com/projects/979776234/honoring-indigenous-poetry-from-north-america/description.

Grounds, Richard A. 2003. "Yuchi Travels: Up and Down the Academic "Road to Disappearance." In *Native Voices: American Indian Identity and Resistance*, edited by George E. Tinker et al., 290–317. Lawrence: University of Kansas.

Grounds, Richard A., et al., eds. 2003. *Native Voices: American Indian Identity and Resistance*. Lawrence: University of Kansas.

Gutierrez, Gustavo. 1973. *A Theology of Liberation: History, Politics, and Salvation*. 15th Anniversary Edition. Edited and Translated by Caridad Inda and John Eagleson. Maryknoll, NY: Orbis.

———. 1984. *The Power of the Poor in History*. Translated by Robert R. Barr. Maryknoll, NY: Orbis.

Harjo, Sterlin, and Taika Waititi. 2021. *Reservations Dogs*. FX Productions.

Harris, Michelle, et al., eds. 2013. *The Politics of Identity: Emerging Indigenity*. Haymarket, New South Wales: UTS.

Hefflinger, Mark. 2014. "Harvest the Hope: Neil Young and Willie Nelson in Concert." August 18. http://boldnebraska.org/concert/.

Holland, Joe, and Peter Henriot. 1980. *Social Analysis: Linking Faith and Justice*. Maryknoll, NY: Orbis.

Horn, Gabriel. 2003. "The Genocide of a Generation's Identity." In *Genocide of the Mind: New Native American Writing*, edited by MariJo Moore, 65–75. New York: Nation.

Huebsch, Bill. 1997. *Vatican II In Plain English: The Decrees and Declarations*. Allen, TX: Thomas More.

Indian Country Today Media Network. 2013. "Cartoonist Marty Two Bulls Profiled by Associate Press." *Indian Country Today Media Network*, June 13. https://indiancountrymedianetwork.com/culture/arts-entertainment/cartoonist-marty-two-bulls-profiled-by-associated-press/.

———. 2016. Indian Country Today Media Network. Accessed June 20, 2016. http://indiancountrytodaymedianetwork.com/department/ask-n-ndn.

Ives, Stephen, dir. 1996. "The West, Episode Eight: Ghost Dance." *PBS*, aired September 21. Accessed November 18, 2017. http://www.pbs.org/weta/thewest/program/episodes/eight/likegrass.htm.

Johnson, Elizabeth A. 2007. *Quest for the Living God: Mapping Frontiers in the Theology of God*. New York: Continuum.

Karalis, H. Lee. 2003. "A Different Rhythm." In *Genocide of the Mind: New Native American Writing*, edited by MariJo Moore, 167–76. New York: Nation.

Keene, Adrienne. 2010. "But Why Can't I Wear a Hipster Headdress?" *Native Appropriations*, April 27. https://nativeappropriations.com/2010/04/but-why-cant-i-wear-a-hipster-headdress.html.

———. 2017a. "Valentino Didn't Learn Anything." *Native Appropriations*, March 23. https://nativeappropriations.com/2017/03/valentino-didnt-learn-anything.html.

———. 2017b. "'I Can't See Em Comin Down My Eyes/So I Gotta Make This Post Cry': Or, How Our Toxic Indigenous Masculinity Is Stopping the Revolution." *Native Appropriations*, October 18. https://web.archive.org/web/20171020022703/https://nativeappropriations.com/2017/10/i-cant-see-em-comin-down-my-eyesso-i-gotta-make-this-post-cry-or-how-our-toxic-indigenous-masculinity-is-stopping-the-revolution.html.

Kidwell, Clara Sue, et al. 2001. *A Native American Theology*. Maryknoll, NY: Orbis.

Killsback, Leo. 2016. "The Revenant Is a Game-Changer." *Indian Country Today Media Network*, January 14. https://indiancountrymedianetwork.com/news/opinions/the-revenant-is-a-game-changer/.

King, Gilbert. 2012. "Edward Curtis' Epic Project to Photograph Native Americans." *Smithsonian Magazine*, March 21. https://www.smithsonianmag.com/history/edward-curtis-epic-project-to-photograph-native-americans-162523282/.

LaDuke, Winona. 2017. "Commentary: 'I Am Tired of Being Invisible to You All.'" *West Central Tribune*, November 13. https://www.wctrib.com/opinion/commentary-i-am-tired-of-being-invisible-to-you-all.

REFERENCES

Leavitt, Peter A., et al. 2015. "'Frozen in Time': The Impact of Native American Media Representations on Identity and Self-Understanding." *Journal of Social Science Issues* 71: 39–53.

Lee, Tanya H. 2015. "7 Apologies Made to American Indians." *Indian Country Today Media Network*, July 1. https://indiancountrymedianetwork.com/history/events/7-apologies-made-to-american-indians/.

Lucci-Cooper, Kathryn. 2003. "To Carry the Fire Home." In *Genocide of the Mind: New Native American Writing*, by MariJo Moore, 3–11. New York: Nation.

Martinez, Donna, et al. 2016. *Urban American Indians: Reclaiming Native Space*. Santa Barbara, CA: Praeger.

McKay, Neil. 2003. "The Spirit of Language." In *Genocide of the Mind: New Native American Writing*, edited by MariJo Moore, 159–65. New York: Nation.

Melmer, David. 2007. "'Bury My Heart at Wounded Knee' Brings Controversy." *Indian Country Today Media Network*, June 4. https://indiancountrymedianetwork.com/news/bury-my-heart-at-wounded-knee-brings-controversy/.

Merton, Thomas. 2007. *New Seeds of Contemplation*. New York: New Directions Paperback.

Metz, Johann Baptist. 2007. *Faith in History and Society: Toward a Practical Fundamental Theology*. Edited and Translated by J. Matthew Ashley. New York: Herder & Herder.

Miller, Susan A., and James Riding In, eds. 2011. *Native Historians Write Back: Decolonizing American Indian History*. Lubbock: Texas Tech University.

Moore, MariJo, ed. 2003. *Genocide of the Mind: New Native American Writing*. New York: Nation.

Morales, Laurel. 2016. "For the Navajo Nation, Uranium Mining's Deadly Legacy Lingers." *NPR*, April 10. https://www.npr.org/sections/health-shots/2016/04/10/473547227/for-the-navajo-nation-uranium-minings-deadly-legacy-lingers.

Morris, Glenn T. 2003. "Vine Deloira Jr., and the Development of the Decolonizing Critique of Indigenous Peoples and International Relations." In *Native Voices: American Indian Identity and Resistance*, by George E. Tinker et al., 97–154. Lawrence: University of Kansas.

Moya-Smith, Simon. 2014. "The Daily Show with Jon Stewart Airs R-Word Segment, Debunks WashPo Report." *Indian County Today*, September 26. https://web.archive.org/web/20170321154939/https://indiancountrymedianetwork.com/culture/sports/the-daily-show-with-jon-stewart-airs-r-word-segment-debunks-washpo-report/.

Nabokov, Peter. 1999. *Native American Testimony*. Rev. ed. New York: Penguin.

National Park Service. n.d. "National Park Service: The Louisiana Purchase." Accessed July 8, 2016. https://www.nps.gov/jeff/learn/historyculture/upload/louisiana_purchase.pdf.

Neihardt, John G. 1979. *Black Elk Speaks: Being the Life Story of a Holy Man of the Oglala Sioux*. Lincoln, NE: University of Nebraska.

Nerney, Catherine, and Hal Taussig. 2002. *Re-Imagining Life Together in America: A New Gospel of Community*. Chicago: Sheed & Ward.

Oceti Sakowin Camp. 2016. "Forgiveness Ceremony: Veterans Kneel at Standing Rock." *YouTube*, December 7. https://www.youtube.com/watch?v=OjotlPIlRqw&pbjreload=10.

Owen, Suzanne. 2008. *The Appropriation of Native American Spirituality*. London: Continuum.
Paul VI, Pope. 1965. *Gaudium et Spes*. December 7, 1965. https://www.vatican.va/archive/hist_councils/ii_vatican_council/documents/vat-ii_const_19651207_gaudium-et-spes_en.html.
Peelman, Achiel. 1995. *Christ Is a Native American*. Maryknoll, NY: Orbis.
Pember, Mary Annette. 2020. "This November, Try Something New: Decolonize Your Mind - Yes! Magazine Solutions Journalism." *YES! Magazine*, November 24. https://www.yesmagazine.org/democracy/2017/11/13/this-november-try-something-new-decolonize-your-mind.
Pensoneau, Migizi. 2014. "Behind the Scenes of Our Tense Segment on *The Daily Show*." *Huffpost*, November 30. https://www.huffingtonpost.com/migizi-pensoneau/1491s-daily-show_b_5907244.html.
Pesantubbee, Michelene E. 2003. "Religious Studies on the Margins: Decolonizing Our Minds." In *Native Voices: American Indian Identity and Resistance*, edited by George E. Tinker et al., 209–22. Lawrence: University of Kansas.
Pratt, Richard H. 1892. "The Advantages of Mingling Indians with Whites." In *Official Report of the Nineteenth Annual Conference of Charities and Correction*, 46–59. Cambridge: Harvard University. Accessed June 20, 2016. http://historymatters.gmu.edu/d/4929/.
Prucha, Francis Paul, ed. 1990. *Documents of United States Indian Policy*. 2nd ed. Lincoln: University of Nebraska.
Rahner, Karl. 1997. *The Need and Blessing of Prayer*. Collegeville, MN: Liturgical.
Rebel Music. 2014. "Rebel Music: Native America | Frank Waln Performs 'My Stone.'" *YouTube*, November 18. https://www.youtube.com/watch?v=zcSQZ-5IvTo.
Reconciliation Australia. 2023. "Stolen Generations Gathering for National Sorry Day." *Reconciliation Australia*, May 26. https://www.reconciliation.org.au/stolen-generations-gathering-in-sydney/.
Red Corn, Ryan. 2015. "20 More Glorious Portraits of Native Americans." *Indian County Today*, June 30. https://indiancountrymedianetwork.com/culture/arts-entertainment/20-more-glorious-portraits-of-native-americans-by-ryan-red-corn/.
———. 2017. "Ryan Red Corn on Building and Creating Things." *NextGen Native*, June 8. http://nextgennative.com/ryanredcorn/.
Robinson, Steven Charleston, and Elaine A. Robinson. 2015. *Coming Full Circle: Constructing Native Christian Theology*. Minneapolis: Fortress.
Roppolo, Kimberly. 2003. "Symbolic Racism, History, and Reality: The Real Problem with Indian Mascots." In *Genocide of the Mind: New Native American Writing*, edited by MariJo Moore, 187–98. New York: Nation.
Rosay, Andre B. 2010. "Violence against American Indian and Native Alaskan Women and Men." *National Institute of Justice*. Accessed October 23, 2017. https://www.ncjrs.gov/pdffiles1/nij/249736.pdf.
Scharen, Christian, and Aana Marie Vigen, eds. 2011. *Ethnography as Christian Theology and Ethics*. New York: Continuum.
Schilling, Vincent. 2018. "Hostiles Movie Review: A Profound Respect for Native Culture, a Gut Punch of Reality." January 11. Accessed January 18, 2018. https://indiancountrymedianetwork.com/culture/arts-entertainment/hostiles-movie-review-profound-respect-native-culture-gut-punch-reality/.

Schreiter, Robert J. 1985. *Constructing Local Theologies*. Maryknoll, NY: Orbis.
Scorsese, Martin, dir. 2023. *Killers of the Flower Moon*. United States: Paramount.
Shapira, Ian. 2014. "'Daily Show' Airs Segment Pitting Redskins Fans against Native Americans." *Washington Post*, September 26. https://www.washingtonpost.com/local/daily-show-airs-segment-pitting-redskins-fans-against-native-americans/2014/09/25/f5d082da-44e3-11e4-b437-1a7368204804_story.html?utm_term=.3784200f8870.
Silko, Leslie Marmon. 1977. *Ceremony: Edition with Introduction by Larry McMurtry*. New York: Penguin.
Simons, Margaret. 2001. "Australia's Churches Call on Nation to Acknowledge 'Stolen Generations.'" *Christianity Today*, June 1. http://www.christianitytoday.com/ct/2001/juneweb-only/6-4-16.0.html.
Smith, Joanna. 2015. "Canada's Residential Schools Cultural Genocide, Truth and Reconciliation Commission Says." *The Star*, June 2. https://www.thestar.com/news/canada/2015/06/02/canadas-residential-schools-cultural-genocide-truth-and-reconciliation-commission-says.html.
Sobrino, Jon. 2008. *No Salvation Outside the Poor: Prophetic-Utopian Essays*. Maryknoll, NY: Orbis.
Southern Poverty Law Center. 2017. "Hate Groups Increase for Second Consecutive Year as Trump Electrifies Radical Right." February 15. https://www.splcenter.org/news/2017/02/15/hate-groups-increase-second-consecutive-year-trump-electrifies-radical-right.
Stephenson, Michele, and Brian Young. 2017. "A Conversation with Native Americans on Race." *New York Time*, August 15. https://www.nytimes.com/2017/08/15/opinion/a-conversation-with-native-americans-on-race.html.
sterlz501. 2009. "New Moon Wolf Pack Auditions." *YouTube*, December 1. https://www.youtube.com/watch?v=BmFxJYFSXyo&t=14s.
Stewart, John. 2014. "The Redskin's Name—Catching Racism." *The Daily Show with Jon Stewart*, September 25. https://www.cc.com/video/189afv/the-daily-show-with-jon-stewart-the-redskins-name-catching-racism.
The Stream Team. 2006. *Voices from the Margins: Interpreting the Bible in the Third World*. Maryknoll, NY: Orbis.
———. 2014. "The 1491s." *Aljazeera America*, March 21. http://america.aljazeera.com/watch/shows/the-stream/the-latest/2014/3/21/-the-1491s-.html.
Sugirtharajah, R. S. 2003. *Postcolonial Reconfigurations: An Alternative Way of Reading the Bible and Doing Theology*. London: SCM.
———, ed. 2006. *Voices from the Margin: Interpreting the Bible in the Third World*. Revised and expanded 3rd ed. Maryknoll, NY: Orbis.
Supaman. "Supaman—Why?" 2015. *YouTube*, September 4. https://www.youtube.com/watch?v=OiVU-W9VT7Q.
TEDx Talks. 2014. "TedX Teacher's College: Changing the Way We See Native Americans." *YouTube*, July 23. https://www.youtube.com/watch?v=GIzYzz3rEZU.
the1491s. 2011a. "Bad Indians." *YouTube*, March 17. https://www.youtube.com/watch?v=3FUgDutdauQ.
———. 2011b. "Hunting." *YouTube*, September 1. https://www.youtube.com/watch?v=70KtyYIIcaQ.
———. 2011c. "Smiling Indians." *YouTube*, February 21. https://www.youtube.com/watch?v=ga98brEf1AU.

———. 2012. "I'm an Indian Too." *YouTube*, September 21. https://www.youtube.com/watch?v=9BHvpWP2V9Y.

———. 2013. "The Indian Store." *YouTube*, December 23. https://www.youtube.com/watch?v=NuzPoidV4nI.

———. 2016. "Wounded White Warrior Savior Photographer." *YouTube*, April 28. https://www.youtube.com/watch?v=rdy5XSdCkzo.

Tinker, George E. 1993. *Missionary Conquest: The Gospel and Native American Cultural Genocide*. Minneapolis: Fortress.

———. 2004. *Spirit and Resistance: Political Theology and American Indian Liberation*. Minneapolis: Fortress.

———. 2008. *American Indian Liberation: A Theology of Sovereignty*. Maryknoll, NY: Orbis.

Tracy, David. 1975. *Blessed Rage for Order: The New Pluralism in Theology*. Chicago: University of Chicago.

———. 1981. *The Analogical Imagination: Christian Theology and the Culture of Pluralism*. New York: Crossroad.

———. 1987. *Plurality and Ambiguity: Hermeneutics, Religion, and Hope*. Chicago: University of Chicago.

United Nations. 2008. "United Nations Declaration on the Rights of Indigenous Peoples." March. http://www.un.org/esa/socdev/unpfii/documents/DRIPS_en.pdf.

Valanos, Olga, dir. 2013. *Generation Red Nation*.

Walker, Bryce, and Jill Maynard eds. 1995. *Through Indian Eyes: The Untold Story of Native American Peoples*. Pleasantville, NY: Reader's Digest.

Waln, Frank. 2013a. "AbOriginal." *YouTube*, October 24. https://www.youtube.com/watch?v=5_1fmbKCMmY.

———. 2013b. "Oil 4 Blood Official Music Video." *YouTube*, February 2. https://www.youtube.com/watch?v=yKh5awjGWSk.

Warrior, Robert Allen. 2006. "A Native American Perspective: Canaanites, Cowboys, and Indians." In *Voices from the Margins: Interpreting the Bible in the Third World*, edited by R. S. Sugirtharajah, 235–41. Maryknoll, NY: Orbis.

Waters, Joel. 2003. "Indians in the Attic." In *Genocide of the Mind: New Native American Writing*, edited by MariJo Moore, 85–92. New York: Nation.

Wilson, Edmund. 1992. *Apologies to the Iroquois*. Syracuse, NY: Syracuse University Press.

Wong, Joseph H. 1995. "Anonymous Christians: Karl Rahner's Pneuma-Christocentricism and an East-West Dialogue." *Theological Studies* 55: 609–37.

Wounded Knee Memorial Motorcycle Run 202+. n.d. Facebook page, accessed January 28, 2024. https://www.facebook.com/profile.php?id=100071413644603.

Index

Abenakis Tribe, 78
"AbOriginal" (Waln song), 80
The Absolutely True Diary of a Part-Time Indian (Alexie), 72
academic honesty, 105–6
academics, actions they can take, 126–133
Alexie, Sherman, 36, 71–73, 96, 104–5
Allen, Paula Gunn, 22, 36, 46, 54
allotment, of land, 52–55
American Indian Liberation (Tinker), 10, 12–13, 43, 44–45, 63
American Indian Movement (AIM), 62, 79n6
American society, remembering Wounded Knee, 144–46
"America's unfinished business" (Tinker), 7
The Analogical Imagination (Tracy), 129
Anishinaabe language (Ojibway, Chippewa), 11
Annie Get Your Gun (musical), 70
anthropologists, 34
"Anthropologists and Other Friends" (Deloria), 4n1, 31
Apologies to the Iroquois (Wilson), 2
Applebee's Indian, 5–6
Aquash, Annie Mae, 84
Arianism, 100n6
"As We See It" (photography exhibit), 71
assimilation, 17, 17n2, 57–58
Australia
  National Council of Churches, 137
  National Sorry Day, 137, 150

avoidance, 153–56
Ayana, S. James, 61

Bachofner, Carol Snow Moon, 78, 97
"Bad Indians" (Red Corn poem), 32
Baldridge, Clifford, 7
Banks, Dennis, 79n6, 83
basileia, understanding, 141
Baudrillard, Jean, 27
Bellecourt, Clyde, 79n6
Benally, Klee, 79n7
Benedict XVI, Pope, 135
Berlin, Irving, 70
Black Elk, Nicholas, 147, 147n2
Black Elk Speaks (Neihardt), 37
blind spots of White culture, 94–99
boarding schools, 57–58
Bordewich, Fergus M., 50, 50–51n6
Bourdieu, Pierre, 94–95, 100, 101, 106, 133
Brave Bird, Mary, 84
Brown, Dee, 138n1, 140, 145, 154
Buber, Martin, 126, 128
Bury My Heart at Wounded Knee (Brown and film), 138n1, 140, 145, 154

Cabot, John, 49
"Canaanites, Cowboys, and Indians" (Warrior), 109
Canadian Catholic Aboriginal Council, 135
Canadian Catholic Organization for Development and Peace, 135
Canadian Conference of Catholic Bishops, 50n5, 98, 135

INDEX

Canadian Religious Conference, 135
Cardijn, Joseph, 4, 16n1
"Career Building through Genocide" (Dunbar-Ortiz), 41
Ceremony (Silko), 40, 97, 116
"The Challenge to Other Churches" (Schreiter), 102
Charleston, Steven
  being indigenous and Christian, 13, 36
  Choctaw tribal affiliation, 10
  Coming Full Circle, 8n9, 103, 105, 107–8, 108n9
  dehumanization of the indigenous woman, 94
  The Four Vision Quests of Jesus, 104, 134
  indigenous covenant with the Creator, 90, 107–9, 108n9, 111–15
  memories from past colonizers, 126, 133–34
  Native and Christian theological insights, 139–140
Cherokee Nation, 11, 21, 50
Chippewa Nation, 11
Choctaw Nation, 104, 108
Chomsky, Noam, 96, 97–98, 99
Christ Is a Native American (Peelman), 99n4, 103, 113
Christian identity, 99–102
Christian missions, 7, 11, 23, 44, 57, 92, 106
Christianity
  in colonization, 90–93
  creeds in Christian traditions, 96, 97–98, 102
  images of God, 93–94
  term usage, 13–14
church in America, 135–37
"the church" term usage, 11
Churchill, Ward, 21, 21n6, 27, 147
cities, first populated by American Indians, 49
Civil Rights Act (1968), 61
civilized cultural erasure, 44–45
Clark, Wesley Jr., 143
Clement, Kelli, 144

Clement of Alexandria, 113
Cliff, Mike "Witko," 76, 82–83, 88
Collier, John, 59
colonization/colonizers, 12, 39–40, 45–48, 91–92, 98
Columbus, voyages of, 50n5
Coming Full Circle (Charleston and Robinson), 8n9, 103, 105, 107–8, 108n9
  See also covenant relationship, with Creator God
communication, linguistic model for, 95–97
competence, language and, 96
Cook-Lynn, Elizabeth, 41, 42
Cooper, James Fenimore, 49
Council of Nicaea (325), 100n6
covenant relationship, with Creator God, 90, 107–9, 108n9, 111–15
  See also Coming Full Circle
Crawford, T. Hartley, 53–54, 57
Creator God, 90, 109
creeds in Christian traditions, 96, 97–98, 102
Crow Dog, Leonard, 143–44
Crow Dog, Mary, 83–84
cultural appropriation, 85–87, 147–48
cultural genocide, 54, 73–77, 79–81
"Culture of Conquest" (Dunbar-Oritz), 47n4
Curtis, Edward S., 71
Custer Died for Your Sins (Deloria), 2, 4n1, 36

The Daily Show, Indian mascots debate (2014), 74–76
Dakota Access Pipeline protest (2016), 66, 79, 80, 85, 143
Dances with Wolves (film), 44n2
David, King of Israel, 119–120, 122
Davis, Gary "Litefoot," 79n7
Dawes Act (General Allotment Act of 1887), 52, 58, 83
"A Day in Court" (Lang), 154n1
"Declaration on the Relationship of the Church to Non-Christian Religions (Vatican II), 113

INDEX

decolonization, 12, 40, 41–43, 44–45, 150
Deloria, Vine Jr.
  on academic honesty, 105–6
  on anthropologists, 34
  "Anthropologists and Other Friends," 4n1, 31
  on Civil Rights movement and racism in America, 6–7
  Custer Died for Your Sins, 2, 4n1, 36
  death of, 63
  God Is Red, 94–95n3, 133
  on Indian identity, 17–18
  influence on young generation, 36, 62–63
  as source for the retelling of history, 40
  vision for Indians, 3–4
  We Talk, You Listen, 65
Dine language (Navajo), 11
Doctrine of Discovery, 43, 49–50, 50n5, 98, 140, 144
Documents of United States Indian Policy (Prucha), 20–21
"Don't Talk, Don't Live" (Bachofner), 78
Dowd, Josephine, 21
Dube, Musa W., 12
Dunbar-Oritz, Roxanne
  "Career Building through Genocide," 41
  on concealing one's Indian identity, 17
  "Culture of Conquest," 47n4
  Euro-American, term usage, 4n2
  An Indigenous Peoples' History of the United States, 9n5, 13, 40–41, 45–46, 45n3
  on Native nations names in own language, 10–11
  on North America as wilderness, 48–49
  "North America Is a Crime Scene," 40
  on reservations, 55–56

Eastman, Charles, 37
errors, we do not see, 119–120
ethnic cleansing, 43–45
Ethnology as Christian Theology and Ethics (Scharen and Vigen), 35
Euro-American, term usage, 13
extermination, 44–45

Fadden, Dave Kanietakeron, 79n7
faith leaders, at pipeline protest, 144
false historical narrative, 81–85
"First Criterion" (Schreiter), 100, 100n6
Fixico, Donald L., 17, 24, 58
Florida State University mascot, 73
Four Sheets to the Wind (film), 87n10
The Four Vision Quests of Jesus (Charleston), 104, 134
1491s comedy group (2013)
  "Bad Indians" (Red Corn poem), 32
  Daily Show, Indian mascots debate, 74–75
  FX on Hulu, 33
  The Indian Store, 20, 32
  logo, 87
  "New Moon Wolf Pack Auditions," 87
  performances arise from Indian identity, 97
  "Smiling Indians" (video), 71
  on stereotypes, 126
  YouTube video artists, 69–70
Fraher, Diane, 63–64, 68
Francis, Pope, 90, 108, 115, 130–33, 135
Francis, Saint, 108, 115
Fuhrman, CMarie, 80–81

Gaudium et Spes (Vatican II), 117n11
General Allotment (Dawes) Act (1887), 52, 58, 83
Generation Red Nation (documentary), 81–82
genocide, 46, 73–77
"The Genocide of a Generation's Identity" (Horn), 73
Genocide of the Mind (Moore), 6n3, 7–8, 10n7, 36, 63, 77
Ghost Dance, 138, 139
God
  Creator, 90, 109
  distorted images of, 93–94

God Is Red (Deloria), 94–95n3, 133
Goldtooth, Dallas, 80, 87
grace, as gift and threat, 141
grammar, critique of performance, 96, 97
Grant, Ulysses S., 52–55
Grounds, Richard A., 43–44, 44n2, 51
Gutierrez, Gustavo, 31, 110, 126

Haaland, Deb, 158
Halbritter, Ray, 82
Harjo, Joy, 3, 36
Harjo, Sterlin, 33, 87, 87n10, 157
Harvest the Hope concert (2014), 88
Haudenosaunee language (Iroquois), 11
hearing, with ears to hear, 119–120
heartful listening, 121
"The Helper-Spirit" (Rahner), 122
Henriot, Peter, 15, 27–30, 67, 128, 149
Ho-Chunk Tribes, Wisconsin, 19n3
Holland, Joe, 15, 27–30, 67, 128, 149
Holy Spirit, 113, 114, 117, 122, 124, 136
Homestead Act (1862), 56
Honor, Caldecott, 73n4
Horn, Gabriel, 17, 30, 73–74
Hostiles (film), 145

imperialism, 12
Indian Child Welfare Act (1978), 3
Indian Country Media, 146
Indian Country Today (digital news publication), 71, 75, 82, 145, 147
Indian Country Today Media Network (website), 36, 137, 158
Indian identity, 19–20, 19n4, 24, 63–64, 68–73, 90–93, 96–97, 99–102, 149
Indian mascots, 73–76, 82, 87
Indian Removal Act (1830), 50
"The Indian Store" (YouTube), 20, 32
"Indians as Mascots" (Roppolo), 5
An Indigenous Peoples' History of the United States (Dunbar-Ortiz), 9n5, 13, 40–41, 45–46, 45n3
"indigenous peoples," term usage, 9
indigenous theologies, 45

IndiJ Public Media, 82
Ireland, indigenous peoples of, 47, 47n4
Iron Eyes, Chase, 79n7, 84, 85
Iroquois Nations, 2, 11

Jackson, Andrew, 40–41, 50
Jasper, Inez (née Point), 67, 76, 88, 102
Jefferson, Thomas, 49, 51–52
Jeremiah (prophet), 114
Jesus
    prayer for unity of believers, 93–94
    on truth, 151
Johnson, Elizabeth, 117–18, 134
Johnson v. M'Intosh (1823), 49–50
"The Judgement of Other Churches" (Schreiter), 102
justified extermination, 44

Karalis, H. Lee, 77–78
Keene, Adrienne, 36, 85–86, 147, 158
Keetowah Band of Cherokee, 21
Kennedy, Joe III, 29
Keystone XL pipeline, Nebraska, 80, 88
Kidwell, Clara Sue, 136
Killers of the Flower Moon (film), 145, 158
Killing the White Man's Indian (Bordewich), 50
Klamath Tribe of Oregon, 60

LaDuke, Winona, 65, 118, 148
Lakota Surrender (image), 70
Lakota Woman (Crow Dog), 83–84
land allotment, 52–55
Lang, John Edward, Sr., 23
language
    grammar, critique of performance, 96, 97
    linguistic model for communication, 95–97
    loss of, 77–79
    tribal names in original language, 10–11
language acquisition model, 96, 99
language theory, 95

INDEX

The Last of the Mohicans (Cooper novel and film), 43–44, 49
Laudato Si (Francis), 108, 115, 115n10
Leal, Melissa, 79n7
Lechusza-Aquallo, Alan, 79n7
"The Lewis and Clark Story, the Captive Narrative, and the Pitfalls of Indian History" (Cook-Lynn), 41
Lincoln, Abraham, 41
linear time, 110–14
listening
　as deference, 146–151
　meaning of, 120–21
listening relationship of power-holders, 121–24
Lobo, Susan, 19n4
Locke, Allen, 84
The Logic of Practice (Bourdieu), 95, 106
The Lone Ranger and Tonto Fistfight in Heaven (Alexie), 72
Louisiana Purchase, 49, 51–52
Lucci-Cooper, Kathryn, 69
Lumen Gentium (Vatican II), 117n11

Manifest Destiny, 91–92, 101, 148
Mark, Gospels of, 109
Marshall, John, 49–50, 98
Martiea, Jarett, 79n7
Martinez, Donna, 49, 64
McKay, Neil, 78
Means, Nataanii, 76, 78–79, 84, 88
Means, Russell, 44n2, 79, 79n6, 81, 83
memories from past colonizers, 126, 133–34, 141, 146, 150–51
Menominee Nation of Wisconsin, 1, 2, 16, 18–19, 21, 51n7, 59–61
Menominee Restoration Act (1973), 60
Menominee Tribe v. United States (1968), 61
Merton, Thomas, 121
Metz, Johann Baptist, 138, 139
Micah (prophet), 94, 107–8
Micmac Tribe, 84
Miller, Susan A., 42, 43
missionaries, 7, 11, 23, 44, 57, 92, 106

missionary "conquest," by Christian missionaries, 45, 100
Missionary Conquest (Tinker), 12n8, 44, 57, 92, 99–102, 116, 148
Missouri Indians, 54–55
Mohawk Band of Indians, New York, 2
Monroe, James, 50
Moore, MariJo, 7–8, 10n7, 77, 79
Morales, Yuyi, 73n4
Morgan, J. P., 71
Morgan, Thomas J., 57–58
Morris, Glenn T., 49
Moya-Smith, Simon, 79n7, 86–87, 88
Muskogee (Creek) Nation, 3, 41
"My Stone" (Waln song), 80

Nabokov, Peter, 52, 154
National Council of Churches, Australia, 137
National Museum of the American Indian, 3, 9
National Wounded Knee Memorial Day, 141, 150
"Native America: 7th Generation Rising" (MTV), 79–80
"A Native American Perspective: Canaanites, Cowboys, and Indians" (Warrior), 32
Native American voices, newest generation of, 65–68
Native Appropriations (blog), 85–86
Native Christian theology, 133–35
Native Historians Write Back (Miller and Riding In), 42
Native identity. *See* Indian identity
Native Lives Matter movement, 76, 78, 83–85
Native theology, 126
Native Voices (Grounds, Tinker & Wilkins), 21, 27, 36, 62–63, 80–81, 133
Nativeappropriations.com (website), 36
Navajo Nation, 11
Navajo Neuropathy, 85
The Need and the Blessing of Prayer (Rahner), 121

Neihardt, John G., 147
Nelson, Willie, 88
Nerney, Catherine, 149–150
"New Moon Wolf Pack Auditions" (1491s), 87
New Seeds of Contemplation (Merton), 122
New Tribes Mission, 23
Nez, Helen, 85
Nicholas, Pope, 50n5
Nixon, Richard, 60, 61–62, 64
"North America Is a Crime Scene" (Dunbar-Ortiz), 40
Notable Native People (Keene), 158
nuclear waste facility, Yucca Mountain, 29
Nuclear Waste Task Force, Nevada, 29

Obama, Barack, 146
"occupancy of title" concept, 49
Oceti Sakowin Camp, 85
"Oil 4 Blood" (Waln song), 80
oil-and-land grab (1920's), 158
Ojibway (Ojibwe) Nation, 11, 21, 65, 78
Omaha Tribe, 78
"One Good Man" (Alexie), 72, 104–5
Ono, Azusa, 64
Osage Nation, 158
Other, term usage, 94, 96, 98
Otoe-Missouri Treaty (1854), 54–55
Owen, Suzanne, 19, 35, 147

paper genocide, 17, 30
Paul VI, Pope, 24, 112
peace, restoration and, 135, 151
Peelman, Achiel, 99n4, 103, 109, 113–14, 134
Pember, Mary Annette, 150
Pensoneau, Migizi, 75
Pesantubbee, Michelene E., 26–27, 28
Pine Ridge Reservation, South Dakota, 81–82, 84, 143
Plumbar, Camille, 82
Plurality and Ambiguity (Tracy), 129
The Power of the Poor in History (Gutierrez), 110
Pratt, Richard H., 17n2, 57, 60

prayerful listening, 121–24
preferential option for the poor, 31
presumptuous errors, 121
Project 562 (work of), 76–77
Prucha, Francis Paul, 21, 58n10

Quest for the Living God (Johnson), 117–18

radical model, for social change, 29–30, 67, 149
Rahner, Karl, 111–13, 121
Rebel Music (MTV episode), 76, 78, 79–80, 79–80n7
"Rebel Voices" (MTV episode), 67
reconciliation, 122, 135–36
Red Corn, Ryan, 32, 70–71, 70n3, 126
Red Star, Wendy, 71
reflective listening, 37–38
religious conversions, 112
Relocation Program, 58–59
removal and expansion, 48–52
Reservation Dogs (FX Hula series), 20, 33, 80, 87, 157–59
reservations, 52–56
The Revenant (film), 145
Riding In, James, 42, 43
Robinson, Elaine A., 103, 105, 107, 108n9, 111
Roman Catholic Church
  Benedict XVI, Pope, 135
  Black Elk, cause for sainthood, 147n2
  Canadian Catholic Aboriginal Council, 135
  Canadian Catholic Organization for Development and Peace, 135
  Canadian Conference of Catholic Bishops, 50n5, 98, 135
  Canadian Religious Conference, 135
  Christian missionaries, 11
  Council of Nicaea (325), 100n6
  "Declaration on the Relationship of the Church to Non-Christian Religions (Vatican II), 113
  Francis, Pope, 90, 108, 115, 130–33, 135

INDEX

Gaudium et Spes, 117n11
Laudato Si Encyclical, 108, 115, 115n10
Lumen Gentium (Vatican II), 117n11
Nicholas, Pope, 50n5
Paul VI, Pope, 24, 112
sacred everywhere, 22
United States Conference of Catholic Bishops, 50n5
Veritatis Gaudium (Apostolic Constitution), 131
Roppolo, Kimberly, 5–7
Royal Proclamation of Reconciliation, Canada, 146
Royce, Irvin, 1, 16, 17, 18
Rudd, Kevin, 137

Sage, Grace, 19n4, 64
Sand Creek Colorado Territory (1865), 154
Scharen, Christian, 34, 35
Schreiter, Robert J.
  "The Challenge to Other Churches," 102
  Christian community identity, 103
  "First Criterion," 100, 100n6
  "The Judgement of Other Churches," 102
  linguistic model for communication, 95–97, 99–101
  "The Praxis of the Community," 101
Scorsese, Martin, 158
"see-judge-act" method, 4, 16n1
Seneca Nation, 103
shared memory, 146
Shoshone Tribe, Nevada, 29
Silko, Leslie Marmon, 36, 40, 63, 97, 116
Simoneau, Yves, 138n1
"Smiling Indians" (1491s video), 71
Sneve, Virginia Driving Hawk, 68–69
Snyder, Daniel, 74
Sobrino, Jon, 31
social analysis method, 27–31, 126
Social Darwinism, 47
social science research,, 34

Songs My Brothers Taught Me (film), 36, 82
Sorry Day, Australia, 137, 150
Southern Poverty Law Center, 128
sovereignty, 60–64
Spider Woman's Granddaughter (Allen), 46
Spirit and Resistance (Tinker), 110
spirituality of community, 20
Spokane language, 72, 104
"Stand With Standing Rock" protest movement, 85
Standing Rock protest, 85, 143–44
stereotypes, 87–88, 126
Stewart, Jon, 74–75
Stockbridge Munsee Band of Mohicans, 19, 51n7
stories, as means of communication, 30
Sugirtharajah, R. S., 9–10n, 12
Supremacy Clause, U. S. Constitution, 61
Sweetwater (Indian carpenter), 104

Taussig, Hal, 149–150
termination era, 17–18, 21, 39, 41, 46
termination policy, 59–60
terminology, use of, 8–14
"The Praxis of the Community" (Schreiter), 101
"The Question of History" (Tracy), 141
They Taught You Wrong (unknown author), 21
Three Mile Island, nuclear reactor accident (1979), 29
Three Stooges, 70
Thunder Boy Jr. (Alexie), 73, 73n4
Tinker, George E. "Tink"
  American Indian Liberation, 10, 12–13, 43, 44–45, 63
  "America's unfinished business," 7
  basileia, understanding of, 141
  as conversation partner, 36
  cultural genocide, 107
  Deloria and, 4
  Euro-American Christian theology, 92–93

(Tinker, George E. "Tink" continued)
   on *Generation Red Nation*, 81
   liberation theology and, 110
   liberation/freedom, as principal goal, 62
   on linear time, 111–12
   on missionaries, 106
   Missionary Conquest, 12n8, 44, 57, 92, 99–102, 116, 148
   Native Voices. see Native Voices
   Spirit and Resistance, 110
   on termination policy, 59
   on theological reconciliation, 105
   on western expansion, 44–45
   on White superiority, 95
To the Finland Station (Wilson), 2
The Toughest Indian In the World (Alexie), 72
toxic waste disposal, 29, 85
Tracy, David, 124, 126, 128–29, 131–32, 138, 141
Trail of Broken Treaties (1972), 62, 82
Trail of Tears, Cherokee Nation, 50, 139, 150, 153
tribal names
   to define Native identity, 17
   in the original language, 10–11
Truth and Reconciliation Commission, Canadian Conference of Catholic Bishops, 50n5
Truth and Reconciliation Commission of Canada, 145–46
Tsalagi language (Cherokee), 11
Two Bulls, Marty, 82
two-way theological evaluation, 102–3

United Nations Declaration on the Rights of Indigenous Peoples, 125
United States Conference of Catholic Bishops, 50n5
Urban American Indians (Martinez, Sage, and Ono), 64
The Urban Indian Experience (Fixico), 17
urban Indian identity, 19n4

"The Urban Indian Identity Crisis" (Fixico), 24
U.S. Army veterans' apology, 143–44

Valanos, Olga, 81
Valentino (fashion designer), 86
Veritatis Gaudium (Apostolic Constitution), 131
Vigen, Aana Marie, 34, 35
Voices from the Margin (Sugirtharajah), 9–10n

Waititi, Taika, 157
Waln, Frank, 67, 79–81, 88, 102, 158
wannabes, 18, 21, 21n5
Warrior, Clyde, 42
Warrior, Robert Allen, 32, 109
Washington Redskins mascot, 74–75, 82, 87
Water Protectors (Dakota Access Pipeline), 143
Waters, Joel, 20
Watkins, Arthur V., 59
"We Ain't Got Feathers and Beads" (Bordewich), 51n6
We Talk, You Listen (Deloria), 4
weeping, as sign, 151–52, 155
The West (PBS film project), 141
Western Shoshone Nation, 29
Wheeler-Howard Act (1934), 59
White culture, blind spots, 94–99
White superiority, 89–93, 107, 110, 116
whitesplaining, 69, 69n2
white-think, 22
Wicazo Sa Review (journal), 41–42
Wilbur, Mitaka, 76–77
Williams, Rick, 141
Wilson, Bobby, 75, 87–88
Wilson, Edmund, 2
Wisdom, Book of, 108
Wolf River Treaty (1854), 61
Wonder Horse (Indian carpenter), 104
Wong, Joseph, 112–13
Wounded Knee, American society remembering, 144–46

Wounded Knee massacre (1890), 83, 137–144
Wounded Knee Memorial Run, 139
Wounded Knee occupation (1973), 62, 79n6, 83–84
"Wounded White Warrior Savior Photographer" (Red Corn), 126

Wovoka (prophet), 138, 139

Yankton, Margaret, 81
Young, Neil, 88
Yucca Mountain, nuclear waste facility, 29
"Yuchi Travels" (Grounds), 43, 51

www.ingramcontent.com/pod-product-compliance
Lightning Source LLC
Chambersburg PA
CBHW071448150426
43191CB00008B/1273